THE REAL LAS VEGAS

The Real Las Vegas

LIFE BEYOND THE STRIP

Edited by David Littlejohn
Photographs by Eric Gran

OXFORD
UNIVERSITY PRESS
1999

OXFORD
UNIVERSITY PRESS

Oxford   New York

Athens   Auckland   Bangkok   Bogotá   Buenos Aires   Calcutta
Cape Town   Chennai   Dar es Salaam   Delhi   Florence   Hong Kong   Istanbul
Karachi   Kuala Lumpur   Madrid   Melbourne   Mexico City   Mumbai
Nairobi   Paris   São Paulo   Singapore   Taipei   Tokyo   Toronto   Warsaw

and associated companies in
Berlin   Ibadan

Copyright © 1999 by David Littlejohn

Published by Oxford University Press, Inc.
198 Madison Avenue, New York, New York 10016

Library of Congress Cataloging-in-Publication Data
The real Las Vegas: life beyond the strip/edited by David Littlejohn;
photographs by Eric Gran.
p. cm.
Includes index.
ISBN 0-19-513070-7
1. Las Vegas (Nev.)—Description and travel. 2. Las Vegas (Nev.)—Social
conditions. 3. Las Vegas (Nev.)—Economic conditions.
I. Littlejohn, David, 1937–   .
F849.L35R38   1999   979.3'135033—dc21   98–43830

Design: Adam B. Bohannon

9 8 7 6 5 4 3 2 1
Printed in the United States of America
on acid-free paper

To all the good people of Clark County and Nye County, Nevada,
who generously shared with us their lives and ideas;
with special thanks to Ed Bayley, Orville Schell, John L. Smith,
and the University of California alumni of southern Nevada.

Contents

Illustrations appear after pages 132 and 180

THE REAL LAS VEGAS

Introduction

THE ULTIMATE COMPANY TOWN
David Littlejohn

PEELING OFF THE STRIP

Las Vegas Valley is a flat—a very flat—stretch of about 500 square miles of dry desert land surrounded by smooth, treeless brown mountains. In 1999 it was home to well over a million people. Projecting into the future the valley's current rate of growth (there were about 400,000 people here in 1980, 700,000 in 1990), the Nevada State demographer envisions two million people living in Las Vegas Valley by 2010. This prospect horrifies some residents, who insist that they will be long gone before the two-millionth citizen arrives, at the same time that it tantalizes real estate developers. These million or two million people are or will be here—whether or not they realize or admit it—because of the Industry, as insiders tend to call it, the way people in Los Angeles refer to the companies that make movies and television films.

The Industry in Las Vegas is casino gambling, which its representatives would like you to call the Gaming Industry. For most people this denotes a four-mile stretch of Las Vegas Boulevard South called the Strip, which occasionally spills over onto side and parallel streets, from Sahara Avenue at the north end to just past Hacienda Avenue at the south, where it bumps into McCarran Airport. The Industry also implies Downtown, a couple of miles north of the Strip, which was once a genuine downtown, the historic birthplace and commercial center of the city. Although more cluttered by urban reality than the Strip, what Las Vegas promoters now call Downtown is a secondary tourist district of ten major and several minor casino-hotels centered on 2,000 feet of Fremont Street, east of the railroad tracks and Interstate 15. In 1995-96, gamblers left behind $3.7 billion at the machines, tables, and sports books of the Strip compared to $683 million Downtown, a fact that gives some idea of the relative importance of the two in the industry that created and still runs Las Vegas.

In actuality, Las Vegas has no downtown, no central business district. Residents shop at a few grand-scale shopping plazas and any one of a hundred strip malls scattered about the valley. There are two upscale retail centers on the Strip—the Fashion Show Mall and the Forum Shops at Caesars—but these depend on visitors for most of their profits. What offices there are (Clark County has about 2,100 attorneys, 1,900 doctors, and 2,600 architects) tend to be strung out along the evenly spaced grid of long, straight boulevards or clustered in a few medium-size high-rises, none of which approaches the height or grandeur of the ruling casino hotels.

Las Vegas can mean the City of Las Vegas proper, which includes Downtown, a cluster of public buildings, and the relatively impoverished West Side but not the Strip, the airport, the university, or most of the residential and commercial development of the past 50 years. Considerably enlarged by the annexation since 1987 of a vast new housing development to the northwest, the City of Las Vegas now encompasses 85,000 acres and had in 1996 a population of 377,000. To anyone except local politicians, voters, and taxpayers, however, it would be absurd to talk about "Las Vegas" and not include the 36 casino-hotels on and just off the Strip, with their 83,000 rooms (scheduled to grow to 91,000 by 2000), their scores of restaurants, their vast meeting and convention halls, their showrooms and spas and arenas and shops, and their more than 500 acres of covered, often lavishly decorated space in which adult visitors are invited to gamble.

In order to include these, the iconic places of Las Vegas, one must define the city more broadly. Many claims for or statistics about Las Vegas actually refer to the county that surrounds it. Clark County, a political jurisdiction considerably more important than the city, *does* include the Strip, the airport, and the university, as well as Nellis Air Force Base and the incorporated towns of Boulder City (where public gambling is forbidden), North Las Vegas, Henderson, and Laughlin, a ten-casino lowrollers' haven at the pointy southern tip of the state. It also includes a handful of other unincorporated settlements, and vast stretches of desert in between. Clark County covers 8,084 square miles (most of them empty) and had in 1997 an estimated population of 1,106,000—60 percent of the people in Nevada. An alternative definition of the city is what the U.S. Census Bureau calls the Las Vegas Metropolitan Statistical Area (1997 estimated population: 1,262,099). This includes not only all of Clark County, but also Nye County to the north and Mohave County in Arizona, which are presumed to fall within Las Vegas's economic orbit.

These distinctions are important. Las Vegas Valley and its dominant industry generate a great many statistics, some misleading, others conflicting. One reason the statistics may mislead is that those generating or citing them often have large axes to grind. One reason they often conflict is that people mean different things when they refer to Las Vegas.

What I mean, and what most people mean, by Las Vegas is the developed portion of Las Vegas Valley: the freeway-linked area west of Lake Mead that includes the four incorporated cities of Clark County as well as the contiguous unincorporated areas of Paradise, Winchester, Sunrise Manor, and Spring Valley. Logically, these areas should have been made part of the city of Las Vegas in 1946, when casino and other property owners successfully fought off the first of several efforts to annex the Strip to the city.

■ ■ ■

Jan Morris once described the effect of the Las Vegas Strip on what can appear—once you move away from the radiance of Las Vegas Boulevard South—to be a decent, bourgeois, conservative, even churchy western town. "It is as though some inconceivable alien organism has fallen upon the old depot town," she wrote, "squatting there athwart the tracks and infecting everything with some incurable, unidentifiable but not altogether disagreeable virus."

It was my intention, in the experiment that led to this book, to pull this alien organism off of the map of Las Vegas—as if one could insert a thumbnail under the Stratosphere Hotel and Tower, just north of Sahara Avenue, and peel off the map everything down to the black pyramid of the Luxor, plus whatever the Circus Circus people end up building across the street. Just-off-the-Strip growths like the Las Vegas Hilton, the Rio Suites, the Gold Coast, the Maxim, the San Remo, the Continental, the new Paris, the smaller Hard Rock, and the defunct Debbie Reynolds casino-hotels would presumably adhere to the lifted Strip and be peeled off along with it.

It would not be as easy, figuratively or theoretically, to remove from the map the fiction of Downtown—the whole Fremont/Ogden Street tourist experience—because indigenous reality (poor people, pawn shops, prostitutes, drug dealers) continues to intrude on what used to be called Glitter Gulch.

But my goal was to examine the city in which 1.2 million Las Vegans actually live, *beyond* the Strip and Downtown. The latter have been written about, photographed, mocked, and marveled over almost to distraction, like the canals of Venice or the skyscrapers of New York. In 1984, I saw an exhibition, called "Dietro I Palazzi" ("Behind the Palaces"), that took the perverse approach of examining Venice's uncelebrated, nondescript buildings and neighborhoods, those hidden behind the tourist precincts, where 60,000 real Venetians—all that were left on the city's lagoon islands at the time—lived, worked, and played. This is what I have aimed to do with Greater Las Vegas.

At first I thought of this project as a possible object lesson for other American cities, counties, states, and Indian reservations that in the past twenty years have hit on the idea of legalized casino gambling as a solution to their economic problems. In this short time the spread of casino gambling in North America has taken on the force of a tidal wave. First Atlantic City, in 1978; then Indian reservations (which can negotiate the building of casinos independently with their states); then, after 1991, several midwestern and southern states as well as individual counties and cities joined Nevada in this latest rush after gold. As of 1998, fourteen states had voted to legalize full-scale casino gambling, restricted in many cases to "riverboats," many of which never leave port. Indian tribes have opened casinos—including the busiest and most profitable casino in the world, Foxwoods in Connecticut—in 23 states. Offshore boats carry gamblers out of territorial waters from ports in Florida, Georgia, and New York.

Originally, I thought of calling this book *Beyond the Strip: Learning More from Las Vegas*, implying both a tribute to and a step beyond *Learning from Las Vegas*, the groundbreaking study published in 1972 by Robert Venturi, Denise Scott Brown, and Steven Izenour, who had worked in conjunction with some of their graduate students at Yale. What Venturi et al. suggested, after their ten-day trip to Las Vegas in 1968, was that the untidy sprawl of the Strip, with its gigantic flashing neon signs—signs more important, both as marketing tools and works of art, than the rather ordinary buildings behind them—represented a legitimate indigenous American art form, which was something more than simply crude, commercial, and non-European. In the decade that followed, other observers of the American scene took up the cause of popular commercial art forms.

Main Street was *almost* all right; Disneyland was the most important architectural landmark in southern California; comic-book and graffiti artists merited gallery exhibitions. MTV taught us a whole new way of seeing.

In Las Vegas, meanwhile, the large, elaborate signs Venturi had admired kept growing larger and more elaborate, often dispensing with neon altogether in favor of light-emitting diodes, in order to compete with the multi-thousand-room tower blocks rising behind them. The biggest sign of all (a freestanding structure 362 feet tall and 192 feet wide), erected by the Las Vegas Hilton in 1993, blew down in a storm the following year.

Meanwhile, strange things were happening to Las Vegas as it spread further out from the Strip and Downtown. For one thing, it became one of the fastest growing urban areas in the United States. In the Census Bureau's estimates of population growth in the five years after 1990, the city of Las Vegas grew by 27 percent; Clark County by 33.9 percent, and the Las Vegas metropolitan area by 33.6 percent. In the same period, the nearest competitor among the nation's 100 largest cities (Aurora, Colorado) grew by 13 percent. Among counties with populations of over half a million, the nearest competitor was Riverside County, California, with an increase of 17.9%.

Between 1950 and 1960, Clark County's growth (165 percent) was exceeded by that of the boom regions of Broward County, Florida (Fort Lauderdale), and Orange County, California. But no U.S. county of comparable size grew faster during the 1960s or '70s and only Riverside County grew faster during the 1980s, when Clark County's growth rates were 115, 70, and 60 percent respectively. Between 1990 and 1997, the Las Vegas Metropolitan Standard Area grew by more than 48 percent—eight percent faster than its nearest rival. Over the 45-year period 1950-95 Clark County grew more than twenty times in size, from 48,000 people to 993,000—a record no other large U.S. county even comes close to matching.

One effect of this astonishing growth is that the second-largest industry in Clark County is construction. In 1995, permits were issued for 29,537 new housing units in the Las Vegas metropolitan area; in 1996, 32,381, almost exactly as many as were issued in the entire Los Angeles-Orange County-Riverside metropolitan area, which had a population thirteen times that of Las Vegas. Greater Los Angeles overtook Las Vegas in 1997, and housing starts in five other metropolitan areas exceeded both of their figures. But all of these areas had populations several times that of Greater Las Vegas, which means that Las Vegas is building new homes at a higher rate than any other city in the country: 32,173 residential unit building permits were issued in 1998.

Another way to look at the housing construction boom is to judge how quickly a city replicates itself. Between 1990 and 1996, Greater Las Vegas increased its housing stock by 45.2 percent—far ahead of the rate of its nearest competitor, Naples, Florida, with 33 percent, and more than double that of Orlando.

Atlantic City, St. Louis, Biloxi, New Orleans, Detroit—any U.S. city may decide to permit casino gambling within its borders or along its shores. But these cities were established on other economic and social bases, and the introduction of casinos will never shape or define them absolutely, the way the casinos of Downtown and the Strip have shaped and defined Las Vegas.

Much of what has happened to Las Vegas in the last ten, twenty, and forty years has been duplicated by other boomtowns of the American Sunbelt, cities like San Jose, Phoenix, Colorado Springs, El Paso, and Fort Lauderdale. "Destination resort" communities in these favored latitudes—notably Disney's Anaheim and Orlando—share many characteristics with Las Vegas. But a sampling of the other claims and statistics often cited in discussions of Vegas may help explain why I have come to regard the city as worthy of study not as an object lesson, but for its own sake. Many of these numbers and rankings refer to Clark County (which is in effect Las Vegas) or to the state of Nevada; but almost two-thirds of Nevadans live in Clark County.

- Nevada currently has the highest suicide rate in the country—double the national rate. This appears to be true for every age group, although fully 40 percent of the suicides in Nevada are committed by people over sixty-five. It is often said that the teen-suicide rate (or, depending on the source, the rate of suicide *attempts* by teenagers) in Las Vegas is the highest in the nation, but I've never been able to verify this claim.
- Nevada has the highest alcohol-consumption rate in the country, (probably due in part to tourists), with an attendant record for incidence of cirrhosis of the liver. It ranks high among American states in rates of abortions, teen pregnancies, and births to unmarried mothers—43 percent of births in 1996, the third-highest in the country. Nevada also has the highest rate of automobile accidents per miles driven, which may have something to do with its rate of alcohol consumption, and Las Vegas has the fifth highest air-pollution index among American cities. Until recently, Nevada had a higher percentage of smokers than any other state, and in 1997 it still led the nation in percentage of female smokers—more than double California's. Las Vegas has far more than its share of deaths from

lung cancer, coronary artery disease, and cardiac arrest; Las Vegas cardiologist Thomas Ahearn explains, "We attract people whose lifestyles are somewhat less healthy than [the] ideal." Casino employees in Las Vegas, like airline flight attendants, are trained to use portable defibrators, in case they need to shock heart-attack victims out of dying on their premises.

- Las Vegas claims to be the number-one tourist destination in the U.S., with more than 30 million visitors a year (although Orlando and New York continue to make the same claim). Terry Jicinsky, the chief number-cruncher for the Las Vegas Convention and Visitor Authority, explained to me the complex methodology behind the LVCVA's statistical estimates. But statistical estimates, however carefully determined, are not the same thing as actual head counts, and leave room for dispute.

- Since convention delegates have to register to attend, on the other hand, it is clear that Las Vegas has become at least the runner-up to Chicago as the leading convention/exhibition host in the nation, attracting about three thousand such events each year for a total of about three million patrons. Its mammoth civic convention center is smaller than McCormack Place in Chicago, but (along with the private Sands/Venetian facility) may surpass it once the current expansion is complete. Las Vegas's annual Comdex, a computer dealers' exhibition held each November, is the world's largest such gathering, attracting more than 200,000 paid visitors.

- Las Vegas has more hotel rooms than any other city in the world (more than a hundred thousand in 1998, with twenty thousand more either planned or under construction), and the highest average hotel-occupancy rate (87 to 90 percent) of any American city. In 1995, the *Zagat Guide* estimated that it offered the lowest average daily hotel room rate of the thirty-three leading U.S. visitor destinations. Las Vegas currently contains nine of the world's ten largest hotels. In 1998, the world's largest was Thailand's Ambassador City Hotel, but that may change when both phases of the new Venetian Hotel are completed on the Strip.

- Nevada's bankruptcy rate (6.3 per thousand people in 1997) was the fourth-highest in the nation, after those of Tennessee, Georgia, and Alabama. The national average was 4.2 per thousand.

- According to the FBI's Uniform Crime Reports for 1995, Las Vegas had the highest total crime rate and the highest rate of crimes against property among all American cities with more than 250,000 people. Police reports for that year placed Las Vegas fourth among

U.S. metropolitan areas of over a million population—after Miami, Phoenix, and Oklahoma City—in the rate of *all* serious crimes; 14.7 percent of these were called "violent." Along with those of Washington and Atlanta, the city's crime rate rose markedly in 1996, despite declining crime rates in most American cities. Although other cities had higher rates of homicide and other violent crimes in 1995, Las Vegas ranked lowest in the percentage of "cleared" violent crimes, i.e., crimes leading to arrests (1,950 of 9,421, or 20.7 percent, against a national average of 45 percent).

- In 1985, Nevada's high-school dropout rate (teenagers 16 to 19 who have not completed and are not attending school) was 25 percent. By 1992 it had dropped to 14.9 percent but was still the highest in the country. The dropout rate for Clark County in 1996-97 was nearly 12 percent, the highest in the state. Recent SAT and ACT scores for Nevada seniors (and the percentage of high-school graduates taking these exams) have ranked around the middle of the national standings; in funding per student, Nevada has risen to thirty-fourth. But fewer Nevada high-school graduates go on to college than those of any other state except Alaska.

- Nevada had in 1996 both the highest marriage rate (ten times the national average, due primarily to out-of-state couples who come to Las Vegas and Reno to marry) and the highest divorce rate (more than double the national average). Although out-of-staters once flocked to Nevada for "quickie" divorces, the numbers now represent primarily local residents. The state's divorce rate has declined markedly since 1980, as other states have relaxed their regulations. "People come here for fresh starts," explained Lucy Rey, a family counselor. "People come here to declare bankruptcy, people come here to lose something or somebody. And they do it successfully."

- According to *Money* magazine, Las Vegas had in 1995 the second-lowest property-tax burden of America's hundred largest cities, after Knoxville.

- Although it is the urban center of the thirty-fifth-largest U.S. metropolitan area in terms of population (1996), Las Vegas has the twelfth-busiest airport in the country, and the ninth-largest school district. It does *not* have a major-league sports team, a nationally accredited symphony orchestra or opera company, a theater company that performs throughout the week, or a major art museum.

- Las Vegans are often blamed for using more water than the residents of any other city in the world: currently 325 gallons per capita per year (down from 360 gallons in 1989), as opposed to half that much or less for other western cities such as Santa Fe, Tucson, El Paso, and San Diego. (Phoenix and Albuquerque use about 250 gallons a day per capita.) Civic defenders often attribute Las Vegas's high levels of water use, as they do its crime rate, to the city's tourists, but their presence increases the average daily population by at most 25 percent. Two-thirds of the region's water use is domestic; in fact, most of that water goes to keep front-yard lawns green in the middle of a desert. The planners of Summerlin, the huge master-planned community to the northwest, are aiming for water-use levels of one-third the Las Vegas norm by maintaining strict controls over "desert-friendly" planting.

■ ■ ■

I do not pretend that all of these claims and statistics are accurate, or remain accurate. Las Vegas is the kind of place that generates urban legends, which then become an ineradicable part of its image, and where other statistics change as rapidly as the population. It is often written, for example, that Las Vegas has the "highest number of churches per capita" of any U.S. city, which, if it was ever true, is certainly not true now: there are more churches per capita in half a dozen cities I have investigated, and probably in others. The National Coalition Against Legalized Gambling, citing a survey of 1998, asserts that 18 percent of bankruptcies are "gambling related"; Nevada casino interests insist the figure is closer to 2 percent. Neither side has come up with any persuasive evidence. The Las Vegas Metro Police tries in vain to kill the persisting myth of tourists being drugged and having their kidneys removed (presumably for sale). Civic boosters (and no city spends more money per resident selling itself to the outside world) come up each year with wondrous new numbers to help them define Las Vegas's magical status. The city's detractors, for their part—in particular, nowadays, people opposed to the spread of casino gambling to other regions—keep discovering or inventing ugly statistics and nasty anecdotes about the lives of Las Vegans, hoping to warn decent Americans elsewhere of the sordid depths to which legalized gambling can lead.

Sixteen of us (and our photographer) drove or flew down from Berkeley several times during 1996-97, then fanned out beyond the ever-more-overwhelming signs, facades, casinos, and showrooms of the Strip and Downtown that had spellbound Professor Venturi's Yalies in 1968. Who, we wanted to know, lived under all the red-tile roofs represented by those tens of thousands of building permits, inside the houses and condominiums and apartment buildings that every day reached closer towards the mountain walls that enclose Las Vegas Valley? Why had they come here? Why had they stayed? What did they *do*, at work, at home, in their spare time? What did they think of their famous, their infamous city? How did they regard, how were they personally affected by the industry that so visibly dominates this, the ultimate company town?

■ ■ ■

Once you peel off the Strip and Downtown from a map or bird's-eye view of Las Vegas, what you are left with is basically a rectangular grid of boulevards spaced at one-mile intervals. (In some areas, the intervals vary. The rectangular grid is broken by a few jogs and wiggles, as well as three major diagonal routes: Las Vegas Boulevard, Boulder Highway, and the northern portion of Rancho Drive. The two interstates fly over everything.) In the 1950s, when they still reached only a few blocks into the desert, the best-known of these boulevards were renamed after the hotels that had been erected at their intersection with the Strip—an early indication of Las Vegas's identity as a company town. San Francisco Street became Tropicana Avenue; Boggs became Flamingo. Half a mile south of Tropicana, where the Hacienda Hotel stood until it was blown up in 1996, was Hacienda Avenue. North of Flamingo, helping to advertise other early resorts, were Desert Inn Road and Sahara Avenue. Once the main roads were taken, the Dunes, Sands, Riviera, Circus Circus, Hilton, and Stardust Hotels had to settle for short streets that ran alongside their properties. Recently, new hotels have given their names to minor access lanes.

The other major east-west lines in the grid, south of Hacienda to the Henderson city line, are Russell, Sunset, and Warm Springs. Heading north from Sahara (the city's southern edge) you cross Charleston, Bonanza, Owens, Lake Mead, Carey, Cheyenne, and Craig. By the time you have reached Cheyenne (the route east to Nellis Air Force Base) these ruler-straight roads tend to be bordered by blank miles of flat desert scrub. Up here, yet-to-be-exploited *terrains vagues* are marked only by occasional signposts stuck among dusty clumps of sagebrush and tumbleweed balls, advertising real-estate developments or candidates running for last year's political offices.

These east-west roads are cut by similar, if less interesting, north-south axes. With a few key exceptions, most local (as distinct from tourist) development took place on the avenues running east and west. Paradise and Industrial Roads, running on either side of the Strip, carry some of its spillover: parking lots and garages; lesser restaurants, casinos, and motels; the sprawling convention center; the Las Vegas Hilton; and a fair amount of urban dreck. The easternmost line in the grid is Nellis Boulevard, which leads south from the air-force base. After Nellis hits the diagonal of Boulder Highway, near the lively Sam's Town complex, the highway demarcates the rest of the valley's edge—although a great deal of new development, including the Sam Boyd Stadium, or "Silver Bowl," and an $18-million Mormon temple consecrated in 1989, has already begun spreading towards the foothills east of Boulder Highway and the grid.

For most of the valley, the western limit of paved roads and habitation (as of today; it will be further west tomorrow) is Durango Drive. Large new housing tracts in the northwest—Summerlin, The Lakes, Canyon Gate—have pushed the boundaries of inhabited Las Vegas three or four miles beyond Durango towards the mountains. Between Nellis Boulevard and Durango Drive you cross, at mile intervals, Lamb, Pecos, Eastern, Maryland Parkway (the most important north-south boulevard, after the Strip); portions of Paradise and Rancho; Valley View, Decatur, Jones, Rainbow, Buffalo, and Cimarron.

Here, then, is an overview of the "real" Las Vegas, stripped of the Strip and Downtown: twelve wide roads, each a mile from the next, running east and west. Every mile, as they cross one of the fourteen similar roads running north and south, stoplights help to guide traffic into shopping malls, gas stations, and fast-food restaurants. Laid across this checkerboard are three major diagonals, as well as the snaking loops of two interstate highways—the means by which people get in and out of town. Along, in-between, and, increasingly, beyond the wide gridlines live more than a million people.

ON PLANNING, COMPANY TOWNS, AND THE HEAVY HAND OF THE INDUSTRY

You might think, from the paradigmatic grid I have described, that Las Vegas was a model of urban planning, like Washington, D.C., or Savannah. In fact, like other Sunbelt cities designed more for automobiles than for people, more by property speculators than by city planners, it often looks an unreadable chaos of non-planning, in which developments emerge like random spores miles from one another, with nothing but empty desert in between. Almost all new building has taken place along the mile-apart roads, leaving the city with vast barren spaces that have yet to be filled in. From the air, the edges of Las Vegas can resemble a chicken-wire fence, with rags and feathers of development caught along the wires, clustering where they intersect. Huge tracts of new housing are approved (Clark County prides itself on how much more rapidly it grants building permits than its California counterparts) even when they lie far from existing road networks, water and sewer lines, fire stations, and schools, because this is where developers are able to find the cheapest federal land. Since 1946, the Strip casinos and other property owners south of Sahara have fiercely resisted absorption into the City of Las Vegas, on the presumption that county commissioners were easier to buy and control than city-council members, and for fear of having to pay for Las Vegas's needs.

Not that the cities of Las Vegas, Henderson, and North Las Vegas have been models of enlightened planning. Eager to annex new industrial parks and master-planned communities proposed for adjacent desert lands, they readily amend their own master plans to satisfy developers and duel with one another to attract new business, which rules out any unified, county-wide planning. The "Fremont Street Experience," an extravagant light-show canopy designed to draw patrons to Downtown casinos (paid for in large part by the Las Vegas Redevelopment Agency and the local Convention and Visitors Authority), and the emergence of new casinos in outlying neighborhoods, indicate that the three cities are no less eager than Clark County to cater to the wishes of the Industry.

Every few years, the county or its cities convenes a series of "strategic planning" workshops and committees, with the intention of devising long-range schemes for improving life in Las Vegas. In 1985, the City of Las Vegas announced plans for a futuristic "maglev" (magnetically levitated) people-mover, including a downtown transportation center where the system's coaches would connect with efficient buses and quaint trolleys. Only one part of the project was ever built; it was then torn down (at a cost of $4 million) after Strip casino magnates objected. Two years later, the Downtown plan was expanded to include a Florida developer's proposed two-square-block "festival marketplace." The casino he opened there (with a generous city subsidy) declared bankruptcy after four months.

In 1989, a group of 300 citizens convened by both the city and the county met throughout the year to draw up a plan called "Las Vegas: 2000 and Beyond." Some of the 110 action items they ended up proposing were either banal or unattainable; but most of them were reasonable, and some were essential. Many of their recommendations have been implemented—except, of course, things like city-county consolidation, or at least coordinated planning; a workable mass-transit system; a scheme for gridlock-free streets; a regional park system; alternatives to suburban sprawl; and, most importantly, a revision in Nevada's gambling-dependent tax structure, which might enable Las Vegas to obtain the billions of dollars it requires for new and improved roads and schools, as well as water, sewer, and power lines.

Eight years closer to the millennium, another meeting was convened (called "Preview '97") at which a dozen high-powered speakers offered dire warnings about the future of Las Vegas. By 1997 "infrastructure" had become a local buzzword, as casino presidents and property developers, seconded by pundits and politicians, expressed common fears that the valley might be growing too fast—though no one wanted to be the first to suggest controls, let alone limits to future growth. "We need to take a look at how many people this valley can hold before it gets dangerous," the gathering was told by Stephen Wynn, president of Mirage Resorts, whose hotels employed at the time more than eighteen thousand of those people. "We can't see if we can fill up every inch of desert with houses and shopping centers." The goal was to get more tax money out of somebody—preferably somebody else—to pay for the essential facilities all these people require (roads, water, schools, some form of mass transit), at a figure then estimated at $7 billion, or $7,000 for each tax-resistant citizen.

In 1983 the county's staff of professional planners drew up drew a comprehensive map (approved by the Planning Commission and reevaluated each year), indicating (1) which sectors of unincorporated territory they regarded as suitable for development; (2) semirural areas where expansion *might* take place, once services were in place; and (3) vast outlying areas they hoped to retain, if not as empty space, at most as equestrian-oriented ranches (or "ranchettes") of an acre or more. The planners' goal was to direct most newcomers to already-populated districts in order to minimize both sprawl and the cost of extending services. But Jeff Harris, head of the county's long-range planning effort, admitted that if sufficient pressure was brought to bear, outlying areas would be rezoned to accommodate large developers. "The Board [of County Commissioners] has been pretty good about retaining our 'no-growth area' right now," he said in 1997, "with the exception of those large, major projects which have economies of scale, and the bucks behind them. Of course, when they do build something, it just blows us all to hell anyway."

The introduction of gigantic new residential projects like Summerlin or Lake Las Vegas obliges planners to rip up their maps and start over. The owners of both of these developments *asked* to be annexed to adjacent cities, which are currently perceived as more hospitable to large, master-planned communities than the county is. Speaking for the county, Harris insists, "We would never have allowed Lake Las Vegas"—a $4-billion oasis of wealth slated to be built around a 320-acre artificial lake with five golf courses and six resort hotels, seventeen miles southeast of the Strip.

Harris may privately harbor no-growth ideals, but of course he can't admit to that and keep working for Clark County. Talking about the so-called second straw—a projected second pipeline from Lake Mead, designed to accommodate imagined future water needs—he confessed, "Part of me deals with the growth side, and says it'd be a great way to control growth—not to put the damn thing in." But he knows it's going to happen. The county, he says, slipping into Vegasese, is "betting on the come": budgeting for a new pipeline on the gamble that water not yet allotted will eventually arrive.

> DL: You say you "assess growth impacts," but then what can you do with your assessments? In California, people can hold up controversial new developments for years with lawsuits, and demands for environmental impact reports.

> JH: We have a different process here, a different philosophy. I take my direction from the board. I have no ability to limit growth.

> DL: You can't tell people not to come, of course. But you can make expansion difficult, as they've done in Portland [Oregon] or Boulder City.

> JH: That's not the board's direction. Their job, and therefore my job, is to accommodate growth in Las Vegas Valley. To sustain it.

> DL: So the two-million population projections—officially that doesn't bother you?

> JH: No. We look to limiting factors. We look to land availability. We've drawn a line we call the Ultimate Growth Boundary—which of course it may or may not be. It's determined by topography, administrative boundaries: Red Rock, Nellis, the bombing range, Lake Mead to the east. Within that area we still have lots of available land.

> DL: And as for water, you buy the water district's argument that "we can get it because we can pay for it"?

> JH: Yes. Money is the only limiting factor. And for many property owners here, money is not a problem. They are willing to invest millions in property and just hold on to it, earning nothing from it, betting on the future. And that tells you a lot.

It is only by metaphoric license that Las Vegas, like Los Angeles or Washington—two other American cities on which the label is frequently pinned—can be called a "company town." This country has a long history of genuine company towns, most of them originally built, owned, and controlled entirely by mining or lumber companies to provide homes and other services for the workers they needed to attract. In *The Company Town in the American West* (1966), James B. Allen describes 191 such towns, some dismantled, some abandoned and in ruins, some sold off to their residents, and some still functioning as company towns at the time, with populations of a few hundred people; these include copper-mining and smelting towns in Arizona and Nevada, lumber-mill towns in California and the Northwest, and coal-mining towns in Colorado, New Mexico, Utah, and Wyoming. In most of these towns, every house, store, utility, and public service was at one time owned by either a local entrepreneur or a large national corporation (Phelps Dodge, Kennecott Copper, Anaconda, Pacific Lumber, International Paper, Georgia-Pacific, Kaiser Steel). Some even issued their own scrip (think casino chips) to serve as money in company stores. Henderson, Nevada—now a part of Greater Las Vegas—began life as a company town; so, in a way, did Boulder City to the north. Las Vegas was originally owned by a railroad. At one time people even talked of Montana as a "company state," so great was the hold of Anaconda Copper over its legislature and newspapers. When the state legislature rejected the company's plans for a reservoir in 1969, one reporter wrote, "No one could remember an impertinence of that order before."

In eastern states, towns and cities grew up under the ownership and control of manufacturing enterprises, whose names they sometimes bore—Pullman, Illinois; Hershey and Bethlehem, Pennsylvania; Corning and Steinway, New York.

With differing degrees of benevolence and occasional gestures toward democracy, the owners of these towns were also their managers and city officials. They determined rents and regulations, hired the police, appointed the school board, and lay down moral codes regarding things like drinking and prostitution. Peddlers and solicitors were banned, and unions were unwelcome—a fact made clear by the Pullman Company strike of 1894, in which federal troops were called in to put down strikers. What is now called paternalism led some of these towns to provide hospitals, churches, and schools, parks and recreation, in addition to profitable company stores.

Allen's summary of the "intangible spirit" of a genuine company town may have a certain resonance for visitors to Las Vegas:

In the company town...there is a somewhat intangible overtone which seems to run through all phases of its life and is definitely connected with the complete dominance of a single company.... It might be described as the complete saturation by the company of the town, its inhabitants, and all its surroundings—the complete dominance of the business of the company in everything that is seen or talked about....

When visiting a typical copper town, for example, a person first drives through miles of barren desert, knowing that at the end of the narrow highway is the sole reason for the road's existence....

In many company towns the whistle at the company plant is a regular part of community life. It not only determines the shifts, which in turn regulate family life, but it also tells time and provides a curfew.... All this is only natural to the long-time resident, but the visitor cannot help observing that this illusive but veritable saturation by company business of everything is a very real and distinguishing feature in the company town.

The term "company town" has been enlarged in recent decades to signify not so much the historic, company-*owned* town—of which very few are left—as the company-*dominated* town, like Rochester, New York (Eastman Kodak), Poughkeepsie, New York (IBM), Flint, Michigan (General Motors), Homestead, Pennsylvania, and Gary, Indiana (U.S. Steel), or Midland, Michigan (Dow Chemical). It also extends to cities virtually created by large government installations, like Huntsville, Alabama, and Los Alamos, New Mexico.

Such cities were in the news frequently between the 1970s and 1990s, because of the disastrous social and economic effects they suffered from slowdowns, cutbacks, and in some cases total shutdowns of the dominant powers. Two hundred fifty American textile plants closed during the 1980s, bringing devastation to many eastern and southern cities and towns. The once-mighty American steel industry laid off 70 percent of its employees between 1950 and 1995, wreaking havoc on places like Steelton and Bethlehem, Pennsylvania. The near-fatal impact of General Motors' shutdown in Flint became the subject of Michael Moore's hostile 1989 documentary *Roger and Me*—Roger being Roger Smith, the elusive CEO of General Motors. Butte, Montana proposed making a grim tourist attraction out of the slag heaps and polluted open pits left after nearly a century of ownership and exploitation by Anaconda Copper and its successors. Many of Rochester's cultural institutions, founded by and kept afloat on Eastman Kodak largess, bear the name of the city's longtime economic protector (The Eastman School of Music, The George Eastman House, The Eastman-Rochester Orchestra), and suffered along with the city when Kodak radically downsized in the 1980s.

■ ■ ■

Las Vegas should most accurately be called a "single-industry town," along the lines of Lowell and Lawrence (textile mills), Brockton (shoes), Pittsburgh (steel), Detroit (cars), Akron (tires), Grand Rapids (furniture), Toledo (glass), Peoria (tractors), or Hartford (insurance). Its dominant industry—gambling, and servicing gamblers—is divided among about a dozen owners or co-owners of major Strip hotels and a few locally based or family-owned off-Strip companies, backed up by slot-machine manu- facturers and similar adjuncts. But single-industry towns are no less vul- nerable to the fickle winds and whims of the global economy than single-company towns. (Detroit is the glaring example, but Houston lost more than 200,000 jobs during the 1980s oil crisis.) As Clark County school superintendent Brian Cram likes to say, "The casinos are our steel mills." This is where his high-school students look for jobs; this is the sacred cow all Nevada politicians treat with deference; this is the industry Las Vegas depends on for its survival.

Because of the horror stories of the 1980s and the legends of industrial tyranny identified with places like Pullman and Lowell, the phrase "com- pany town" has become a term of abuse. Few grown-up cities want to be thought of as single-company (or even single-industry) towns. Economists and bankers advise them to "diversify" as a cushion against future shocks.

"The company town is a fundamentally flawed economic organism," wrote a *Business Week* reporter of Poughkeepsie in 1995 ("The Town IBM Left Behind"). "Dominant employers foster dependency in their commu- nities, dulling the incentive to take risks." "Company towns," wrote William Fulton ("On the Manifest Destiny of Vegas," *Governing*, October 1995), "only grow beyond their roots when the politicians stop giving the company everything it wants."

■ ■ ■

Las Vegas's best-known newspaper columnists, Jon Ralston and John L. Smith of the *Review-Journal* and Mike O'Callaghan (a former two-term governor) and Jeff German of the *Sun*, are not afraid to take on the over- whelming political influence of the Industry, and the timidity or impo- tence of most elected officials in addressing it. In fact, like many Las Vegans, they sometimes seem almost cynically resigned to both situations. "There are a few forces in the city, but the one that moves the mountains, the one that makes the sun rise, is the gaming industry," says Smith. "The Industry is ubiquitous. The movie industry doesn't have one-tenth the clout in L.A. that the Industry has here."

Does the gaming industry control an excess of political power in Clark County? In the spring of 1997, I posed that question to a number of well-educated Las Vegans.

"Ask the state's governor, Steve Wynn, what he thinks. Of course gaming controls an excess of political power in Clark County!"

"The gaming industry controls the political system, absolutely. Thus, it is responsible for most of the negative manifestations of life in Clark County."

"Oil controls Alaska as gaming controls Nevada, and that will never change."

"The gaming industry not only controls an excess of political power in Clark County, it has spread its behind-the-scenes tentacles to such entertainment and basic household resource centers as favorite NFL-team sports bars and supermarket slots."

"Obviously. Politicians support contributors, resulting in gaming having significant control."

"The fact that the city won't press annexation of the county and take responsibility for the Strip is evidence that the city doesn't believe it has the power or strength to impact the industry."

Others cited non-gambling constituencies that held what they believed to be equal or comparable political influence and power: the Mormons, the unions, the mining interests. "I believe the land developers have a firmer grip on local politics than the gaming corporations, which are often remotely headquartered."

Still others regarded the proposition as true, but in no way surprising, unique, or even improper. "Why not? It's the major industry." "Unfortunately true; where there is money there is power." "Money talks." "Although not admirable, it is hardly surprising."

"Our economic base is gaming and tourism. Without it we cannot support the community, there would be no reason for Las Vegas."

"Obviously: without gaming Nevada would be the poorest state in the Union. Except for gaming all we have is a little farming, ranching (BLM [The U.S. Bureau of Land Management] controls the vast majority of land), mining, military (particularly bombing and gunnery ranges), and, perhaps, nuclear-waste disposal."

"Yes, it is true—but he who pays the piper calls the tune—see Detroit and automobiles, Bay Area and hi-tech industry, Portland and timber, etc. Why would it be any different here? Gaming is the reason this city exists and the political landscape is heavily influenced by gaming. Is it excessive? No, in my opinion." (From the vice-president for public relations at a major casino-hotel.)

Letters to the editors of the local daily and weekly papers suggest that many Las Vegans are suspicious of the political clout of the casinos, just as citizens elsewhere are suspicious of the power and influence of wealthy businessmen and corporations in their communities. But apart from such predictable expressions of opinion, is there any evidence that the gambling industry does, in fact, exert the kind of control over Las Vegas one identifies with the proprietors of a company town?

■ ■ ■

Businesspeople from outside Nevada are often surprised to learn how quickly and readily building permits are granted in Las Vegas for multi-thousand-room hotels and additions, with little or no demand for the kind of "environmental-impact reports" their builders would be obliged to offer elsewhere. Although regulations and inspections were tightened after a series of disastrous, image-blackening hotel fires in the early 1980s, these thirty- to fifty-story towers are still approved, erected, and opened for business with remarkable speed. New hotels, moreover, seem consistently able to persuade the county planning commission to build new access roads for them, to condemn lesser properties to accommodate them, to alter building codes, or to block off or reroute existing streets.

The struggle for control of the sidewalks along and intersecting Las Vegas Boulevard South offers an interesting illustration of the power of the larger hotels. In 1993 MGM Grand persuaded the county commissioners to declare the sidewalk alongside its hotel private property in return for an easement guaranteeing public access—an agreement the hotel has felt free to amend in order to keep away "undesirable" members of the public, such as strikers, sidewalk vendors, and sex-industry leafleters.

In 1994, the hotel demanded that Culinary Union picketers be arrested for trespassing on its sidewalk. Obliging the hotel, Metro police arrested more than five hundred strikers. When a Nevada deputy attorney general protested these provisions as unconstitutional, he was asked to resign; when he refused, he was fired.

In 1992, Mirage Resorts asked for and obtained from the county planning commissioners permission to build bleachers on "their" sidewalk (in front of the Treasure Island Hotel) to accommodate viewers of the popular "volcano," which erupts every 90 minutes after dark—despite the bottleneck it would create in pedestrian traffic. "Someone else will have to worry about the traffic," owner Steve Wynn told the pliable commissioners, who later narrowed the busy boulevard for a pedestrian path behind the bleachers so that people could still walk by during eruptions. Three years later, Mirage Resorts got the state Department of Transportation (backed by the Attorney General) to relinquish control of the sidewalk altogether so that they could ban T-shirt vendors and leafleters who might compete with their show, or lower the tone of their piece of the Strip. Las Vegas hotel-security forces have the right to detain people they regard as obnoxious from *in front of* as well as inside their properties. In 1997, the owner of the former Sands Hotel property (now the Venetian) asked the planning commission to declare the sidewalk in front of *his* planned hotel private as well. It is hard to imagine department stores, theaters, office buildings, or hotels in New York or Chicago being allowed to negotiate agreements like these.

In general, the "understanding" between the major casino-hotels of Las Vegas and the city and county police appears to favor the former automatically in any disputes with people they regard as bad news. After nine hundred strikers were arrested during a two-month strike against the hotels in 1984, one union leader protested, "From judges to cops, the state was completely aligned with the casino owners." Casinos have the right to eject or bar anyone from their premises for any reason (including being clever enough to win regularly at blackjack) and to detain undesirables in their own lock-up rooms until the police arrive. The state attorney general will pursue visitors accused of cheating at cards or writing bad checks across state lines on the casinos' behalf in efforts to obtain repayment or extradition.

In almost every Las Vegas-based political race in recent years—for city, county, state, or national congressional office—casino owners have provided about half the campaign funds for winning candidates. The point, insists Richard Bunker, chief spokesman for the major casinos since 1987, is not to influence legislation directly, but to buy access. "When I interview a candidate, I don't say, 'You must vote for me on every issue that I bring to you. I want you to know that my contribution to you gives me one thing, and that's access. I know the time constraints in Carson City [the state capitol, where the legislature meets only for five months every other year]. I want to be able to tell you I need ten minutes, or thirty minutes. If I cannot persuade you of the merits of what I'm doing in that time, I do not expect you to support me.'"

And yet Bunker also declared that the Nevada Resort Association—the casino owners' lobbying group, of which he is president—is about to get tougher with what it perceives as unsympathetic politicians. "Early on, if people were really objectionable to what we're trying to do, we would try to defeat them in elections," he says. "And we were successful." He described the ways by which his late, legendary partner, lobbyist Jim Joyce, used to apply muscle to legislators and "take care" of candidates—which sometimes meant taking them out of office. "The ninety-seven session has brought me to the reality that it was time to go back to playing the way we had to play before. We've already put the word out with the two state senators that we will not support them. And I believe that because of that, to a large measure, one of them is talking about running for something else, and one of them is talking about not running."

Although the Nevada Resort Association does not itself make campaign contributions, it will be very explicit in its advice to its member properties—which include almost all the major casino-hotels in Nevada—about where *their* donations should go. "We are going out and taking a very firm position in any number of races," Bunker said.

Of course, other interested groups, like the Culinary Union and the Southern Nevada Homebuilders Association, do the same thing, but no other group has the resources or persuasive powers of the assembled owners of the casino-hotels. In 1996, the Culinary Union mounted a successful campaign to defeat an incumbent state senator who was also an anti-union hotel owner; in 1998, the union's efforts were influential in a number of races. But the general perception in Clark County is that *no one* has a chance of winning or holding onto elected office without the support of the Industry. Even offending an industry leader like Stephen Wynn (whose sensitivity to offense, and taste for litigation, have helped make him one of Las Vegas's more colorful overlords) can spell the end of a political career. "In Nevada," wrote columnist John L. Smith in his biography of Wynn—for which his publisher was sued—"a few politicians survive more than one campaign without the blessing, and the financial backing, of the state's largest industry." He cited the case of Jan Laverty Jones, the mayor of Las Vegas, who decided to run for governor in 1994. "She criticized a couple of gaming people—gaming attorneys—for the so-called 'fixed' nature of the system, and said some things that I consider quite accurate. But she changed her tune very shortly. She was basically hounded into silence, and ended up losing the election by a very large number." (Mayor Jones lost another race for governor in 1998.)

The Nevada Resort Association expects the positions of elected officials (including judges) to mirror its own as closely as possible on such issues as gaming taxes, building permits, hotel and casino regulation, traffic access, and keeping the Strip (and at least the relevant blocks of

Fremont Street) clear of undesirables—picketers, prostitutes, drug dealers, teenagers, vendors, beggars, and leafleters. In recent years, association lobbyists have persuaded the state legislature to vote for a strict limit on the punitive damages that can be awarded to guests injured in their premises, and to restrict the number of new casinos that can be built, with exceptions for casinos currently proposed for properties owned by their members and friends. With the help of a congressman from California, the association won in 1997 a long-sought $160 million interchange at Barstow (a notorious bottleneck for tourists from southern California). It is always pushing for expanded terminals, gates, and runways at McCarran Airport. Both of these efforts are intended to ease and increase the flow of gamblers to Las Vegas. But the association remains ever alert against the imposition of new taxes or regulations. It lost a fight against a ¼-cent raise in sales taxes to pay for new water resources in 1996-98.

■ ■ ■

Each of the chapters that follow was intended to examine one aspect of life in Las Vegas away from the Strip and Downtown. But no matter how far removed the subject, reference to these places often turned out to be impossible to avoid. It is on the Strip, after all, that many immigrants from Mexico find jobs. It is here that teenagers cruise; that union members work or picket; that security guards keep watch. When all the reports were in, I was struck by the degree to which the heavy hand of the Industry controlled virtually every area of life in Las Vegas Valley.

Most of the crimes committed (or deterred) inside casinos are under the control of the city's hundreds of private security guards, who compose an army four times the size of the county police force. But the burdens placed on the Metro Police are considerably increased by the nature of casino visitors, both criminals and their victims. In no other American city does so much actual cash float so freely about. In her essay on police and security guards, Heather World describes a popular trick played on tourists at McCarran Airport, in which a pair of thieves surrounds an unwitting victim at the X-ray conveyor belt and delays the tourist long enough to snatch a suitcase or bag. "This is Las Vegas!" detectives Kevin Johnson and Keith Blascoe of Metro's tourist-safety unit exclaim in unison. "People come here to gamble," says Johnson, "to double their money. They've always got a couple of thousand U.S. on them."

Teenagers are not legally allowed to gamble, or even to linger on the sidewalks of the Strip after 9 PM. If they risk either diversion, they may find themselves hustled out of casinos by vigilant security guards or sent on their way by cruising Metro police. But those whose job it is to worry about local teenagers claim that their problems are intimately tied up with the unnatural work hours, the transient workforce, and the unusual values of a gambling-based city. Young residents often feel that Las Vegas is so fixated on selling adult entertainment to adult customers that it doesn't even want them around. A local family therapist told Marie Sanchez, "People come here to work and get caught up in gambling very early. This is what we do best here and it's very seductive. Adults gamble, lose money, then lose their job in this right-to-fire town. Then their family goes. That's what causes a lot of suicide and depression...."

"This town assimilates its own. A twenty-one year old client of mine was thinking of getting out. But his mother, who is high up in a casino here, got him a job as a valet parking cars. He's making sixty thousand dollars a year—to park cars! I don't see him leaving. Las Vegas kids will grow up and become part of the industry, and they'll continue to perpetuate generations of Las Vegas kids who grow up and assimilate back into the structure. They'll continue to perpetuate the things this town needs to support its economic base" ("Growing Up in Las Vegas").

Although many older Las Vegans we talked to—particularly the better-off and better educated—insist that they have nothing to do with the city's casino culture ("We sometimes go for the shows"), many residents admit that neighborhood casinos have become the senior centers of choice for thousands of local elderly people. As Michelle Ling explains in "Bingo!," small-stakes gambling, particularly at bingo, video poker, and quarter slots, has become an essential part of life of a great many Las Vegans over sixty-five. It provides them with friendly company, free transportation, cheap food, and a degree of entertainment and excitement that to them seem worth every quarter they lose, infinitely preferable to the county's senior centers or staying at home watching TV. One well-known professor at the University of Nevada at Las Vegas (UNLV)—whose aged mother loved taking the free shuttles to Sam's Town—insisted that the greatest value of many neighborhood casinos was, in fact, their function as social centers for old people living alone. He told me of one old dear who had become such a pet of the dealers, runners, and waitresses at her favorite casino that many of them showed up at her funeral.

Neighborhood casinos, which remain largely unknown to visitors familiar with the legendary establishments on the Strip and Downtown, have become a substantial part of the Industry. In 1997, the larger neighborhood casinos—particularly the Boulder, Palace, Sunset, and Texas Station Hotels, along with Sam's Town to the south and the Santa Fe to

the north—were showing greater profit increases than many of their better-known brothers. The casinos at Sam's Town, on the Boulder Highway,
and at the handsome new Sunset Station, in Henderson, are larger and
more profitable than most of their counterparts in town. In late 1997, billboards along I-95 tempted locals to a new neighborhood casino by asking,
"Are you Tired of the Strip Too?"

The Hispanic immigrants who throng to Las Vegas in search of work,
as Bill Dauber points out in "El Pueblo de Las Vegas," have rarely been
able to break into high-paying building-trade union jobs, let alone upper-
level, high-visibility positions in the big hotels. But they now represent
the largest single group among the tens of thousands of low-echelon,
back-of-the-house hotel workers: maids, porters, dishwashers, bus boys,
janitors, stock clerks, laborers, and the like. Such jobs may be looked down
on by unemployed black or white workers, but they usually represent an
economic step up for Mexican Americans and their neighbors from south
of the border.

Those who report on such groups as labor unions, homeless people,
teenagers, and the city's black population learned how Las Vegas's all-
absorbing concern for its "image" can affect such people's lives. They
learned of the degree to which politicians, police, and hotel managers will
collaborate to keep the Strip "visitor-friendly," which means, among other
things, cleared of panhandlers, protesters, and local teenagers—particularly black and Hispanic teenagers—who might frighten out-of-town
gamblers away.

A counselor from a community health center said, "Ninety percent of
my clients have gambling and alcohol problems. Drugs, meth, cocaine.
Heroin is starting to come back. Gambling is one of the ways to raise
money for this. Just being around the casinos they have access to free alcohol." Those who work to find jobs for the poor worry that the first day's
wages will be lost to the lure of the casinos. "All you need is four or five
bucks converted into quarters and there's this fantasy of hitting the jackpot" (Malcolm Garcia, "Down and Out in Vegas").

Other phenomena covered in the pages that follow are related not so
much to the gambling industry as to the remarkable fact of "boomtown"
growth itself, a condition Las Vegas shares with a number of other cities of
the American Sunbelt. These include such issues as the rapid surge in new
residential housing; a school system unable to cope with tidal waves of
troubled new students; the fundamental problem of providing water for
millions of people moving into a desert; and new nondenominational
churches that are trying to supply everything these people have lost, or left
behind.

So although most people in this "company town" do not work for the company, and may even pretend to ignore it, is obvious that the economic power of the gambling industry lies behind both Clark County's extraordinary growth and the combination of prosperity, misery, and chaos that has come in its wake. If nothing else, the constant public clamor to have the Industry subsidize a greater share of growth-related costs suggests that local citizens regard its role as central, like that of the all-powerful courts of seventeenth-century England and France. This is where the power and wealth are centered; so this is where decisions must be made. Many people believe that "casino values" have affected tens of thousands of people who have never set foot in a casino. The establishments aligned with the Nevada Resort Association and the Fremont Street Experience have made major efforts to rid their sidewalks and premises of prostitutes; and yet most Las Vegans still regard the gambling industry and the sex industry of Clark County as intimately related.

THE VOICE OF THE MIDDLE CLASS

One risk of this project was that, in focusing on what seemed to us especially interesting groups of people (adolescents and old people, sex workers and the indigent, Westside blacks and north-side Hispanics), institutions (like the new non-denominational "megachurches"), or problems (the 24-hour work cycle, overstretched schools, an endangered water supply), we would end up ignoring the opinions and concerns of the majority of Las Vegans. Within this majority are a great many contented middle-class citizens who insist that, apart from the Strip and Downtown—which are really "just for tourists"—Las Vegas is a "town like any other," full of good-hearted, hard-working family people who are active in churches and community organizations, who work for a great number of good causes, and whose children join the Scouts and play Little League ball. Except in angry letters to the editor written in defense of their city—and few people I have met in this country are as defensive as the Las Vegas middle class—such people are rarely heard from in articles or books about the city. We hear from Steve Wynn and the hookers, Wayne Newton and Local 226, Mike Tyson and the high-rollers who fly into town for his fights; but very little from the people who fill up the new housing projects, golf courses, shopping malls, and churches.

Most of us did talk to civic leaders and satisfied citizens. But a deep-rooted hostility to or suspicion of Las Vegas was not always easy for us to overcome. In an attempt to counteract this, and add some balance to our report, I wrote early in 1997 to some four hundred Berkeley alumni residents in Clark County, describing our project and inviting their participation. About a hundred replied, including (with their spouses) fourteen attorneys, eight UNLV professors, seven doctors (and a medical-center manager), seven real-estate brokers or appraisers, five reporters or writers, five school teachers or counselors, three engineers, three people in the insurance business, two clergymen, two Howard Hughes executives, two casino executives (and a retired blackjack dealer), two architects, two family therapists, a psychiatric nurse, a stagehand at Cirque du Soleil, an artist, a banker, a Department of Energy scientist, an ostrich farmer, a librarian, a medical secretary, a golf-course marketer, a computer salesman (specializing in casino sales), a geologist, a retired air-force officer, an "investor," and a deputy district attorney. Among these were a large number of retired people and housewives active in volunteer roles. In March we met with fifty of these people at the Gold Coast Hotel.

Even among these willing aides, graduates of our own university, we encountered the suspicion of and hostility toward outside examiners that might be expected from the citizens of a maligned and often caricatured city. One attorney warned us in advance, "We Las Vegans tend to be somewhat skeptical of participation in such projects because we have been the subjects of so many studies by outsiders intent on ratifying their predetermined conclusions…. Your students may love us or hate us, but they will not be able to ignore the vibrance and potential we presently enjoy." "Remember," wrote a native-born civic leader, "real people live here!"

Several of these people complained about the distorting fixation of the national media on casino-hotels and gambling, and Las Vegas's persistent Sin City image. "No, we don't all live on The Strip. No, we don't all have a gambling problem. Yes, we do put up Christmas lights. Basically, this is a normal community with all the problems and pleasures of any large city."

There seems to be no question that living in Las Vegas generates a kind of prickly defensiveness against criticism from outside—even though, as we shall see, locals are quick to criticize the city themselves. Decades of movies, TV shows, and popular books and articles about mobsters, crime, gross taste, and sleazy sex have created an international image that even new residents of Las Vegas have to deal with. One public-interest attorney, who moved here after 34 years in San Diego, listed as one of the major problems facing Las Vegas "gaining social acceptance from outside Nevada." When presented with some of the statistics cited above (on crime, suicide, child abuse, bankruptcy, divorce, and other signs of social dysfunction), many Las Vegans simply countered that things were no better elsewhere, and often a great deal worse. (The cities most often cited as "worse" were New York, Washington, Chicago, and Los Angeles.) These people may well have been unaware or in denial of the facts, or extrapolating from their own relatively safe and comfortable enclaves. "They [the ignorant reporters from outside] don't realize that in the suburban neighborhoods it may as well be Phoenix, Tucson, Albuquerque, or any other southwest city." As for the sneered-upon excesses of the Strip, these may come down to nothing more than a difference in taste. "Las Vegas's tackiness," wrote a UNLV professor, is "worn as a badge of pride."

"We have none of the problems of older cities with inner-city generations of social problems," wrote a particularly defensive civic booster (Cal '63), director of a large neighborhood casino-hotel and former regent of the University of Nevada. "Most of our problems with violence are imported from Los Angeles gangs looking for new markets for drugs.... The high-profile characters who come to town for sporting events draw undesirables who add to our negative publicity (e.g., Tupac Shakur).... All of the negative attributes given to Las Vegas are found in all other large cities in the U.S." "The city without high crime, prejudice, and dysfunctional government should cast the first stone," wrote a retired artist who once lived in Manhattan, where she felt the effects of street crime and racial prejudice. "New York has these problems in spades. Almost every big city has such problems."

What is it that drew them to Las Vegas, and what keeps them here, these proud and sensitive middle-class Las Vegans? My respondents ranged in age from about twenty-five to eighty-two; their median graduation year from Berkeley was 1969. There were very few natives, but then Las Vegas had a population of only about twenty thousand when my average respondent was born. The reasons most of them moved here initially (other than to retire) were almost always job- or income-related. Their companies or government agencies had transferred them, or downsized; the architecture (or building, or banking) industry had dried up in San Diego or Honolulu; they were eager (or desperate) for a new job; they could earn more money (teaching, selling insurance, practicing law) in Las Vegas than they could in their previous home. A few cited the heady challenge of working in a wide-open, go-ahead town. The basic attractions most often cited were the climate; the lower taxes and cost of living generally; the "excitement" and available entertainment; the friendly people; the positive attitude towards business; and the ease of escape to other places.

Almost everyone talked or wrote about the weather. Warm winters were stressed by retirees from the East and Midwest. A former Bay Area resident raved about the warm summer evenings, when she could float in her pool by moonlight. A desert-loving artist—who obviously lives some distance from the Strip—grew poetic in praise of the atmosphere:

> Las Vegas has well over a hundred magic days each year—i.e., little or no humidity with a temperature that could be up to 85 and still be comfortable. Fully 80 percent of the sunsets are wonderful. The air is still; it's so quiet you can hear the chirping of the critters as dusk approaches. The sky goes from pale blue to deepest blue black; the moon is huge and just over there, and you can actually see a sky full of stars.

Interestingly, almost as many people—often the same people—listed the appalling summer heat (105-110° days are not uncommon) as one of the least attractive aspects of life in Las Vegas: a good reason to visit relatives back home, or at least stay indoors with the air-conditioning on high.

Almost everyone who answered my questions cited "lower taxes" as a major reason for moving to or remaining in Las Vegas. Nevada has no state income tax (a situation enjoyed by residents of Alaska, Florida, South Dakota, Texas, Washington, and Wyoming as well). Its 7-percent sales tax, however—something one rarely hears mentioned—is the fifth-highest in the nation (seven states have no sales tax at all). Homeowners almost inevitably insist that they pay comparatively low property taxes, get more home for their money than homeowners elsewhere, and enjoy a generally lower cost of living; but that depends on what they're comparing themselves with. Las Vegas is indeed cheaper for most people to live in than Los Angeles, San Diego, or San Francisco; but in 1995 the American Chamber of Commerce found the cost-of-living index and the average price of a new home higher in Las Vegas than in most other southwestern cities.

Along with Las Vegans' professed pleasure at their low tax burden goes their realization that the casinos are paying most of their public-works bills. A 6.25-percent tax on gambling profits—a rate far lower than any other state's—pays more than a third of Nevada's annual expenses. A number of people I talked to conceded glumly that taxes would probably have to be raised soon, if Clark County was to pay for many desperately needed things—primarily water, schools, better roads, and improved local services made necessary by the runaway growth of the last twenty years. But they are of several minds on the question of where those revenues should come from.

> Our property taxes are lower than they would be without gaming. But it would be better if our government and schools were LESS dependent on gaming and we had higher taxes.... At some point, homeowners will have to pay more.

The ultimate beneficiary, the gaming industry, should bear the burden…If gaming wants to be the only game in town, let them pay…. There will have to be a modest general increase in hotel-casino tax support.

Make builders pay impact fees for new developments' roads, schools, sewers, fire and police…. Make all new growth pay for its own infrastructure…Longtime residents resent increased taxation to pay for growth they don't want, schools they don't want.

To some degree, the same ambiguity underlies praise for what new residents—particularly former Californians, who make up more than 40 percent of them—regard as the more "affordable" cost of housing, food, and other things in Las Vegas. They praise the casinos, in particular, for providing inexpensive meals and entertainment, subsidized by the gambling losses of others. But when I asked them if my wife and I should consider leaving Berkeley and moving to Las Vegas when we retired, many local citizens were taken aback. Retiring to Las Vegas, they felt, made sense primarily for less adventurous or less imaginative older people on fixed incomes, who were able to sell up in California and get more house for their money in Vegas: for them, the warmer weather, the lower taxes, the cheaper housing, the golf, the sense of security, and the cheap entertainment were enough. "But if you can maintain your life style in San Francisco in a satisfactory manner, I cannot see why in the world you would want to live here…. I wouldn't cast aside anything you are comfortable and happy with until you are sure you would be as happy here." This banker from Northern California added, "I know of some people who retired here from the Midwest and hated it so much they eventually went back to their snowdrifts and tornadoes."

Although a surprising number of the business, professional, and retired people we met insisted that they never gamble, and try to avoid the Strip altogether, others admit that they love the excitement, the 24-hour lifestyle, the entertainment provided by the casinos. "It's a lot of fun living here," wrote a sixty-three-year-old housewife and substitute teacher. "There are not enough hours in the day to take advantage of all the fun things to do, many of which are free. And then there so many exciting personalities coming to town to entertain."

Bishop Daniel Walsh, who came here in 1987 to lead the Catholic diocese of Las Vegas after twenty-five years of service in California, admits that he misses the convenience of 24-hour stores when he returns to San Francisco for a visit. Like the Convention and Visitors Authority, some citizens really do believe that Las Vegas is "the entertainment capital of the world," and are thrilled by the presence of so many resident and visiting performers. Some recreational gamblers are candid about the joy they take in the ready availability of their favorite games, and the added plea-sure of getting free meals or shows in return for their investments. But most of those who cite gambling as one of the city's "attractions" insist that they are not among those attracted.

A few of the Berkeley alumni in Las Vegas agreed with what we had heard from local social workers, teachers, counselors, and psychiatrists: that the city's constant influx of new residents, its constant rebuilding and expansion, its gambling-based economy, and its huge 24-hour service-sec-tor workforce made it difficult to maintain or establish any sense of "com-munity."

> We're nearly all from somewhere else [wrote a 38-year-old Strip casino executive from Northern California, who had lived in Las Vegas for six years] and have family ties, loyalties, etc. in other states and cities…. Our community is adding people at such a furious rate, it is tough to come together. When people are unsure how long they will stay, whether they'll like it or find success here, I believe roots are put down in a very tentative way, and may not really be sunk for years—or until another generation of family grows up. Time will tell. I suspect California was much like this a hundred years ago.

But many of our sample group disagreed. The civically active director of an off-Strip casino was especially adamant: "There are probably more 'community' organizations in Las Vegas per capita than in any other city in the U.S.," she wrote. "This is probably one of the most community-minded and generous cities in the *world*. This city doesn't know the mean-ing of the phrase 'We can't do it.'" She went on to list a wide and active array of service clubs, volunteer programs, sports activities, and churches. There is, she insisted, "no better place to live, work, and retire." We were frequently told how generous and open Las Vegans were—*away* from the tourist center. "People away from the Strip fairly outdo themselves to show you just how friendly they are." (And yet, this same person wrote, you may scarcely know your next-door neighbors, because they come and go so often.)

There remains among residents a wide, even bitter division of opinion on this question of community. We held a dinner in December 1996 at an off-Strip French restaurant to hear opinions on the city's problems and prospects from local journalists, politicians, and professors. The discussion over coffee and dessert exploded into an angry dispute over whether or not Las Vegas had a "soul." ("This city has a black hole where its soul ought to be," declared one local writer/reporter—a comment that drew down the wrath of Myrna Williams, a feisty county commissioner who had lived here for thirty-seven years.) Master-planned communities like Summerlin and Green Valley clearly work hard to create a sense of community within their walls (one has only to read their chirpy newsletters) but not everyone enjoys that kind of regulated neighborliness. Residents of long standing feel, or perhaps have created around them, a far greater sense of community than newcomers. One old-timer, in fact, blamed "all these new people from the East" for destroying the traditional Nevadan-Western frontier ideals of hospitality and politeness. Retirees, day-shift workers, and people who feel settled in their homes and jobs obviously see this issue differently than swing- and night-shift workers (of which Las Vegas has so many); workers insecure in their jobs; or people who change addresses—and watch their children change schools—every year. Some cite the presence of Nellis Air Force Base, UNLV, even "Saturday-night craps at your favorite neighborhood casino" as valuable nodes of community building in a transient, ever-spreading town. The local Boy Scout council, with 22,000 scouts and 5,500 volunteer adult leaders, is one of the largest in the nation; 9,500 children participate in Boys and Girls Clubs, 7,250 in Girl Scouts, and many more in the athletic programs of the Clark County Department of Parks and Recreation.

We heard over and over of the vitality of the churches of Las Vegas—in particular, of "my" church or synagogue, which for many recent residents (see chapter 9) has become the single most important force in their lives. Although most of those who identified their denomination were mainstream Protestants, a sense also emerged that the presence of so many family-centered and morally disciplined Mormons and Catholics helped to create the strong sense of community they craved.

People in business praise Las Vegas (as they do Clark County and Nevada) for its "excellent business climate," by which they mean fewer taxes and regulations than they would have to put up with in California or Arizona—a point the Nevada Development Authority makes with hammering insistence when trying to entice businesses from elsewhere to relocate in Clark County. "The thing that really makes Las Vegas great," one small businessman told our spring banquet, "is its entrepreneurial spirit." He was proud of the hundreds of strip-mall shops, he insisted, and the hundreds of small-scale building contractors, because each one indicated a brave new adventurer in the free-market sea of Clark County. "The government is off your back, the mindset is open to new ideas, the elected officials have a vision of economic progress."

Many residents blessed Las Vegas for being easy to escape, and within ready reach of more-attractive places. These desirable other places range from nearby attractions like Lake Mead, Red Rock Canyon, and Mt.

Charleston to the ski resorts of Lake Tahoe, Mammoth Mountain, and Utah; Grand Canyon and Zion National Parks; other southwestern desert regions; and "real" cities like Phoenix, Salt Lake City, Los Angeles, and San Diego. (How many people living in these cities, I wonder, would list as one of their advantages their proximity to Las Vegas?) On the other hand, residents of other cities might well envy Las Vegans their easy access to a large and reasonably efficient airport, and the number and relative cheapness of daily flights to and from so many U.S. destinations—a boon provided by and for the resort and gambling industry, of course.

Among other reasons cited for moving to or remaining happily in Las Vegas were the cultural and sports opportunities, about which opinions differ; the unlikelihood of floods, earthquakes, tornadoes, blizzards, and snow; the "safe, secure neighborhoods" (some retirement communities, like Sun City-Summerlin, have particularly passionate advocates); the golf courses; the school system ("A lot of parents complain, but they should try other school systems!"); and the city's "small-town" feeling.

■ ■ ■

There is no reason to suspect or distrust these claims of contentment. Those who say they enjoy the job opportunities and low taxes of Las Vegas, the natural as well as the economic climate, the churches and schools and libraries and cultural events and community activities, are not fooling themselves, or speaking in bad faith: they are telling the truth. You can live a reasonably happy life in Las Vegas, whether or not you make use of the tourist center.

One rhetorical excess to which these good people are often driven, however, is to assert that, precisely because of its churches and schools, its Boy Scout troops and Little League teams, Las Vegas is "just like any other city." It is not. If not precisely a company town, Las Vegas still very much a one–industry town, not all that different from Detroit or Pittsburgh in their heyday. As the industry goes, so goes Las Vegas.

It seemed arrogant at the time, but Steve Wynn was right to mock the pretensions of "economic diversification" represented by the opening of the Levi Strauss distribution center in 1996, of which the Development Authority seemed inordinately proud. "You would have thought the Hoover Dam was being built again," he said. "The party they threw was so disproportionate to the amount of people hired, but everybody was so happy. And the rolling thunder that accompanied the arrival of

Citibank—oh, my God, it was like, Hallelujah!" Levi Strauss hired about four hundred people. Citibank's credit-card operation in Las Vegas hired sixteen hundred employees. Mirage Resorts Inc. has more than twenty-five thousand.

Like every thinking Las Vegan, Steve Wynn knows perfectly well what makes Las Vegas different from other American cities. He knows who pays the bills and who (therefore) calls the shots. Every doctor, lawyer, architect, clergyman, banker, real-estate developer, teacher, grocery clerk, carpenter, prostitute, and drug dealer in Las Vegas ultimately depends for survival on the people who lose their money gambling on the Strip and Downtown—and, increasingly, in outlying neighborhoods as well. In most cases, the ordinary—or at least ordinary college-educated—citizens I talked and wrote to were as quick to find fault with their city as any prejudiced and unthinking outsider might be. "Basically," wrote one candid citizen, "the 'Sin City' perception is not a mislabel. Gaming (greed), sex, and alcohol dominate the community."

The most serious problem confronting the city and county is what most residents regard as totally unplanned growth. The growth is not, of course, totally unplanned, as we have seen: both city and county have large staffs of dedicated and conscientious planners. But their best advice and intentions are frequently overridden by elected politicians and the two industries—casino-hotels and property development—politicians attend to with greatest respect. A minority of my respondents profess to find the rapid growth "exciting," a way to keep the economy "vibrant." Most free-market businesspeople resist the idea of placing any controls or limits on growth, like the "ring around the valley" proposed (and killed) in the state legislature in 1997. Such measures would be "inconsistent with the spirit of entrepreneurialism." (How quickly Las Vegans pick up the word "entrepreneur" and its derivatives!) Others may dream of growth limits but concede that they are politically impossible given the power structure of southern Nevada—"the last outpost of the Wild West," as one person called it. "Nothing but the marketplace will ever limit the growth of casinos." Most educated Las Vegans simply rail against the runaway expansion of the last ten years, without any clear idea how to stop or control it. "Where else does the phone company publish two phone books a year in an effort to cope with turnover?"

We can't manage growth.... Too many people too quickly spells disaster.... The government can't keep up with the infrastructure and other problems.

I believe the raging growth will only be brought under control by some unanticipated disaster. Las Vegas is a desert and will not change because of development efforts.

The city's greatest problem is handling the phenomenal growth rate and the subsequent problems that creates: traffic, schools, water, public services, etc.... Population growth must be halted until these problems are solved.

Growth is out of control, first in gaming, which brings in lots of low-income workers, secondly in retirees, who don't want to support schools, parks, roads, utilities, police, etc.

The attitude that growth pays for itself—which it does not—will be our major problem in the long run.

The chaos of the last ten years drove us back to California.

So far as I know, no Las Vegas daily newspaper, no city-council member, no county commissioner, no labor union, and no major industry or professional group has ever dared publicly suggest setting limits on growth in Clark County. County commissioners lobbied aggressively against the "ring around the valley" proposed in 1997. "Any idea of 'controlled growth' is treated by the political elite as being on a par with communism," wrote one Las Vegas architect. Some people who appear to have thought seriously about growth-related problems hold out hopes for limiting them by better coordinated and more thoughtful long range planning; raising the price of water; charging developers realistic impact fees; maintaining stricter zoning requirements; and consolidating city and county governments.

The one result of Las Vegas's record growth that almost every resident mentions with disgust is the increase in traffic congestion, a complaint that may simply represent a longing for the simpler and smaller city of the past. At the right times of day, using side roads and detours, I found Las Vegas no harder to get around than, say, San Francisco or Los Angeles. But traffic tie-ups on the Strip and the major east-west boulevards can be time-consuming and frustrating; and the automobile domination of Los Angeles is precisely what many people came here to escape. The solutions proposed (better public transport; more and wider freeways; better traffic-flow management; and a monorail down the Strip, between Downtown and the airport) are unlikely to relieve a situation in which (according to a 1997 study cited by Mark Smith, former president of the Las Vegas Chamber of Commerce) eighteen new north-south lanes, and twenty new east-west lanes would have to be built by the year 2015 just to keep traffic congestion from getting *worse* than it is today. Even if such an imperial roadbuilding project made sense economically, there is simply nowhere to build that many new lanes.

The second-most-common area of complaint (or fear for the future) among local citizens regards natural resources, specifically, water and air. With regard to the continuing availability of water for this essentially bone-dry city, many citizens I spoke to cited the now-standard doomsday prediction: available sources of water (underground or Colorado River) will run up against the population wall around the year 2005, and Las Vegans who refuse to face that fact are simply "in denial." Others accept the Southern Nevada Water District's assurance that water in the West will always go to whoever is willing to pay for it, and that Las Vegas will always be wealthy enough to cut deals with ranchers and farmers, other western states, and the federal government in order to get all the water it needs. Given the latter attitude, it is not surprising that some people believe that "[Water-] conservation efforts in the state are a joke." One attorney declared, "Las Vegas lacks a community ethos that would support conservation"—and local government the guts to impose conservation rules on residents and hotels.

Air pollution and smog (the city was placed on a "severe" non-compliance alert in 1997, which could lead to major cutbacks in federal highway funding) are obviously an outgrowth of the astonishing number of cars on the roads. Although county planners I spoke to insist that the situation has improved markedly since 1990, some local residents still rail against the city's general carelessness about environmental (and the related human) realities. An architect who moved to Las Vegas in 1995 wrote,

> It has all the worst attributes of the L.A.-Orange County syndrome, i.e., Strip city with total dependence on the automobile, sprawling "slurbs" with no sense of place or belonging, high violent crime rate, energy inefficiency—total dependency on air conditioning for five-plus months; physically non-responsive to the realities of the natural environment.

Many people cite Clark County's beleaguered public schools as another major problem. They regard the local schools as inefficient, overcrowded, or simply not good enough, and fear that the situation will not improve as long as so many of their fellow citizens remain "indifferent to the importance of a quality educational system." Many simply fear that the county cannot build *enough* schools, fast enough. "Some of them are on double sessions from the first day they open their doors. Youngsters are tired of being rezoned so often [that] they go to a different school every year." Others regard Las Vegas as generally "unfriendly to children," and blame the gambling industry for high-school dropouts and low SAT scores.

> Gaming doesn't require an education beyond high school for most of its jobs, therefore quality education has a low priority.... Jobs are so easy to get [that] it is hard to keep a lot of kids in school long enough to graduate...If you earn $70,000 parking cars at a hotel (and don't pay tax on most of it), why would you encourage your children to get an education?

The question of "cultural deprivation" depends on what you regard as culture, and how important it is to your life. Some local residents accustomed to the cultural offerings of older cities profess themselves discontent. "The city badly needs a cultural center"..."[there is] a lack of cultural activities within a 200 mile radius." But to people content with Siegfried and Roy, the Liberace Museum, and the National Finals Rodeo, remarks like these may sound like the whining of East Coast or California snobs. A number of respondents professed themselves delighted with the county's new libraries and the university's classical-music series.

Snobbery does seem to underlie a number of people's critical remarks about their fellow citizens. One man complained of the "low intellectual level of the population, most of whom work in the service industries," and said that he found it "hard to meet intellectual peers." Others were disdainful of their conception of the typical residents of "adult" subdivisions, people they regarded as limited in imagination, bored and boring, obsessed with thrift, security, gossip, and their health problems. Residents of master-planned communities were regarded as isolated, self-centered, and burdened with intolerably restrictive codes designed to homogenize their building, decorating, and behavior.

> Educated persons have something of a challenge living in Las Vegas, because so many of the cultural icons appeal to the obvious and the vulgar. The professional class has in effect to isolate and inoculate itself in order to survive.

> This is basically a very blue-collar town, which could be positive or negative, depending on your perspective. It is a little more blue-collar than I would like to see.

Finally, a number of these middle-class, churchgoing Las Vegans expressed a disgust at the "low moral tone" set by the gambling industry—as if its existence came as a great surprise to them after they chose to move here.

> For those with no interest in gaming it is necessary to ignore—or actively, mentally oppose—the messages of the fast-buck culture.

> The moral tone set by the gaming industry is one of complete sleaze. It encourages people to throw away their money on the illusion of quick riches.

> People who have a weakness for gambling, who are seeking escape from unfulfilled lives, do not do well in any community where gambling is so vigorously promoted. Family life is bound to be adversely affected.

> Fundamentally, I think the industry is not eager to see improvements in the quality of life because it may detract from their operations.

It's sad to stop at a 7-11 for gasoline at 4 a.m. and see people with their quart of milk and loaf of bread going sour and stale as they put in another ten dollars.

My hope is to get out of this hellhole within the next five or ten years.

■ ■ ■

As I wrote at the outset, I originally envisioned this project as our effort to "learn more from Las Vegas"; to offer a series of lessons for other U.S. cities contemplating the turn towards a gambling-based economy. I no longer regard this as useful or even possible. Las Vegas, I have concluded, is unique, and may therefore have no lessons—economic, social, or ethical—to pass on to the rest of the country. Although incorporated in 1905, the city we see was essentially created in 1931 by and for casino gambling. Monte Carlo or Sun City, in southern Africa, may have similar stories to tell. But you cannot fairly compare the situations of Atlantic City, Biloxi, Detroit, or New Orleans; all of these cities had long histories of a mixed social and economic base, before reaching out to casino gambling in recent years. Gambling has been the *raison d'être* of Las Vegas for two-thirds of a century.

Over and over, I heard two commonplaces about Las Vegas that I now regard as equally and fundamentally wrong: first, that Las Vegas is at heart "just like any other city," and second, that the legalizing of casino gambling in some other city will turn it into "another Las Vegas." Not a chance.

THE NEVADA ATTITUDE

Beneath the uniqueness of Las Vegas lies a century-old "Nevada Attitude," or complex of attitudes, that has permitted or encouraged not only casino gambling but also legal prostitution; do-as-you-will marriage and divorce laws; a hostility to taxes or regulation; a brazen defiance of the federal government, not unlike that of Brigham Young in 1857; an indifference to environmental concerns and the downside of uncontrolled growth; the most positive possible climate for entrepreneurs of every sort, from nail polishers and strip-club owners to home builders and telemarketers; unusually free-wheeling land speculators; brazenly commercial doctors and lawyers; three decades (from the mid-1940s to the mid-1970s) of virtually unchecked dominion by organized crime; a tradition (shared by other cities) of pliant or corrupt elected politicians and police; a defiant resistance to any kind of planning; lax building codes and inspections; and an unusually cynical approach to sports, from amateur basketball to professional boxing, thanks to which people like Jerry Tarkanian and Don King have been elevated to local heroes almost on the level of Bugsy Siegel, Del Webb, Howard Hughes, Liberace, Frank Sinatra, Wayne Newton, Elvis Presley, Steve Wynn, and Siegfried Fischbacker and Roy Horn.

Many people I talked to, including native born Nevadans as well as newcomers, boast freely of this "Nevada Attitude." It is vividly demonstrated in the final chapter of this book, which deals with the anti-federalist rebel ranchers who live just north of Clark County. What interests me about this phenomenon, and hence about Las Vegas, is the broad range of feelings and beliefs it is able to encompass, few of which are exportable out of state. Insofar as it exists, the Nevada Attitude seems to include a "Don't Tread on Me" hostility to any kind of outside interference; but also a "can-do" spirit that involves a willingness to take risks and work hard, in the belief that even the most intractable problems can be solved. It embraces both a defiant acceptance (or at least a blind-eye toleration) of legalized gambling and prostitution, unfettered property speculation, and unrestricted smoking and drinking—and a social conservatism often identified with the Mormon Church.

It was the spokesman for another church, however—formerly a teacher at my old high school, near San Francisco—who expressed to me most ardently what Las Vegans admire about the spirit and energy of their fellow citizens. I will let Bishop Walsh have the last word.

Las Vegas is the finest community I've ever lived in. The nicest people I've ever met are right here in Las Vegas, the most generous people I've ever met, the most community-minded people I've ever met. This is a wonderful city, a wonderful town. It's frontier, it's new, it's like I'm sure San Francisco was like at the turn of the century, such a dynamic place. San Francisco was built on gold, and silver from Virginia City. We're building a community here on a different sort of mining. But it is a dynamic community, full of wonderful people....

The city cut our budget for housing emergency shelter by thirty thousand dollars. Well, that means that for two or three months we'd have to close the shelter. I can't make that up, nor can Catholic Charities. I made public our need, and Elaine and Steve Wynn came forward with thirty thousand. They're not of our faith, but they saw the need, and boom!

I think that's the general spirit: a can-do city. It is such an exciting city, and I find the people wonderful. Our local parishes are so totally engaged.

Of course the great challenge is growth. But I would much rather be worrying about building churches than closing them, the way they are in San Francisco. I wish you could fly a few of those surplus churches down here. With the growth we have experienced here, we built ten new churches in the last nine years—all of which the parishioners have to pay for themselves, one-third in cash, one-third in pledges, one-third as a loan from the diocesan bank which they have to pay back....

Our parish communities are *alive*; the people are alive, they're involved! I've had people come from San Francisco, and they say, 'My God, I'd like to bring my children down here—I mean, to see a real church, a vibrant church!' Most of the people are moving in—they're not native sons and daughters, there are very few of them: so there's a vibrancy in our communities, an outreach to newcomers. We had our diocesan celebration of the feast of Our Lady of Guadalupe for the Spanish-speaking community yesterday at the Shrine [the Shrine of the Most Holy Redeemer, just off the Strip, opened in 1992], and we had about fifteen hundred people there. Such a wonderful community.

■ ■ ■

Many of the interviews and much of the research for this book were conducted between December 1996 and June 1997. Although several of us have returned to Las Vegas since, and made efforts to update facts and statistics, the ages and situations of most of the people we talked to have been left as they were when we encountered them. The stately pace of book-publishing is outrun by the frantic changes of urban life, especially in a city that re-creates itself as often as Las Vegas does. But I believe that our pictures of the city remain fundamentally true.

Down and Out in Vegas

Malcolm Garcia

I follow Alan to the park. We emerge from the soup kitchen and cross the parking lot to the corner of Owens Avenue and Main Street. The afternoon glare of the Las Vegas sun hurts my eyes, and the dry air constricts my throat. Alan squints at the ground, stopping from time to time to inspect sudden flashes of light. Loose change or an aluminum-foil gum wrapper? He carries a plastic shopping bag steaming with wet clothes. We wade through sheaths of heat in what was once a shopping mall but now resembles a reservation for outcasts.

Weary-looking men and women trudge past us, accompanied by their children wedged into overstuffed shopping carts. Plastic trash bags filled with donated pastry turning green inside cellophane wrappers molder under the hot sun. Arms and legs stick out the windows of parked cars, the temporary refuge of the unemployed.

Lines of heat shimmer above the slumped bodies at rest beneath the one sign identifying this outpost: "St. Vincent's Plaza. Catholic Charities." Alan and I pause in the narrow shadow provided by the sign before we continue toward the intersection. The four corners, he calls this place: the nonprofit Strip of Las Vegas.

Most of the city's homeless services stretch around this barren township, and Alan and I join the estimated eighteen thousand homeless Las Vegans who eventually gravitate to this desolate spot. The Salvation Army operates a shelter one block up on Owens. Its motto (An Inner Voice Tells You Not To Drink Or Use Other Drugs) hangs on the wall. The MASH Crisis Center bumps against St. Vincent's men's shelter (No Shaving Or Bathing In Bathroom Sink. If Caught You'll Be 86 For The Night). The Key Foundation, a veterans' organization, opens its doors across the hall from St. Vincent's employment project (Look In The Mirror: Would You Hire This Man?), and tucked away at the intersection of Owens and Main stands Shade Tree, a women's shelter.

Traffic passes us heading south to Downtown. Most people in Las Vegas regard a car as a necessity, but with these services so centralized, we have no need for a vehicle: no reason to go anywhere but right here.

■ ■ ■

Seven years ago, the Las Vegas Metropolitan Police made sure homeless people stayed away from the Strip by routinely arresting them for offenses such as standing in front of casinos or refusing to show identification. When the city built a new library on North Las Vegas Boulevard in 1990, administrators instituted an anti-smell policy to eject homeless people hanging out in the library whose body odor was considered offensive.

You didn't need to be homeless, though, to be hassled by Las Vegas city officials, as John Farrell learned in 1989. Farrell was then working for Catholic Charities as a mental-health counselor at St. Vincent's. One weekend he and a group of friends decided to play basketball at a public court outside town.

"One of the guys went to the library and asked for a cigarette," Farrell recalled. "That's what triggered it. Someone complained and the next thing we know the police lined us up against the wall and asked for I.D.'s. They didn't take us in, but we were told to call ahead the next time we wanted to play.

"But you didn't have to go outside of Las Vegas to know what was going on. Every Friday afternoon along Fremont Street, Metro would stop home-less people. No I.D., you went to jail. You were held Friday night through Sunday to avoid the weekend tourist crowd. It was amazing."

That was then. Now, the city has translated its overt hostility into a tightly controlled containment policy. The homeless bounce between agen-cies within a limited geographic area far from the Strip and Glitter Gulch.

"Listen," said Steven Switzer, a homeless advocate who worked in Las Vegas in the early 1990s, "Las Vegas is first and foremost a tourist town. They want to create a fantasy, and they don't want any reality creeping into it."

In 1989, the ACLU brought in a dose of reality. The organization challenged the city's loitering and vagrancy laws with a lawsuit claiming they were unconstitutional. The test case involved three Franciscan friars and a lawyer, who were arrested and convicted of loitering after they questioned police officers who had arrested several homeless people in a Las Vegas city park. A federal judge struck down the loitering law as unconstitutional.

"They came in bulldozers to get rid of homeless camps," recalled Louis Vitalie, one of the Franciscan friars who was arrested. "We sat down in front of the bulldozers and were arrested. And then everybody who got arrested and charged with loitering would bring in their citation and challenge the city in court. Once we overwhelmed the court system they stopped citing people, and negotiated with us so the problem wouldn't get too much publicity."

But to some advocates, these victories were only tentative first steps, taken grudgingly by a city that remains antagonistic toward the homeless.

"For all practical purposes Las Vegas does nothing," said Terry Whitacker, director of the Community Health Center. "People are just warehoused. We're twenty years behind the times just in terms of dignity. Everything is based on tourism. There can be nothing wrong here."

Emboldened by their successful lawsuits, about 180 homeless people led by Switzer and other advocates gathered on the steps of City Hall in the fall of 1991 and confronted newly elected mayor Jan Laverty Jones at her first council meeting.

The *San Diego Union* reported at the time that "suddenly the homeless are getting more headlines than Engelbert, Wayne and other entertainers who have been canonized here with first name only treatment."

"All they wanted was someone to listen to them," Mayor Jones recalled. "The marshals came in and said there are all these people outside and they want to see you. You can't go out there. Of course I can, I said. Two marshals and a councilman accompanied me."

The upshot of the mayor's impromptu meeting with the homeless was the Mobile Assistance and Shelter for the Homeless program, called MASH for short. MASH Crisis Center opened in 1992 and MASH Village, a transitional-housing program, opened in 1994 with much fanfare and one significant stipulation: MASH was for people who "wanted help." So what of the continuing presence of homeless people on the street five years later?

"They're the chronic," Jones said matter-of-factly. "They want to be homeless. Hobos, bums, they want to be bums. We have to question how much responsibility we have to them."

MASH critics think differently. "Everyone really pushed for MASH," recalled Michael Powlack, director of the Economic Opportunity Board, a nonprofit agency based in West Las Vegas. "It was supposed to be a state-of-the-art emergency shelter, but they shifted focus to transitional housing. So, we're still back to the problem of the need for emergency shelter.

"What they need is a general, spartan facility. The homeless are not going away and they're not going into programs. We need to be prepared to maintain people, and we're not."

■ ■ ■

The light turns green, and Alan and I cross over to a pebble-strewn lot where an abandoned station wagon sags over a narrow trench. Empty liquor bottles clutter the ripped seats and lizards scramble over the rusted wheel hubs.

"How's your stomach holding?" Alan asks.

"Fine," I say.

Earlier, I had thrown up after two spoonfuls of St. Vincent's soup. My throat tightened, my stomach lunged, and I stumbled to the bathroom and vomited into a toilet that appeared not to have been flushed for months. I walked back unsteadily to my table and sat down.

Small circular tables and cracked plastic chairs filled the dank, yellow dining hall. A collage of dried swirls scarred the brown-tiled floor, marking an intersecting trail walked nightly by volunteer janitors enrolled in the organization's work program.

Two men sat at my table. One, a younger guy in jeans and a stylish orange shirt, glanced at me, picked up his tray, and moved to another table. The other man, who later introduced himself as Alan ("Don't call me Al. I'm not hip to abbreviations"), eyed me for a moment and then asked how I was.

"Not very well. I got sick."

"Soup'll do it to you the first time," he said.

He looked about fifty and his voice ground like gravel. He sat slouched over his bowl of soup, sipping slowly. He had on a gray windbreaker partially zipped over his bowling ball-shaped stomach. His face was darkly tanned, and his gray hair slicked hard to one side.

"It's like the first drink in the morning," he said over his bowl. "You get sick, but then you can finish the rest. Get yourself another bowl of soup, son."

I did. The bowl was much like the previous one. Floating globs of congealing grease mixed with noodles, carrots, and lukewarm water. Two women tugged on elastic hospital gloves and served the soup with a slice of white bread. I sat back down and sipped at it slowly. My throat constricted, but I swallowed. I kept working at it sip by sip. I closed my eyes. It stayed down. I looked across at Alan. He stared at a noodle dangling off his spoon and nodded his head slowly without looking at me.

"Hold your breath, son. You don't want to taste it."

Alan pushed his tray to the center of the table and relaxed in his chair.

"So where you from?" he asked.

"California. You?"

"Out east. Boston. Came out here four years ago and ran out of money like everybody else."

"Is this the only place that serves food?"

"Salvation Army, but I wouldn't recommend it. The Rescue Mission has good food. Beans, but it's good. If you get there early enough you can get a whole fruit pie. I ate there last night, but I missed the pie."

"How's about a place to stay?"

"I got a camp. I got a good place that I store my blankets. St. Vincent's is all right, but they got critters. If you get a shower and not too many bugs dig in you can make out all right there. You can go to Sallie's [Salvation Army] at ten and the nurse there'll give you something to get rid of them. Sallie's is a good place to sleep. You'll have to shower. They don't turn away first-timers."

"What about jobbing?"

"There are day-labor joints up here on Bonanza if you want work. You about done there? There's a park near here where you can crap out. Figure you need it."

■ ■ ■

The park sprawls around a housing project down the street from the Salvation Army shelter. We follow a narrow dirt path, stepping over dark splashes of dirt stinking with urine.

A man defecates ahead of us. He leans forward and scrapes his butt back and forth against the wall of an abandoned building—a rough substitute, I can only suppose, for toilet paper. We walk past without comment.

The park teems with people crowding picnic tables or sitting in small groups on the grass. A family camped near the path has grouped three shopping carts loaded with clothes and blankets into a U shape. Two small children play in the center of the U, restraining a third from sneaking off.

We wind our way through the mix of bodies, backpacks, and bedrolls to a row of dumpsters.

("I've been here five days and live in my camper. To find myself in this position, I never dreamed of it. I'm fifty-five years old. Mechanic. I can do three to four sets of fifty push-ups. Three sets of five three-hundred-fifteen bench presses. See what I looked like?")

("I'm from Council Bluffs, Iowa. Just a farmer's wife. My husband had a brain tumor and died. My daughter lives in San Antonio. I stopped here on the way down to see her. My husband and I used to come here. Got into a poker game and just didn't give a damn.")

Alan removes a stash of cardboard tucked into the branches of a tree and arranges the pieces on the grass. He spreads the wet shirts from his plastic bag out on the ground and lies down. He washed the shirts when he showered at St. Vincent's. He figures they'll dry in an hour in the afternoon heat.

"Grab yourself some cardboard," he says. "Behind the dumpster there're always boxes you can break up."

I sit on the grass.

A brown Volkswagen van with JESUS IS SWEET painted across it parks on the street, and three women emerge and start serving the homeless beans and cornbread. Ten teenage girls tumble out the side doors and adjust stereo speakers on the hood. Loud rap music competes with static as a tape plays "Space Jam." The girls dance in unison, rolling their hips in wide circles as they drag their hands slowly across their chests and stomachs.

"Shake it girls, oh, shake it!" shouts one of the dancers. "You all smooth!"

None of this makes an impression on Alan, or on anyone else, for that matter. When the song ends the girls look at each other and smile, and one of them flips the cassette. The homeless, their faces flecked with cornbread, concentrate on their bowls of beans.

■ ■ ■

I didn't know it at the time, but the police were planning a homeless "sweep." A fire in an abandoned house one block away would prompt Metro to clear the park two weeks after I met Alan.

Even without the fire, it was only a matter of time before this "squat" attracted the attention of developers, who push the homeless out even as they meet the housing demands of the more than five thousand people who move here each month.

"With growth, more and more homeless areas are being done away with," says Michael Powlack, the Economic Opportunity Board director. "The housing authority wants to develop the park. My bet is that in another year there'll be an apartment complex or a senior center here."

I looked out the window of Powlack's Jeep Cherokee and stared at the vacant park. I glanced over at the tree where Alan stored his cardboard. Its branches were empty.

"It's a tough town," Powlack said. "Very little public space, and what there is tends to get overused. No once accepts that these people are here. No one asks what can we do to make their and our lives better."

■ ■ ■

The homeless certainly have no expectations.

"This is just like any other city." Alan folds his knees under his chin and closes his eyes. "You'll do all right. It's not ideal. It's a matter of working your way out of it. A lot of guys feel stranded. Everyone's always going back home. I'm going back, they'll tell you, but they're trapped. They never seem to get it together. There's always that possibility: I've got twenty dollars burning a hole in my pocket. I'm going to get lucky, I'm going to get out of here."

"And then they blow it."

He rolls over onto his stomach and jams his arms under his head. I wait until I hear him snore, and then I get up. I walk back toward the path and dig into my pocket for my watch. A wad of bills and a credit card emerge along with it.

I didn't want to tell Alan, but I had a room.

■ ■ ■

My room, one of several I had found listed on a housing-referral sheet tacked to the office wall of MASH case worker José Sanchez, looks out at the Strip through mildewed curtains. The Motel Regency: one hundred dollars a week. The toilet runs continually and dried urine rots the chipped tiles. A single light bulb on the ceiling casts a pale hepatitis yellow over the cracked walls.

I know of four alternative shelters not on José's housing list: the Gold Spike, Union Plaza, Western, and El Cortez casinos. Long on odds but easy on the pocket, these casinos boast penny slot machines and serve 24-hour breakfasts that offer three eggs, sausage, and toast for as little as ninety-nine cents. Even the most down-and-out can afford these prices, particularly if they have blood to sell.

Four downtown clinics offer money for blood. First-time donors wait seven days for their blood to be tested and approved, and then they receive thirty dollars. Limited to three donations a month, the donor earns thirty-dollars with each visit.

I was unable to give blood because I was not a Nevada resident, and I couldn't show proof of any permanent address. The reason for these regulations, a nurse informed me, was to prevent the clinics from becoming magnets for the homeless. It was hard to believe that people deliberately move to Nevada to earn, at most, ninety dollars a month; and given that thirty percent of the city's homeless have been in the state five years or more, it seemed a moot point in any case.

In no position to argue, I left the clinic and wandered up to the Gold Spike. Despite doors open to the street and two ceiling fans, the casino had a stale, musty smell, like a room that had been recently cleared of mothballs. A blackjack table took up the middle of the floor. The dealer sat on a stool wearing a wrinkled white shirt and a thin black string tie loosely knotted and crookedly off-center. He cupped his chin in one hand and a rolled a chip in the other.

I bought three one-dollar penny rolls and sat down at a slot machine. Beside me was a prostitute, who told me she was "not working." Next to her a woman in a beige business suit and high heels balanced a cellular phone against her left shoulder and counted a handful of pennies.

On my other side, a scraggly-looking man I recognized from St. Vincent's sat holding a plastic bag stuffed with shoes. He seemed to win a stream of coins with every fifth throw. I asked him if he had a strategy.

"Don't niggle with your money," he explained. "You can't win playing one penny at a time. You got to put in at least five." He said he could make a dollar last an hour, and at that rate stretch thirty dollars over three days. To finance his gambling, he either sold blood or found day labor.

"I almost had three sevens one time. I got up to use the bathroom and these old ladies come in. It's around six thirty in the morning and they got the sevens. I had just got up too."

A waitress walked over, asked what I was drinking, and brought back a free beer.

"Tip her every third time if you want to keep drinking," the man advised me.

I put in five pennies and pulled the lever. Twenty cents tumbled into the tray.

"Just keep putting it back in," the man said. "Stick to this. Don't play the poker slots. I never had no luck on those. If you want to try it—your money. If you get a straight you get fifty dollars."

I'd almost used up one roll of pennies when on the last pull I won five dollars. The stream of pennies clattering into the metal tray seemed to run forever.

"Say, honey," the prostitute said, "you did pretty good. Want a suck?"

"No, thank you," I said.

She turned back to her machine.

"You gotta love this town," said my friend from St. Vincent's.

■ ■ ■

José Sanchez knew that an informal homeless network existed in some casinos, but said he had never seen it himself. A case worker with MASH Crisis Center for three years, José moved to Las Vegas in 1994 so he and his wife could care for his wife's ailing aunt.

"I get the feeling people are attracted by gambling and the life," he said examining a file. "Free drinks, all kinds of action. Find the odd quarter and turn it into a fortune. There's not much help. Vegas is not really hospitable. But they always come back."

José leans back in his chair and waits for Greg Abernathy, a Veterans' Administration representative who works at MASH twice a week, to finish his interview with Gloria, an army veteran and a client of José's. Gloria was thrown out of MASH Village for smoking crack. The Village, José tells me, doesn't tolerate drugs.

■ ■ ■

Surrounded by a tall, black, spiked security gate and pleasantly landscaped in southwestern style, MASH Village, a pink, square building across from St. Vincent's dining hall on Main Street, has three hundred beds for families and single women. A gold "donation tree" hangs on the wall of the reception room, with each leaf representing a donor: Mirage Resorts, the Glidden Company, Good News Inc., and many others. Behind the reception area, staff offices and client quarters spread down two hallways. With the hazy glow of fluorescent lighting bouncing off the shiny, tiled floors and yellow wall, the Village reminds me of a hospital.

Clients enter the Village for either four months or two years. The shorter program prepares clients for the longer one, which offers intensive case-management services: drug counseling, job placement, and remedial education, among other things.

My guide, Mary, is fifty-two. A native of Nevada, she lived briefly in California until she suffered a back injury at a restaurant in Santa Monica and lost her job. "I really didn't know anyone in California," she explains. "But I knew people here. I knew the system."

She lives in a large, crowded dormitory where she and another woman share a bunk bed. Clothing stuffed into their narrow quarters spills onto the floor. Wrapped in a bathrobe, her barefoot bunkmate pushes past us, jostling rows of stuffed animals perched on a divider. Body odor permeates the room, as it does other shelters I've visited. Despite the availability of showers, deodorant, mouthwash, clean cloth and laundered linens, the sheer volume of people squeezed into one cramped space creates a noticeable funk.

Groaning loudly, Mary raises her arms and stretches. She explains that she worked at her job at a printing company until 5:30 this morning.

"I got in at six AM, just as they turned the lights on for wake-up," she says stifling one of many yawns. "I've made all my important calls, I'll go out for recreation. They don't want you out gambling, but the reality of the thing is this is Las Vegas. If you play a game of bingo that doesn't make you addictive. Three or four times a month I play one session of bingo for three dollars."

As Mary walks me through the quiet halls, I notice cameras in the ceiling. She explains that staff observe the residents around the clock.

"Private time is real scarce around here," she says.

■ ■ ■

"José!"

José and I enter Greg Abernathy's office and sit down. Abernathy, a bald, heavy-set black man wearing a blue polo shirt and jeans, rests his elbows on his desk and looks at José. He wants to hear from him before he offers his opinion on Gloria's case. "She says she tested positive because she was around people with crack," José says.

Abernathy shakes his head. "She knows she smoked it, and is just coming up with an excuse," he says.

"She's got one dirty urine analysis already," José says. "Two UA's and you're out of there."

"Can she stay if she goes into a program?"

"We can't advocate for them. She'll have to advocate for herself."

"Can't advocate for your client? What is that? Change number forty-five?"

"They say: 'You're Crisis now. We're the Village. Hands off.'"

"She has been in the program since February," says Abernathy, protesting.

"She can't reapply for sixty days if she's thrown out."

"She'll have to bounce around a little bit. Shade Tree, Salvation Army, Rescue Mission."

Abernathy examines Gloria's file. Diagnosed with Post-Traumatic Stress Disorder resulting from what Abernathy suspects was a sexual assault, her clinical history suggests another option.

"She could go through the Salvation Army alcohol program or get into their mental-health project with the PTSD and into alcohol treatment through the mental-health program. Or the Key Foundation; they have housing for vets," says Abernathy.

José nods, thinking.

■ ■ ■

Gloria folds her arms and rolls her head against the waiting-room wall as the two men debate her fate. Her black hair falls evenly over her shoulders, and her pressed jeans and white blouse contrast sharply with the worn thrift-store apparel of her peers.

Half a dozen people wait silently for their case managers in the dimly lighted room. The pea-green walls, cluttered with faded flyers of missing persons, absorb what little light shines from the stuttering bulbs in the ceiling. Ron, a pleasant but bored security guard in an ill-fitting brown uniform, slouches carelessly at a metal desk. He wakens a man asleep in a chair.

"No sleeping," he says.

A door leads from the waiting room to the crowded reception area. In a cubicle similar to a bank teller's, a woman stands behind a window grill and faces a line of men and women standing unevenly in front of her.

"You can try Catholic Charities," I overhear her say through the wall.

"I was told to come here," a man complains.

"We're not a financial-aid agency."

"I need a health card, too."

"Try Salvation Army."

"But I was told…"

"We're strictly a referral agency. We screen, assess need, and refer out."

A mouse scrambles across the floor, interrupting my eavesdropping.

"Damn!" a man shouts. Half a dozen people swing their legs up and cock their heads to one side.

"Wait till the whole family runs through," Ron deadpans.

Gloria smiles briefly before her face resumes its hard expression. She has just finished seeing Marta Valenzuela, an alcoholism counselor from the Community Health Center who works at MASH Crisis Center on Tuesday mornings. Her session, she says, was unproductive.

"Whenever people first meet me, they jump to conclusions and want to lecture me," she complains. "The last thing I needed was a lecture. She had to lecture me: 'One day at a time.' I don't want to hear her lecture. She didn't care."

She repeats this to José when he calls her back into his office.

"Is that the impression you got?" José says.

She nods.

"Well, what about the Key Foundation? They work with veterans."

Gloria rests her head against José's desk.

"Anything," she whispers. "Where's it at?"

José tells her and she leaves. I watch her go and hear José say, "That's sad." I turn around. He has already picked up another file.

■ ■ ■

That afternoon, back at her office in the Health Center, Marta Valenzuela won't comment on Gloria's case directly. Instead, she explains the difficulties she faces working with addicts in a "twenty-four-hour town."

"Ninety percent of my clients have gambling and alcohol problems. Drugs, meth, cocaine. Heroin is starting to come back. Gambling is one of the ways to raise money for this. Just being around casinos, they have access to free alcohol. They'll be talking about their drinking and then they'll say, 'I was dropping some quarters.' Today I had a man drop eleven hundred dollars worth of quarters. It comes up in conversation.

"This town is Disneyland. They want people to come. Any vice you want you can do here. There's got to be some ethics in this. There is a nothingness coming over this city. We are fighting nothingness."

■ ■ ■

Marta suggests I see Julia Occhiogrosso, who works full-time for Catholic Worker, a lay Roman Catholic activist movement. Julia, Marta says, "unconditionally" loves homeless people. I jot her name down, then hurry out of Marta's office to beat the line for the Salvation Army shelter.

I arrive at Sallie's at four in the afternoon. Although the shelter opens at five, the line for beds begins much earlier. Women can stay at the shelter indefinitely, but men, restricted to a seven-day stay every six months, move in and out constantly. Divided into two sections, the shelter separates not only the sexes, but children from their parents as well; when his week is up, even a father with children on the premises must find shelter elsewhere.

("We're from Chicago. My wife and my kids are at Shade Tree. We recently got married and moved out here to make a new start, but my wife's purse was stolen at Lady Luck with twelve hundred dollars in it. It wasn't a regular purse, it was a planner, a calculator. We'll never do that again. I be like sleeping in the park. Things have not been working out right.")

We gather outside on benches surrounded by our bundles of clothing, rolled blankets, suitcases, and backpacks. A large, outdoor storage area provides a place for us to toss our things, but a sign saying STORE AT YOUR OWN RISK suggests what could happen if we used it. The Salvation Army rents sixty lockers at five dollars a month, but the long waiting list prevents all but the most determined applicants from getting one.

Glen, a member of the shelter staff, holds a clipboard marked "Extended Shelter Stay Registration." For three dollars a night, men can reserve one of forty-two bunkbeds in the T Dorm. Originally, these beds were for homeless men who had recently gotten jobs and needed temporary (T) inexpensive lodging until they earned enough to rent a room; now, T Dorm provides indefinite shelter year-round for anyone who can pay for it.

Glen stands outside and calls the names on the clipboard. A thick coating of dust covers the hair, face, and patterned dress of a five-year-old girl watching him. She sits beside her parents, both dressed in overalls and huddled over two suitcases held together with twine.

"Kennedy!" Glen bellows.

The girl jumps up imitating Glen's stance and shouts, "Kennedy!"

"Franklin!"

"Franklin!" the girl pipes up.

"Miller!"

"Miller!"

The girl's father grabs her hand, sits her down, and orders her to stay put.

Her face crumbles, but she does not cry. Her expression withdraws into a blank poker face. Dull-eyed, she looks at Glen, mouthing softly the names he continues to call.

Back inside, Glen tells his coworker John that none of the people on the waiting list showed up for the T Dorm. Glen drops the clipboard on a desk, grabs a fistful of "lodging cards," and walks back outside.

First-timers get priority in the shelter. Glen punches the number one on a card, hands it to a new client, and lets him inside. The man stops at a desk staffed by a volunteer and blows into a breathalyzer. A family follows behind him; the children beg to blow into it too. When the man tests negative, John issues him a mat.

The line moves rapidly. John types into a computer each person's name and the number of nights they have stayed in the shelter.

"Kennedy! You were called for T Dorm."

"Yes, sir."

"You still want it?"

"Yes, sir."

"See the man outside," he says pointing toward Glen. "Next in line!"

A couple steps forward with a small boy.

"How many kids you got?"

"One."

"Who's watching them?"

The couple hesitates.

"Paul," the mother says to her son, "Stay with me unless you want to stay with Poppa."

The boy holds his father's hand but reaches for his mother.

"I need to know," John says, "so I can put a family mat down for one of you."

The boy stays with his mother.

Another couple with a baby stand next in line. "Hey John, we switching," the woman says. "I'm taking the baby for a change."

A man tries to slip in without stopping. John yells at him to stop at the desk.

"I like it," John says to me as he types the man's name into the computer. "This job's a hundred miles an hour for me. That's what I like. I was selling condos in Florida, but I blew my money. I came out here and blew more money on drugs and gambling. When I got to this shelter I heard about day-labor jobs and signed up. The next day I break my arm in a construction job. So, I'm in T Dorm with a busted arm and I talk to Glen. He's from Daytona, so we had Florida in common. He says, Can you use a computer? And I get this job."

The shelter fills to capacity, with seventy men and fifty women. People watch television or shuffle cards. Two women sit by themselves and play video poker on pocket calculators next to a makeshift nursery where couples juggle crying infants, plastic bottles, soiled baby clothes, and dirty diapers.

■ ■ ■

Above the noise, Glen rattles off the shelter rules: showers after chapel, lights off at ten, staff not responsible for stolen items, absolutely no alcohol or drugs, mandatory church services at seven PM.

The short walk to chapel that evening allows for a cigarette break. We smoke and move slowly toward a small white building about two hundred yards ahead. A man pushes a woman in a wheelchair up a ramp, and I follow them inside. Three rows of pews form a half circle around a square podium. A large, red crucifix hangs off one wall beside a clock.

The woman sitting next to me complains about the "asshole" beside her, who is slumped in his chair, snoring softly. Shifting away from him, she shimmies onto the edge of my chair, and we make ourselves as comfortable as possible. In a short while, she falls asleep against my shoulder.

Children squirm in their parents' arms, and mothers hurry them outside. People without children give up their seats and stand by the door like ushers pointing families toward empty pews.

Above the infants' squalls, a man in a red turtleneck sweater and pressed green slacks introduces himself as this evening's preacher. He implores us to give up our lives to "Him who resides above in heaven."

"Jesus paid a debt he did not owe for us. We're not nice people. We're all sinners. We needed someone to wash our sins away. For that he was tried, sentenced, and hung. The Jews wanted to see him hung. The Jews believe in vindictiveness. Jesus did not believe their pagan religion, and he defied them and rose from the dead."

The preacher paces back and forth, lips pursed intently.

"Three weeks ago, I lost a check for eight hundred and fifty dollars," he says dragging his hands through his hair. "I was a little stressed out, as you can imagine. I looked everywhere and couldn't find it. What was I doing wrong? I was thinking of myself. I had stopped sharing my life with God. I was focused on mortal trappings. I had abandoned Him. I got on my knees and wept. I begged His forgiveness. Then I heard a voice. It said, Look between the front seats of the car. There you'll find the check."

He stops and looks pointedly at each of us. The knot of people at the door murmurs in hushed tones.

"God spoke to me!" says the preacher.

He crouches, clutching his fists across his chest. His face reddens and he shakes on trembling legs. Squinching one eye open and then the other, he waits for his truth to reveal itself to us, but we lost sinners turn away and look at the clock.

■ ■ ■

Julia Occhiogrosso prays while she works in her kitchen on Las Vegas's economically depressed Westside. She scoops globs of peanut butter and strawberry jelly into small Styrofoam bowls and sets them on a tray next to loose stacks of bread. Her husband, Gary, lugs buckets of steaming coffee to a truck parked outside. He spent yesterday grinding bag after bag of coffee beans for this week's free feed; now, standing beside the truck, he uses colander holders to scoop up coffee grounds that have settled in the bottom of the buckets.

Every Wednesday, Thursday, Friday, and Saturday, Julia, Gary, and several volunteers drive the short distance to Ethel Pearson Park to feed the homeless. "We try to do what's good for them," Julia says. "Establishing a relationship with them is a big part of it. We're taking people and saying: you belong to a family."

The Catholic Worker movement was begun by Dorothy Day in the 1930s amid the unrest of the Great Depression. The movement, which has no official connection to the Church, serves as a conscience for mainstream Catholics, according to Julia.

Having joined the Catholic Worker movement in Los Angeles in 1982, Julia brought the movement to Las Vegas four years later.

"Las Vegas was just starting to grow again in nineteen eighty-six," she recalls. "It was kind of like a small town. St. Vincent's had a shelter, and you had the Rescue Mission and Salvation Army. Those three were the main providers at the time.

"We talked to street people. They advised us to start bringing coffee for when they were turned out of the shelters. We started to do that at six-thirty in the morning. When we started, it was maybe seventy guys. Now it can be as many as three hundred to three hundred fifty people."

Our cars form a small caravan that inches toward the park. Gary drives slowly so as not to spill the coffee. I am in charge of cups, and drive ahead.

By the time I arrive, about one hundred homeless people have gathered in the park. They mill around quietly, forming a line on the curb. I hold my cups and wait for Julia and Gary to arrive. Everyone in line watches me.

"You're new to cup detail?" a man asks. He extends a tentative hand and I give him a roll of cups. He opens the wrapper and passes out the cups to the impatient line.

"See, they'll come with the coffee and we just serve ourselves."

He smiles and assures me I'm doing just fine. The coffee break feels like a communal picnic, and when Gary and Julia pull up, everyone pitches in and helps carry collapsible tables and trays of bread, peanut butter, jelly, and coffee.

Julia watches the people eat. She watches birds hop between their legs, pecking at crumbs, and hears the buckets slosh with coffee, the trays scraped clean. "There's a wanting and longing for community with each other," Julia says. "A wanting of something deeper. You kind of think of that when you think of where you want to die as you get older. These people here, many of them, are going to die alone."

■ ■ ■

Despite the good works of Julia and others, some homeless people want nothing to do with charity. They have untangled themselves from the city's safety net and fled to its outer fringes. Squats fill ravines and dried river beds bordering the edges of Las Vegas, like third-world outposts. Living a cat-and-mouse existence, the people in these encampments are part of a Darwinian standoff, with developers one step behind.

I help Julia clean up after the feeding, then drive across town to meet Shawn, a twenty-nine-year-old self-described "sand rat," living in Flamingo Wash. Shawn's camp lies at the intersection of Decatur and Tropicana, where Decatur deadends into desert. Shirts and pants cling to the branches of thorny brush, and smoke drifts casually from a smoldering camp fire. Plastic shopping bags bounce across the ground, wrapping around discarded radios, watches, televisions, teddy bears, pizza boxes, bicycle parts, backpacks, and sleeping bags. Stones and scrap metal form squares defining sleeping areas.

"Everyone's out canning," Shawn explains.

We sit down in his "lot" and share a cigarette. Shawn lives in a large square hut pieced together from plywood and corrugated cardboard. I push back the blanket door and see the sleeping bag, paperback books, and plastic water bottles that comprise his home. An old copy of *Hustler* magazine protrudes from beneath the sleeping bag. Behind the hut stands a makeshift kitchen, where two stacks of bricks support a shorn metal trash barrel. Shawn lights a fire between the bricks and cracks an egg on the barrel. The egg slowly sizzles. He flips it once, twice, scoops it up on a spatula, and slides it into his mouth.

Shawn came to Las Vegas in 1995 to be a poker dealer. He has a different plan now. "I'm going to save money to get my own place, and then I want to start an advertising company on the Internet. When I'm back on my feet I'll get a computer. I've already saved two hundred dollars."

I ask him if he has considered enrolling in St. Vincent's job program. After all, I say, you'd be guaranteed shelter, three daily meals, and regular opportunities to work.

"I've never asked help from anybody," he responds with a hurt look. "If I can't make ends meet on my own, they won't be met."

Shawn has lived at this site for three months, ever since he lost his job at Lotus Scenic Tours. Unable to pay rent, he came out to the desert. "I've been an outdoor person all my life. I was originally further out in the desert near the airport, but over here there's an office building that lets us in to take sponge baths."

He gets odd jobs through Labor Express, a day-labor referral agency downtown. He used to walk three hours to their office, getting up at two in the morning, before he bought a bus pass.

When our conversation ends, Shawn crawls into his hut and between the covers of his sleeping bag. I can see only his eyes. Shawn watches me, a nocturnal animal concealed in his den.

■ ■ ■

In the office of Ed Ficker, the director of St. Vincent's job program, a large bust of Mark Twain sits squarely on a bookshelf filled with anthologies of the writer's work as well as a copy of *Huckleberry Finn*. A slip of paper taped above the bust bears the line, "I have been an author for twenty years and an ass for fifty-five."

"Mark Twain is one of my heroes," Ficker explains. A tall, trim man with a shock of white hair rolled back from his forehead, Ficker talks in a soft midwestern drawl that rolls words like candy.

"I got hooked on Twain by my dad. I started off with O. Henry. Then Jack London. My dad liked *Call of the Wild*. It's a metaphor. It's about comfort, struggle, the wild, and returning to responsibility.

"Henry Ford said charity does not cure poverty. Only work does. When the government told Sitting Bull they'd provide for him and his people on a reservation, he told the government to go to hell. Went to Canada instead, where he could live and work without dependence on the government.

"I'm sort of in the recycling business. I deal with a race of people who are almost nonfunctional. I have to build up their integrity and their will to work."

Ficker shows me a photograph of a homeless man with an unkempt beard and shaggy long hair. Expressionless, he carries a backpack and stares at the ground.

"He's broke, doesn't have I.D., as low as he can be on the pole, right?"

Ficker holds up another photograph. A clean-shaven man with short hair and a wide, toothy grin beams back at me. He's developed a pot belly, and looks like just one of the guys in a red-striped polo shirt, jeans, and tennis shoes.

"Same man three weeks later. He has his own place and can buy goods in the community, like you and me."

The program serves four hundred men at a time. In 1996 eleven hundred participants found full-time employment, and thirteen thousand offerings for casual labor were taken.

"I send guys out, and at the end of the day they wind up with forty-six dollars in their pocket," says Ficker, who worries about the lure of casinos. "Am I concerned? Sure I'm concerned.

"Las Vegas is extremely unique. The guy on the street can still dream. No other city in the world could he still dream. All you need is four or five bucks converted into quarters and there's this fantasy of hitting the jackpot. Cash in hand can mean a thousand dollars or absolutely nothing."

■ ■ ■

Five o'clock, lights out, offices closed. MASH, the Key Foundation, St. Vincent's with its employment center and dining hall sink into shadows. As caseworkers and administrators unlock their cars, security systems shriek. In a few minutes the parking lot is empty, except for two vans and a station wagon hunkered in for the night.

Bearded old men, amputees, and discharged hospital patients bandaged or with crutches sit on the curbstone waiting to enter St. Vincent's men's shelter, a program limited to senior citizens and the disabled. As at Salvation Army, no personal belongings are allowed inside. Like a ticket scalper, the driver of a pickup truck parks outside the shelter and offers overnight storage for "a dollar a pop."

("Can't carry property in here," a volunteer tells me.

"It's just my jacket," I say.

"Put it on.")

Volunteers from St. Vincent's job program make up the shelter staff. They sit in a small living room near the entrance and watch TV, or play mahjong on a computer. Two sofas and several chairs form a circle around a bookshelf that holds a coffeemaker and cups.

Two hundred bunk beds fill the hall, of which seventeen are reserved for the disabled. Some of the beds don't have mattresses, so the staff throws black rubber floor mats over the box springs. Each bed has a blanket, but no sheets or pillows. With only one toilet available, I take care of business outside, along with several others.

Once the beds are set up, the shelter opens for the night.

("Am I spinning my wheels kicking out someone who's fifty-three?" asks a volunteer.

"I didn't make the rules. Fifty-five and older is what we're told," the shift supervisor says.

"He said he talked to you."

"Talked to me? No one talked to me. Who is he?"

"Hey, with the red shirt. Come with us.")

Eight PM. Lights out. In the dark I hear horrendous snores and farts, furtive whispers, obscene jokes. I get nervous. One of Terry Whitacker's staff caught tuberculosis working here, and I am surrounded by coughing people. The more I think about it, the more worried I get, until paranoia finally propels me out the door.

"You won't be allowed back in," the supervisor warns me.

Outside, masked in the glow of a bare bulb, volunteers swat at gnats and smoke cigarettes. Volunteers not on duty hang out, too. They have no place to go except their own bunk beds, in a stuffy, windowless dormitory at the other end of the plaza, ripe with sweat, stale breath, and dirty clothes.

("This blanket has critters!" I hear someone shout.

"What have they ever done to you?" a volunteer yells back.

"Shut up."

"Keep it down or everybody's gonna want one.")

I attach myself to Robert, a volunteer. A Vietnam veteran, Robert spends his days at the shelter running errands.

"Aren't you expected to get a job?" I ask.

"You don't have to look for work as long as you do their work," he says.

Robert doesn't want to return to his bunk, but he doesn't want to remain at the shelter, either. He paces back and forth until finally he wanders toward Main Street and I follow him into Gabe's, a nearby bar adopted by the volunteers as their personal retreat. Robert recognizes some of his cohorts; they appear to be drinking soda or cranberry juice, but he assures me there's vodka in each glass. The bar has three video-poker games and two pool tables. A sign above the video games reads, "The Rules Are Real Simple. You Must Buy A Drink Not Off Sale To Play Slots Or Pool Tables." Another sign, posted behind the bar and above two shelves of liquor bottles, warns, "If You Can Keep Your Head In All This Confusion You Don't Understand The Situation."

Robert sighs, drumming his fingers on the bar. He suggests another place, the Silver Saddle, a strip joint not far away. We walk into the pitch-black and nearly empty bar and order beers. A red-headed, freckle-faced woman comes in behind us and asks about work. Slightly built, she looks barely out of her teens, and I can't imagine what she's doing here. She says she lives in a transitional-housing program and has worked strips before. The bleached-blonde bartender tells her to come back Thursday for an audition, which means she will have to wait a week.

The seventies hit "Staying Alive" provides music for a stripper dancing on a huge circular table in another room much larger but equally dark. She appears to be in her forties and clomps across the table wearing nothing but a blue silk shirt, pink panties, and black platform shoes. She slowly unbuttons her shirt, shaking her breasts at a man sitting nearby. Then she turns around, bends over, and, with her head between her legs, slaps herself hard on the ass.

"Who wants an ass sam'ich?" she shouts between her legs.

She rolls her hips above a man who offers her a dollar bill, and squeezes the bill between her breasts. She wraps herself around a gold pole that rises up through the center of the table, spinning in a slow circle. Suddenly she sneezes, once, twice, three times in rapid succession. Unable to stop, she presses the dollar against her nose and hugs the pole. Static overwhelms the speakers and the music cuts off, providing her with a temporary reprieve. She shouts at the bartender for a cigarette and a Kleenex.

"May I join you, honey?"

A stripper pulls up a stool and settles down beside Robert. She leans against the bar and lights a cigarette, revealing her chest through a loosely knotted bathrobe. Her body sags against the bar in rolls.

"I'm just drinking coffee," Robert says.

"You ain't about shit, are you, honey?"

■ ■ ■

We walk up Owens past the empty park, the silent projects, and the Salvation Army shelter to an overpass beside a set of railroad tracks running deep into darkness. Beneath the bridge lie coffin rows of sleeping people. Robert points to a man whose shaved head, crossed with stitches, shines in the moonlight.

"Some guys beat him with his shopping cart," he says.

Robert suggests we stay here. He has no desire to return to St. Vincent's Plaza. He describes his fellow volunteers as pigeons who, granted a little authority, have turned into hawks. He doesn't think he will stay in the program long.

■ ■ ■

Four o'clock in the morning. I wake up and lurch to my feet, stiff with cold despite the blanket someone threw over me. Robert stirs beside me, as does another man who plans to walk to a casual-labor outlet. I have my car back at St. Vincent's and offer him a ride. He rolls up his bag and we stumble down the hill, scrounging for cigarettes.

In an hour, Owens will experience a pedestrian rush hour, starting with the Salvation Army, which awakens its clients at five. The homeless who have slept in bushes, under bridges, and beside railroad tracks join these sheltered homeless in a dawn march to St. Vincent's for donuts and coffee at six, a ragged band tinted red in the sunrise, steamed and weaving down the street.

Robert, Joe, and I get in my car. I drive onto Main Street, but suddenly Joe asks me to turn down Las Vegas Boulevard toward the Strip.

"It's been a long time," he says.

Bingo!

Michelle Ling

It is barely 8 AM on Sunday and the thick desert air is already on the edge of uncomfortably warm. Marjorie Miller stands at the front of her bungalow-style senior citizens' apartment complex, patting her silver hair and fiddling with the gold crucifix at her breast. Her casual green polyester slacks and white sneakers fit the all-purpose dress code for Las Vegas retirees. The words "Ten Commandments," printed on her T-shirt, peek out from her zippered sweater.

She checks her watch, but not in the manner of someone who is late. She isn't. Her bus isn't scheduled to arrive for another fifteen minutes.

"It gets here at about eight-ten. They say eight-fifteen, but it's usually eight-ten—never after eight-twelve. I think they come early so everyone has a little extra time, and they can help people with walkers and things," she says.

Marjorie should know. She has been taking this shuttle every Sunday morning since she moved to Las Vegas ten years ago. "They don't actually start until nine, but they get you there a little early so you can chat with people you know—even pray a little beforehand!" she giggles. "There's a group that I always see, of course, and we always sit together, save each other seats. Of course, you don't talk while it's going on. Otherwise people can't hear."

It's a common enough scene, one you might see in any American town: a little old lady waiting for the bus to Sunday-morning services. But this isn't just any American town, and Marjorie isn't going to church. The Ten Commandments printed on her T-shirt, revealed after she takes off her sweater, are the Ten Commandments of Bingo. One of them reads, "Thou shall not shout 'Aw, Shit!' when thy neighbor wins."

This Sunday morning, Marjorie is going where she goes about four times a week: to the casino.

■ ■ ■

Ask them anywhere, from the upscale Mediterranean-style houses of the Sun City retirement havens, through the mobile homes on Lamb Boulevard and the many seniors-only condos and apartments, to the low-income housing projects. Ask old people why they moved to Las Vegas, and you get the same answers. They like the weather. The cost of living is lower than it was where they lived before—especially if they came (as many have) from southern California—whether they're talking about the mortgage in their new retirement community or the rent on their mobile home. (In fact, the composite cost of living index for Las Vegas, though lower than that of most southern California cities, is higher than that of Albuquerque, Denver, Phoenix, or Tucson.) And Nevada has no income or inheritance tax, they will tell you. (But its sales taxes and property taxes are comparable to those in California, and higher than those in most other Western states.) Many old people say they moved here from other retirement magnets because the clean, dry air is kind to their arthritis or emphysema. Some purposely avoid the seniors-only communities; others, without family or community ties, seek them out. Gertrude Coco, in Sun City/Summerlin; Primrose Sommerville, in her mobile home on Lamb Boulevard; and Thelma Vanaman in a county housing project reserved for seniors all say they like their new homes for the same reason: they are clean and quiet, and there are no kids running around.

■ ■ ■

But the paradox created by Las Vegas's astonishing growth becomes more frustrating every year. As more people move to Las Vegas (more than 70,000 in 1998, one-sixth of them over sixty-five), the reasons to retire there disappear. The awesome traffic, which reminds them of L.A., is the first thing older Las Vegans mention, with pollution and the crime rate not far behind. "We came to escape the traffic and pollution and crime—

and it followed us out here!" exclaims Emma Kovitz, 77, who retired with her husband Ray first to Orange County, California, then to Sun City/Summerlin when "it got so bad."

"The houses were cheap in the beginning," says Ruth Closky, 81, who bought the 77th home in Sun City/Summerlin (home to more than thirteen thousand seniors in 1998) seven years ago. "Now, I don't think we could even afford to get a home here."

The absence of state income and inheritance taxes is still regarded as a plus. But many seniors grumble that as the city's need for more schools, roads, and police becomes chronic, Clark County is asking them to help pay the costs of Las Vegas's growing pains, through bond measures that add up to billions of dollars.

■ ■ ■

For all the complaints, Las Vegas still has one advantage over Fort Lauderdale, Palm Desert, or Phoenix: this is, after all, as civic boosters still remind us, the "Entertainment Capital of the World."

For many seniors, "entertainment" means the more than two dozen golf courses (especially for those well-off enough to live near one), or water sports on Lake Mead, or hiking on Mount Charleston. Some retirees mention community and college theater and dance productions, the county's libraries, or UNLV basketball. But many old people lack the wealth or the health or the inclination to indulge in these things.

"I've worked my whole life, why do I want to do more gardening?" "Hiking! I'm too old for that." "No, there's no ballet or theater, but even when I lived in New York I didn't go see those things." "My husband and I used to have a boat, but after he died, I sold it." "We used to bowl a lot, but my arthritis is so bad, I can't do that anymore." A surprising number of older people who live next to golf courses don't golf, and don't intend to. The executive director of the Sun City/MacDonald Ranch development south of town was puzzled when, in 1996, only 21 percent of a sampling of new residents professed any interest in using the green fairways their homes all surround.

So what is it that draws old people to this desert city, out of the places where they have often lived all their lives, away from their family and friends? What do they mean when they talk about "entertainment"?

The one source of entertainment that all the old people I talked to in Las Vegas mentioned, without exception, is the one that distinguishes this city from any other retirement haven in America. It is also the one industry in Las Vegas that has done more than any other to reach out and cater to seniors: casino gambling.

■ ■ ■

In a survey of Clark County residents conducted for the Las Vegas Convention and Visitors Authority in 1995-96, 72 percent of all Las Vegas adults questioned admitted to gambling at least "occasionally"; 34 percent said they gambled at least twice a week, spending forty to sixty dollars each time. The frequency of gambling rose markedly for older respondents with no children at home, who tended to gamble (primarily on quarter slots and video-poker machines) off the Strip, in neighborhood stores, bars, and casinos. They disliked the tourist traffic on the Strip, they told interviewers, and found Fremont Street dirty and unsafe.

Most of these older gamblers had never taken a chance on more than the occasional small-stakes church bingo game or state lottery ticket before they arrived in Las Vegas. The gambling industry is well aware that over-sixty-fives in Clark County—who numbered almost 150,000 in 1996—are not only a burgeoning part of the county's population; they are also the most regular and committed gamblers of all Las Vegas residents.

The reason is simple, says Whittier College law professor I. Nelson Rose, who has been studying the national increase in gambling. "For the first time, there's a large percentage of the population that doesn't have to worry about how it's going to pay for food, shelter, and clothing." Retirees as a whole have the two most important things needed for gambling, he says: money and time.

■ ■ ■

Gambling is not, of course, the only thing to do in Las Vegas. But with free door-to-door casino buses, cheap buffets, and the myriad of other promotions offered to resident seniors, it is certainly one of the easiest.

"There's no art films here, only Hollywood trash. In San Francisco, New York, L.A., you can see anything," complains Fred Hill, 81, who (like many other seniors) says he doesn't gamble much. "The first thing promoted here, it's the buffets, it's the casino deals. They don't want you to go to the movies; they want you to go to casinos."

Elaine Kiely, 73, plays slots and bingo, mainly at Arizona Charlie's, four times a week, and doesn't have any illusions about winning it big. "Every now and then, they'd give me a couple of bucks, and then I bring it right back to 'em." And how often does she lose? "Too often," she chuckles.

Although Kiely says she's "a gambler," many others like her simply consider a gambling visit every other day the norm for people of their generation. Indeed, most of the hundred or so seniors I talked to over several days at Arizona Charlie's and Boulder Station said they came three to five times a week. "I'm not a gambler," says Lillian, 73, while waiting for the next bingo session to start. She plays bingo, and yes, okay, sometimes the slots, three or four times a week. But she sticks to a loss limit of twenty to fifty dollars per visit.

For many seniors, and for Las Vegans in general, the itch to gamble is tickled by the ubiquitous opportunities to do so. Sometimes there seem to be slot and video-poker machines in every bar, restaurant, grocery store, and laundromat in the city. Emma Kovitz says that although she doesn't go to the casinos much, "When you go down there to the market, if you have quarters in your pocket—they're gone. It's crazy."

The seniors I talked to at the two neighborhood casinos all seemed aware of the limits of their fixed incomes, and insisted that they keep their gambling expenditures under control. Although many told stories of friends or people they'd heard about who blew their retirement money gambling, no one I met at Arizona Charlie's or Boulder Station seemed to be an addictive gambler. But perhaps this depends on the definition of "addictive." Twenty to fifty dollars, changed into quarters and shoved into the slots three to five times a week, can eat a big piece out of a Social Security check.

■ ■ ■

A few downtown casinos, like Binion's Horseshoe, offer occasional shuttle-bus service. But neighborhood casinos are the ones that have concentrated on locals—and, to judge from the riders I met, on locals over sixty-five. Almost all the casino-hotels that offer bingo provide free bus service. Arizona Charlie's, a West Las Vegas neighborhood casino-hotel built on the site of an old bowling alley and across from a shopping mall, is the leader in free shuttle service, which it has offered ever since it opened in 1987. While other outlying neighborhood casinos such as Boulder Station, Texas Station, and Sam's Town send shuttles to about a dozen locations once a week, Arizona Charlie's sends its fleet of air-conditioned vans and large buses, all wheelchair-and-walker-accessible, to fifty or sixty senior apartment complexes, retirement homes, mobile-home parks, and senior centers throughout Clark County from 8 am to 11 pm seven days a week, picking up about 8,000 customers each month. If the bus doesn't come to your house, says Brent Jones at Arizona Charlie's transportation department, you can call and request one. "If you can get a couple other people, and can commit to using the shuttle, like, once or twice a week, we can probably set it up."

Pam has been driving an Arizona Charlie's bus for four years. She talks about her clients, and former clients, as though they were family. "There was Candy Berry. She lived at Fleming. They called her Candy because she was always giving people candy—and she was so sweet, too! She came in every day, and everybody knew her. It was difficult understanding her, but she was a doll."

Did she have an accent? "No, she just didn't have any teeth."

The clients aren't all nice. "There was this mean old broad. Heaven forbid anyone should get off the bus before her. She'd hit 'em with her cane!"

Pam loves her job, she says, but it has its downside. "The depressing part of this job is when people just don't show up anymore, y'know?" Most of the time, she hears about what happened to them later.

"One lady burned forty percent of her body, when, well, you know, some people just don't have common sense. She was smoking with her oxygen tank on!" The woman died last week.

■ ■ ■

Valley View Village, A Carefree Living Center, is our first stop. Three folks in casual slacks and comfortable shoes are waiting in front of the pastel-and coral-colored main building.

Pam opens the door and steps out.

"You're late!" an old man greets her cheerily.

"I'm not late—you're early," she says, grinning.

"Oh, I know," he says. "I'm just seeing if you're paying attention."

Pam gives each person a voucher, a raffle ticket, and a hand up the steps as they board. Riders cash three vouchers in for a free buffet; the raffle ticket is a chance for a free dinner at the casino's Yukon Grille, or an Arizona Charlie's jacket.

"Hi, sweetie!" she says to a tiny, white-haired woman, handing her a raffle ticket.

"If I don't win that coat this year, I gotta go south for winter!" she exclaims in reply.

The next stop is Clark Towers and Clark Terrace.

"You look kinda spiffy there, kid," Pam says to a woman as she steps up.

"I washed my hair today so I'd look beautiful!" the woman beams.

"Edna! How are you?"

"How-dee!" Edna replies, taking a seat up front.

The bus is filling up, and the mood is decidedly festive.

"If anybody sees Rosie, I want her recipe for what she puts in her cream pies," Pam hollers as she drives.

"She said she promised you," Edna remembers. "They are the best."

Everyone on the bus loves Arizona Charlie's. "It's our home away from home!" Edna's neighbor cries.

"It's a family reunion every day we're out there. Except it's not family," Edna adds.

"We come here all the time," another woman says proudly. "We really appreciate the bus drivers, Pam and Joyce. These girls are always so wonderful. And *not* all of them are," she says, mouthing the name of another casino.

"It's nice to have an arm to hang on to," Edna agrees.

After picking up another group at Sunrise Gardens, a studio complex for single seniors, Pam heads back to Charlie's. The bus schedule is carefully planned so that riders arrive in time for the next bingo session, and perhaps spend a little time on the slots while they wait. The bus usually returns four hours (two bingo sessions and a buffet) later. At very popular locations like Sun City/ Summerlin, the bus will make another round trip in the afternoon. Some buses go to Sun City three, four, or even five times a day.

"Come on, we gotta hustle!" shouts a man in the back.

Pam laughs. "I'm going, I'm going!" She looks at me through her long rear view mirror. "He says that every time."

Despite all the worrying, the bus arrives in plenty of time for the 1 PM bingo session. "I've never been so late that they missed one. But I don't know what would happen if I did!" Pam laughs. "They're so into it. They got their lucky daubers, and they'll kill you over their lucky bingo seat."

■ ■ ■

Some bingo halls in Las Vegas look like converted ballrooms, with chandeliers high above long rows of convention tables and vinyl upholstered chairs. But such accoutrements are extraneous, quite incidental to what really matters in bingo. "I don't need any of that," a graying bingo pro says to me, waving her arm disdainfully around the room. "Just show me the numbers! And then," she says with a grin, "show me the jackpot!"

Arizona Charlie's is a favorite. It's the only casino in town that offers new bingo games every odd hour, 24 hours a day. Like blackjack or poker (or any other casino game that can also be played elsewhere), casino bingo in Las Vegas tends to be more complicated than the domestic variety, with specific procedures and codes of etiquette that are not explained until they're breached. The basic concept, known to millions of Americans through church halls or American Legion fundraisers, is simple. Five letters (B,I,N,G,O) are called out in combination with numbers from one to seventy-five. You cover the numbered spaces on your card as they're called out, until someone completes a five-space row and yells, "Bingo!"

In Las Vegas casinos, however, you are offered a multitude of variations: progressives, bonus packs, special card patterns with names like "Crazy T,L, and U," "Hardway," "Triangle," and the high-stakes "Coverall," in which the player must fill all twenty-five spaces. Games are played in one-hour sessions. Before each session, everyone buys a pack of four to six sheets, each with four to six cards on it; players have to deal with all cards simultaneously. Most seasoned players buy at least a few packs, which they play at the same time (eyes darting from one card to another) in order to double or triple their chances.

Bingo payouts in Las Vegas have come a long way from the charity pot at church, and are also more complex. Some halls offer "bonus" or "bonanza" cards that must be played separately, sometimes with numbers only printed on them, which can pay out as much as $50,000. One man told me about a million-dollar bingo jackpot paid out at an Indian reservation game. "And that was all at once—not over twenty years like in the lottery," he said. (Gamblers' lore is full of such legends, most of them impossible to verify.)

Many halls will pay higher stakes for a bingo called out within, say, eighteen numbers of the start. Pots may grow progressively larger if no one gets bingo within a certain number of calls, and consolation prizes go to those who call bingo on the next number after the first bingo is called. Bingo is legal in every U.S. state except Utah and Hawaii (which permit no form of gambling whatever), but Las Vegas is one of the few places in the country, along with some Indian reservations, with no legal limits on any kind of wagering or jackpots. It is probably also the only place that offers free door-to-door service to and from bingo games.

Lillian is a sweet-looking lady whose smiling eyes belie a surprisingly sharp tongue, developed over twenty-five years of cocktail waitressing in Las Vegas showrooms. Having lived here since 1963, she is an old hand at bingo, and has graciously agreed to serve as my mentor.

Any Vegas bingo hall worth its balls is equipped with enormous number boards that light up each number as it's called, as well as monitors hanging from the ceiling with close-up views of each numbered Ping-Pong ball after it has been sucked out of the hopper.

Arizona Charlie's is a bingo player's bingo hall, seating four hundred. The long, Formica-topped tables are made specifically for the game, with a small partition in the middle, not too high to chat over but high enough to provide a little privacy and aid concentration. The first thing a player has to do is stake out a lucky seat. As in most of the bigger halls, Charlie's posts yellow half sheets on which players circle all the sessions they intend to play, then sign their names to reserve their places. Many sheets have been decorated with ink daubs to name the places permanently, like the bronze plaques affixed to church pews in honor of benefactors. The most serious players at Arizona Charlie's have created works of genuine folk art out of dauber ink on goldenrod Xerox paper. Diana's is a moonlit night scene with an eerie weeping willow under the stars and a witch flying overhead. Bart has drawn a cheerful spring day with a cat sitting under trees and blue skies. Paul's and Rubie's cards have been decorated with blue and pink dauber ink with every session time circled, and then laminated in rigid plastic for posterity. Lillian has a permanent seat marker as well, decorated in typical pink and blue dauber polka dots.

"Here," she says, pulling a seat marker out of her bingo bag. "Just fill it out regular for now. We've got to get in line before it gets too long."

I scribble in my name and follow her to the cashier's cage where the cards are sold. There seem to be four prices for packs; the more you pay, the more you can win. "Well, what'll it be?" the cashier asks me, impatiently. The line behind me is snaking through the room. It's about five minutes before the hour. I am at a loss.

Lillian finally pushes me aside, with a reassuring "It's okay. You're new." Leaning into the window, she tells the woman, "I need one three-dollar, two sixes, and one nine."

Armed, we return to our seats to find a few of Lillian's friends already there. Agnes and Jean are wearing the same crepe plaid shorts set (Agnes in red, Jean in blue) and exactly the same orthopedic shoes. "Hey!" Agnes greets Lillian. "You're late! We wondered what happened."

"I was in line. It just took longer today," Lillian answers, shooting a look at me.

Agnes and Jean look me over. "Where's your stuff?" she asks me.

Lillian explains. "She's never played before."

Knowing "Ohhhhhs."

"I, I couldn't figure out what I wanted…." I stammer.

"Yeah, well, you can buy more packs when you're ready. But if you're starting out, you just better stick to one," Agnes says. "It's okay, Lil, you can share my Orange Julius until you can get to the snack bar."

Daubers are the plastic ink bottles with flat fabric tops that players use to mark winning numbers in most Vegas bingo halls. All daubers must imprint a clear and unmistakable dot covering the number, but not with ink so dark that it makes the number illegible. Casinos distribute their own, sometimes from vending machines, imprinted with the casino logo. They come in every color, including fluorescents and glow-in-the-dark; some inks sparkle, and some are metallic. The bottles are thin and round, flattened for an easy grip, or molded into novelty shapes like stacked balls or teddy bears. Lillian carries all her bingo equipment, including Scotch tape, moist towelettes, and a clipboard to hold the cards up, in a drawstring bag decorated with bingo cards that has holsters all around the outside to house daubers.

Choosing the color, shape, and style of dauber to use for each game usually involves a mixture of strategy and superstition. Of course, I have no dauber, so Lillian lends me a green one. "I used green yesterday, so I'm not gonna use it today," she says.

Lillian is a fury of activity, lining up her rainbow of daubers and Scotch-taping pages together for easy scanning. Agnes and Jean have surrounded themselves with bingo packs, an array of pastel "Horseshoe Casino" daubers, a Dr. Pepper, an Orange Julius, a bottle of Evian, a foot-long hot dog apiece, popcorn, Snickers bars, and a pack of long, skinny More cigarettes. These women are professionals.

The din in the hall immediately ceases when the caller announces the start of the session; it is replaced by a hush and a palpable tension. The room is packed, mainly with older folks, most of them women, most of them white, but the single-minded anticipation permeating the place seems to transform all classes and races into a huge, multiheaded, faceless mass. Three Hell's Angels in black leather vests and motorcycle boots sit in one corner, but they don't stick out. Nearly everyone smokes. No one speaks.

One by one, the balls dancing around the air hopper are sucked out. "B-11. B-11," drones the caller up front. "Chicken legs!" someone shouts. Giggles and groans ripple through the ranks. Agnes whispers that some people also blow a whistle at I-22 or O-69. "If you come a lot, though, it's annoying," she says.

"B-34. B-34." Everyone hunts, the lucky ones daub; everyone waits for the fateful shout.

Finally, it comes. "Bingo!" we hear across the room. A rumble of comments rises up from the mass, and heads begin to peer up to see who it is. The attendants go over and check the numbers, calling out each one.

"B-52? B-52. I-31? I-31. N-29? N-29. G-15? G—uh, I don't…"

The din rises suddenly—the woman was mistaken! Redemption for everyone! The caller concedes that there is, indeed, no bingo. "Rookie!" is shouted from various parts of the room. "See?" Lillian pokes me. "You better be careful."

Soon afterward, however, someone else calls bingo and gets it. The rumble turns to a grumble as people tear off the top sheet and get ready for the next game. The competitive instinct runs so high that it's easy to see why some halls give away "good neighbor" prizes for the people immediately to the left and right of the winner.

■ ■ ■

Anyone who has caught bingo fever but doesn't have the right gear can go to Bingo Novelty World, on Industrial Road, which has everything bingo imaginable. Bingo tote bags in every size and color, bingo seat cushions, neck fans for comfort, bingo-ball key chains, bingo software, bingo card pendants and earrings, bingo sports bottles, bingo clocks, bingo ashtrays with dauber-shaped lighters, bingo daubers with troll-head tops, and the "Lorena Bobbit" penis-shaped gift pack. There is an array of T-shirts with bingo prayers ("Now I lay me down to slumber, I pray that they will call my number…."), and slogans like "Keep Grandma Off the Streets, Take her to Bingo!"

In Las Vegas, America's favorite retirement destination, every kind of public and commercial service for the elderly is available: clinics, clubs, senior centers, senior discounts, special tours, free college courses; subdivisions, apartments, and trailer parks reserved just for them; special exercise classes, golf carts and golf courses, medical-supply stores and pharmacies open 24 hours every day, meals on wheels and home visitors; more than seventy home-health services; more than eighty licensed nursing homes.

But the most valuable senior service of all may be those little cards, each gridded into twenty-five squares and imprinted with someone's lucky numbers. Every day, thousands of elderly Las Vegas flock willingly to the bingo halls of the city's casinos. Whatever the cost, these gambling halls have become for them the most comfortable and congenial social centers in town.

Growing Up in Las Vegas

Marie Sanchez

Airy homes garden sculptures glass-and-tile schools palm-
lined streets parks fountain courtyards Shakespearean actors
families al fresco dining upscale shopping—a sense of community pride and traditional family values.

The new Green Valley neighborhood offers "a sense of
community pride and traditional family values along with the cultural
awareness and conveniences often found in larger cities." The developers
strive to "make sure their communities thrive for decades to come [since]
many home buyers want to feel a sense of community and belonging to
the area in which they live." Scenes of happy family life illustrate the
brochure. The builders, we are told, have created a strong social setting
with such amenities as a "lushly landscaped Paseo [which] meanders
through the community...craft and art fairs and concerts which are all
free...a Town Center, a thriving 'centertainment' hot spot with restaurants, a theatre and shopping...and more intimate concerts in their
acclaimed interactive fountain courtyard area."
Families have lived in the Las Vegas valley ever since Brigham Young
first tried to colonize it with Mormon farmers in 1855-57. Molded in part
by the apparent rush and abandon of the city's dominant industry, in
part by the enduring values of the Old West, and in part by the lingering

influence of its family-oriented Mormon founders, what is the contemporary Las Vegas family like? How are the children of Las Vegas growing up today?

■ ■ ■

In 1997, Nevada ranked second in the nation in teen pregnancies per capita. Clark County (Greater Las Vegas) accounted for most of those. Lately, programs to reduce this rate among thirteen- to seventeen-year-olds have shown some success; the rate is dipping among the more than fifty thousand teens in the county. But now the number of teen abortions is soaring. School buses for some high schools in Clark County come equipped with baby seats.

In 1996, the national Center for Disease Control and Prevention reported that Las Vegas teenagers led the nation in drug use and violence. The Las Vegas Metro Police Department has identified 150 gangs within the city limits, gangs that have organized the drug trade with firepower and violence. "There isn't a single neighborhood without a gang," said one police spokesman. In a move unique in the United States, Nevada has made class sessions in suicide prevention a requirement for high-school graduation.

What has gone wrong?

Talking with Las Vegas teens themselves provides some clues. Whether the young people you talk to profess to love the city or loathe it, a few persistent themes cut across social, economic, and racial lines.

■ ■ ■

> Black silky hair brushing slender hips long legs sparkling almond eyes olive skin plum mouth—I would do anything.

"I would do anything," says Anabel Granados, 17, who might have been the model for Disney's Pocahontas. "Sing, dance, or play violin. But I prefer Selena's music." We are watching videos of some of Anabel's onstage performances, organized to showcase her versatility. In the first, she's dressed in the red uniform of a Matachine Indian, playing the violin at Caesars Palace while fifty members of the Apache tribe sur round her chanting, dancing, and playing ancient and modern musical instruments.

In the next video she's wearing the snug-fitting, braid-trimmed black uniform of Mariachi Mi Tierra while the seven-member group serenades an audience at Nellis Air Force Base. Another shows Anabel during a Catholic ritual before the high gilded altar in St. Christopher's Church, which serves part of Las Vegas's large Spanish-speaking community. In the last one, at her sister Marlyn's *quinceañero* (fifteenth birthday celebration), Anabel wears an upswept coif, heavy makeup, and floor-length blue velvet-and-chiffon while she sings "Wind Beneath my Wings"—Marlyn's favorite song—to a hushed crowd of more than five hundred.

Anabel and her sister Marlyn, 15, curl up in two overstuffed royal-blue chairs in an uncluttered, white-walled, white-tiled living room. Anabel is wearing cutoffs and a red-flowered blouse that stops just above her narrow waist; she folds her slender legs onto the cushion. A lifelong Las Vegas resident who wants to stay in the city and perform in hotel showrooms, she claims that only a recording contract from Los Angeles could uproot her.

Anabel brings out her performance costumes and spreads them on the blue sofa. She and her mother sew them after she and her sister design them. The Matachine costumes, one red and one beige, are ornately fringed, sequined, beaded and heavy. Anabel spent a full year working on the red one, reserved for special religious ceremonies. Other costumes—medium-short swirly skirts and conservative halter tops—come in silver and black, accented by bowties and cummerbunds in black, red, and white. Coordinated hot pants complete the ensembles. "I want people to pay attention to what I do, not how I look. All I've wanted, ever since I can remember, is to perform—and for other people to enjoy it almost as much as I do."

At the moment, when Anabel performs in the occasional show, she makes $25 an hour, a wage few other cities can offer to seventeen-year-olds. Las Vegas's 9-PM weekday curfew (which bans teens unaccompanied by adults from the Strip and Downtown) doesn't affect her: she's an entertainer, in a city that still likes to call itself the Entertainment Capital of the World.

In public, Anabel carries herself with the bearing and confidence of a queen. Her favorite pastime—not exactly typical among American teenagers—is watching the big shows in the Strip hotels: Siegfried and Roy at the Mirage, EFX at the MGM Grand, Cirque du Soleil at Treasure Island. "I could never see things like that anywhere else. And they let me into the Hispanic clubs, but not into the others. I'm not old enough. Still, every casino I know has at least one bar or lounge I can go to."

She also loves to dance. She dances to tropical music at the Gold Coast, Mexican music at Camilo's Ballroom, the Sinaloense and El Rey Clubs, sometimes till four or five in the morning, though not every weekend.

After some reluctance, almost everyone in Anabel's family, including her parents, has come to support her dreams of becoming a big-time performer. "I think this is my chance," she says breathlessly. "When you get a chance, that's it. Either things happen or they don't. You don't usually get a second chance. You have to be prepared." Her voice drops off, as if she is afraid of jinxing her good luck.

Even the moderate measure of success she has won so far has changed her personal life. "Some friends aren't friends anymore. And guys look at you differently. Now when I go out, I wonder why they're seeing me. But you have to be willing to go through all that, and want it badly enough. And be prepared for the ups and downs." Anabel has run into another problem in her chosen field: "The hard part of the music business is there's lots of drugs involved. It attracts a lot of people from out of town who are looking for a change. When things don't go right for them, there's a loneliness thing. They have money and they get tempted.... There's cocaine, Ecstasy, and a lot of rave parties. At school it's so easy to get it."

And, of course, there's the Las Vegas sex industry. "College girls strip for tuition," she says. "Sometimes I wonder how bad things would have to get before I did something like that. There are places where you strip down to a bathing suit. I would look into that if things got really bad."

Anabel dismisses the typical outsider's view of life in Las Vegas. "Everyone assumes that you walk around the casinos all the time, and that there's always this temptation. They assume that I go to the Strip every day." Although her cinderblock row house is only a tumbleweed roll away from Sam's Town, a big neighborhood casino on Boulder Highway, she believes she can insulate herself from the casinos and the problems associated with them. "There's the casinos and there's the other side of Las Vegas, with real problems just like other towns." But she is concerned about the effects of gambling on the city's younger residents. "I live far from the [Strip] casinos, but they still influence us a lot. Things are more liberal here, and that leads to growing up a bit faster. We're exposed to more things than a lot of towns are. And it's easier here to be bad than to be good."

Growing up in North Las Vegas, where most new Latino families start out, Anabel saw firsthand the "real problems" of Las Vegas—"drive-bys every night, drug busts every night." But "it didn't affect me that much," she insists. "Then we moved to a better part of town."

"Now at school there's lots of violence and a lot of racial conflicts. I would think that would be gone by now—by high school you're supposed to be at a more mature level. Last year it was Mexican Americans against African Americans. Then it got all out of hand, not just gangs, but drugs, sex, things in general. And Chaparral is a nice school."

Another "real problem," Anabel says, is teen pregnancy, which is rampant among her friends. "Most of my friends have children. One had two children by age fifteen, another had one at age sixteen, and another had one at seventeen. They decided they were mature enough to have sex, but didn't think about the consequences.

"Our schools don't teach us about sex. We don't have condoms in schools. If I hadn't read a book, I wouldn't know certain things could happen to you." Strong Mormon and fundamentalist Christian influences have helped to keep sex education out of public schools in Clark County. Many of Anabel's friends live with the father of their children in the house of one parent or another, three generations under one roof.

Whatever her peers do, life for Anabel's will probably continue to be different from that of her family and friends. "I decided that if I didn't get married at eighteen, I wouldn't do it until my career either took off—or it didn't."

■ ■ ■

Advanced Spanish class, Chapparal High. Some of the students (most of them Hispanic) have distant looks, nodding heads; others have glazed eyes; a few keep their heads on their desks the entire class. About a quarter of them are visibly on drugs, but the homeroom teacher tells me she has been advised not to mention this.

At the teacher's request, I talk to the students about careers in journalism. After a few polite questions from two students, I ask the class to tell me what *I* should know about growing up in Las Vegas. The energy level climbs, although only a few students participate. Gradually, they start talking about pregnancies, gangs, drugs, suicides.

Then more students join in: There is nothing to do. We're discriminated against. Suddenly many of them are talking at once. I live for the dances. A girl I knew killed herself, she was eighteen, pregnant, her boyfriend left her. I can work in a casino, why should I care about school?

Anabel warned me that many kids don't value education. "Don't take it personally if you don't get anywhere with them," she said. "Try to get them to answer questions." Now we sit on a wooden bench under an emerald pine that filters out the hazy March sun in the school's central courtyard, next to a statue of a cowboy mounted on a bucking bronco.

Anabel is dressed in gray slacks and a fitted black jacket, both of which match the dark circles under her eyes as she tells me about her schedule. "There's so much pressure right now. Things are happening way too fast."

She plans to play and sing her way through the University of Nevada at Las Vegas, thanks to a violin scholarship from the University and a grant from the Hispanic Chamber of Commerce. "I'm still filling out scholarship applications. The thought of college is so scary." She lets out a trembling breath. "But it's really going to happen. I'm also trying to be a manager at McDonald's and I haven't even started to read the manual. I have to get pictures in makeup and costumes this week, and cut a demonstration CD with three songs next month. There'll be so much rehearsing. Then there are newspaper interviews and stuff. Everything they write, I have to live up to." Her shoulders sag under the burden.

Chirping birds pierce the sound of Anabel's agitated voice as she describes how she's managing this stage in her life. "Either I sing or go to youth group at church. Or it builds up until I have a nervous breakdown. Then I cry a lot and then it goes away. I haven't been to youth group for three weeks."

From a loudspeaker, a foghorn sound summons her back inside for class. It's choir practice, the last period before spring break. Fifty-plus students form a crescent across a low stage, and a student conductor begins the rehearsal. Their voices send Latin, German, and English phrases into the warm, stuffy air. Most of the kids concentrate, bodies stiff, hands clenched at their sides. Chins and lips project like songbirds' beaks; eyebrows are stitched in concentration. A few in the back laugh quietly or talk, elbowing each other. Anabel stands near the center, rapt and focused. The choir, which receives high marks at festivals, sounds very good.

The foghorn blares again. Small groups of students amass and disperse. Anabel says goodbye and rushes off to her job.

A few minutes later, at the tiny, original-style McDonald's on Eastern and Tropicana (one of thirty-eight in Las Vegas), Anabel is taking orders. She hands me a Coke and invites me inside for a behind-the-counter tour of her workplace. She reviews the day's sales on a personal computer, checks supplies, and goes back to taking orders. With fluid, efficient movements she rotates from register to fries to burgers to soft drinks. She's dressed in an unglamorous navy-blue polo shirt and slacks, her ebony mane in a top knot that pokes through the navy cap emblazoned "McDonald's."

Anabel is hardly typical of Las Vegas youth. She doesn't drink, smoke, swear, or do drugs. "I don't drink because it has such horrible consequences. My uncle killed someone because he was driving drunk. Hurt himself, too. My mom smokes and it affected my immune system. I get sick easily around smoke—I get sniffles and feel weird."

The Catholic Church and two strict parents have given Anabel strong and deep roots. There was no dating, no makeup, no high heels until she turned fifteen. While I visited, Anabel's mother was in Mexico caring for her own sick mother. When she decided to lengthen her stay, Anabel and Marlyn had to keep the house running back in Las Vegas. In spite of the respite provided by spring break, Anabel had little time for herself. She canceled her photo shoot, a youth-group meeting, the premiere of the Selena movie, a weekend dance, and a trip with a friend to a California beach in order to stay home and wash dishes, do laundry, mop the floors, and cook for her father, a chef at Ricardo's Mexican restaurant on East Tropicana. She couldn't meet with me on Sunday, she said, because "Sunday is family day."

In spite of everything she's seen, Las Vegas is still Anabel's town. "It's weird in other towns. You go out at two AM and it's empty, or people are doing things they shouldn't be doing. Here the Strip is so beautiful."

■ ■ ■

Volmar Franz, who came to Las Vegas in 1983, works as a family therapist. He tries to shed some light on my story of a seventeen-year-old girl from a Mexican Catholic family who performs in casino hotels. "You've got a strange mix in Las Vegas. There's a Mormon influence in the town that is very heavy. Beyond the Mormons, there's a heavy-duty Christian influence.

"Then there's the image of the town: get rich quick and indulge in fast and easy sex, everything here's free and loose." The strict ethical principles of the religious groups clash with the Sin City appeal of Downtown and the Strip. "It's disorienting. It's a constant contradiction in terms. It takes a lot to figure it out, and I can't say after sixteen years that it makes a lot of sense to me.

"I see some of that as being an attempt to balance what's going on here. On the one hand, the casinos crack down on prostitution; on the other hand, we've got some of the wildest strip clubs in the country. You can come here and lose everything. But don't get too drunk, or someone will go to the gaming-room floor and you'll disappear. Don't get too bawdy about finding yourself a whore. If you make too much noise or are too overt, they will take you away. Do not get involved in drug use. Possession of any amount is a felony—a seed of marijuana is a felony! They are not loose about drugs at all, although it is pervasive. If you get caught, they will prosecute you. You will fall."

The subtleties of Las Vegas's conflicting rules for survival can be lost on teens. And for those who aren't as rooted as Anabel, the conflicts can create major problems.

"It's a problem for kids trying to find an identity," says Franz. "It slows down their development. They're less prepared to go out and do something."

The problems that affect Las Vegas children include overcrowded schools that run daily double shifts; the fewest parks of any major U.S. city; and a general lack of recreational activities. For many teenagers—who can quickly be made to feel unwanted anyway in this "adults-only" town—these can combine to create a sense of being superfluous and ignored, and a stress-filled, unhealthy, dangerous space in which to grow up.

■ ■ ■

On this rainy, windy night I am trying to follow the directions I have been given to meet a group of teens in a hard-to-find community, master-planned and guard-gated, the pride and joy of its residents. I attempt to follow my hostess's directions, but the identical houses in all-but-identical subdivisions leave me bewildered. Road signs are difficult to spot, as if residents did not want outsiders to find them. I stop at stores to ask for directions; sales clerks stare at me with blank faces.

In the middle of the downpour, I call my hostess and get more detailed directions. It's still no use. Finally, she comes to pick me up at the pay phone I am using. I am forty-five minutes late by this time, and thoroughly wet.

I sit in a warm, white living room under a beamed ceiling and try to dry myself out (along with my tape recorder, which has fallen in a puddle). Six teens sit in modular furniture of pale beiges and deep creams. They've been eating chips, pretzels, and nuts and drinking soft drinks while waiting for me. They tell me how they got lost the first time they visited here, too. One girl says she drove around for almost an hour.

They range in age from fifteen to nineteen. After some initial wariness, they start to talk about their hometowns. All but one have come to Las Vegas in the last two or three years, when their parents were lured here by money and jobs. They plan to go to college and become journalists, businesspeople, medical assistants, doctors. They are all white, well-to-do students at Durango, one of the county's "better" high schools. (It boasts two modern gyms, one of which seats 3,500.) 82 percent of its seniors graduate.

At my urging, the students' meandering talk soon turns to the subject of what it's like to grow up in Las Vegas. These are some of the things they told me, as we talked long into the night.

On drugs:
"Over half the kids at school use them. Mainly crystal."
"I lost forty pounds on them."
"I loved all the energy it gave me for school, household chores, and then my night job."
"People are always offering them to me."

On sex, prostitution, and teen pregnancy:
"The popular girls wear shiny leather miniskirts, high-heeled pumps, and big hair to school. They look like whores."
"If girls need cash, [prostitution is] always on the back of their minds, especially at the end of the month or at Christmas."
"My friends are careless with sex. They say 'Let's go get drunk or high or something,' then…they have stupid, irresponsible sex and get pregnant…or worse."
"My friend married and divorced by the time she graduated from high school."
"I get HIV-tested to get free condoms."

On violence:
"I know someone who was raped."
"My friend got his throat cut. He was an innocent bystander. He was twenty and he survived."
"Someone tried to kill my brother by running him over with a car."
"My friend got a gun pulled on him six months ago."

On suicide:
"It's pretty fucking intimidating here. The kids have Mercedes, nice clothes, and all that."
"A football player I knew committed suicide. He got all A's and was popular, with a pretty girlfriend."
"When you sit there with nothing to do, nowhere to go, you feel really alone—like a speck of salt in a sea of sand."

On alienation:
"People move in and out. You lose your friends."
"It's hard here, usually because you feel you don't fit in. This is a small community."
"No one talks to you. I went up to my neighbor and said, 'Hello.' He ran inside his house without a word."

On families, and the twenty-four-hour lifestyle:
"My parents are the only ones I know of who are still together."
"My mom works two jobs."
"That's why kids use drugs. We can get everything done then: school-work, cleaning our rooms, after-school jobs, and partying."

And how do these affluent, reasonably balanced teens who want to leave Las Vegas for "someplace greener," or any college but UNLV, handle the anything-goes atmosphere of Las Vegas?
"In a twenty-four-hour town, there's a lot of things you can do impulsively. You have to grow up sooner."
"You have to harden yourself to protect yourself."
"Vegas attracts a lot of bad people. You have to really be selective."

■ ■ ■

Jack Diamond, a marriage and family therapist, believes that in Las Vegas, the 24-hour way of life is probably the single most destructive element for families. "Shift work creates a lot of problems with relationships. If one parent works day, and the other graveyard, then the couple stops doing things together." Marriages break up. One-parent families proliferate. "Many kids don't have much supervision, and no extended family to watch out for them if their parents work."

Residents, he believes, develop addictions in response to the city's bounty of temptations. Diamond provides a sketch of family life in Las Vegas based on his own clientele. "It includes gambling, alcohol, and drug addictions. And then marriage problems, half of which end in divorce. For children, on top of everything else, it reflects the dysfunctional family's problems, as well as their own."

These addictions can destroy adults, thus compounding their effects on teenagers. "The younger the subject's age, the faster the various addictions form. That makes it more difficult for normal developmental processes to take over. Kids are more juvenile and less socialized. If they drink or take drugs before age twenty-one, then these activities keep them in a pubertal state longer. They react instead of act. And their behavior remains impulsive."

Gambling is the most common addiction among Diamond's clients. "They started gambling before they were twenty-one. Some started as teens. But the gambling addiction really manifests itself in adulthood. It takes time to develop."

Even if they manage to avoid most temptations, says Diamond, children who grow up in Las Vegas are at higher-than-normal risk for erratic behavior and personality disorders. They see "people who come here to work and get caught up in gambling very early. This is what we do best here and it's very seductive. Adults gamble, lose money, then lose their job in this right-to-fire town. Then their family goes. That's what causes a lot of suicide and depression. Others move here, and the temptations overcome them.

"By growing up exposed to all this, kids think they are growing up faster. They're just losing their innocence sooner. The growing up comes later. And it comes most often for the children in the upper economic strata, where parents are better educated and have the money to get the help their children need to overcome whatever addiction or disorder they develop. Other kids must parent themselves. And they do it poorly. The teens most at risk are near poverty level, especially if parents are not involved in their lives, or if they don't have organized athletics or interests in their lives."

Allan Pulsipher, a management analyst with the county's Family and Youth Services Division for juvenile offenders, paints the face of the town from a different angle. "Nevada's always been an outlaw state," he says. "The vast barren desert cannot support a state government. We've legalized activities that are illegal elsewhere to attract industry and tourists. It makes things more wide open than other places. It creates a culture where more is possible. It's living on the edge." The result, he says, is too many people and kids and too few services. "Our juvenile jails are overcrowded. We have mattresses on the floors for kids to sleep on. Our schools are overcrowded. Our streets are packed. We lurch from one crisis to another."

Diamond guides me through other points of interest on the Las Vegas social landscape: "We are the second-highest state for beer consumption per capita. We have more DUIs ["driving under the influence" arrests] than any other state. About five percent of the people here are addicted to gambling; nationwide it's half as high. Ten percent of the people here go to A.A."

> Freckle-specked porcelain skin blue-gray eyes flaming-red hair pouty vulnerable tough shy rebellious at risk. I was shaking, I was sweating.

"I was shaking at the time, and I was sweating," says nineteen-year-old Anne. Anne is talking about the night she denied to her foster mother that she used marijuana, when she was actually strung out on speed. "It was really, really bad—the fact that I had to lie, and on drugs, and being on a drug worse than she could ever imagine that I was doing. I love my foster parents more than anything."

That was the start of her recovery, almost two years ago. Anne had alighted in Las Vegas the year before. Her decline began almost as soon as she arrived in Speed City. "My first rail of speed was a couple of weeks after I moved here. The crowd I was with, these two girls, they were into it. Maybe I did it to belong or to do something different.... Here drugs aren't a problem of the inner city. It's a worse problem in the suburbs.

"With speed, you're so spun for, like, seven hours—even more. And when you're down, you do another line. The down is sooo hard. It's like you get the flu—you're sluggish and you don't want to move. You're upset at people and you're angry.

"I would do a line before school. Halfway through I'd go to the bathroom and do another line. I'd go home and sleep all day. I'd wake up in the middle of the night and do another line, and then go to school.

"My grades were really good. I had flunked my freshman year at high school in Colorado. I had a one-point-eight as a sophomore in Ohio. But I came here and was getting straight A's; the speed kicked me off into the mode where I wanted straight A's. You always wanna be busy, and you don't want to sleep or sit down. You just want to do everything. I cleaned my room top to bottom. I'd dust all the little cracks of my room. I'd do my homework in an hour."

In a 24-hour town, where energy is a big lure, speed is fast becoming the most prevalent drug in high schools. But its snare began to frighten Anne.

"I think speed is the biggest drug that will change people inside. It will make people not want to do the things they've always wanted to do. I started not to care about my family. People started looking at me different. I was classified as a 'tweaker,' people who don't take care of themselves. They're not good people.

"I thought I'd take care of myself, but five or six in the morning would roll around and I'd still be up and would just take a shower. I'd always thought personal appearance shows a lot about a person.

"One time I passed out in the parking lot. I had been up for a couple of days. I'd go days without eating. Then I'd get really sick and sleep the whole day. One day after being violently sick, I just said, 'I don't want to do this anymore.'"

And she hasn't, she says, although she admits she'd do coke if she had the money. "The downs aren't as bad with coke."

Anne views Las Vegas with the perspective of an outsider. "Reality is really sad here. This town brings out the worst in people: crime, pornography, gambling, homelessness and desperation. It's a really sad city. All the mobile-park homes and kids growing up with fathers and mothers that are alcoholics and addicted to gambling. I know people who have grown up basically without parents, because they're compulsive gamblers, which has left them with nothing.

"It brings out the greed. People want to be high rollers—bigger and better. Vegas is like a mirage for something deeper than what it really is. I don't think Vegas is real. There wouldn't be such crime and poverty in Vegas without this whole idea of 'come to Vegas and get rich and famous.'

"There's a lot of opportunity in Vegas, but I don't think there's a lot of things to do because of the whole twenty-one thing. When kids look around and don't find anything to do, there's crime. My best friend had a gun pulled on him six months ago. My twelve-year-old foster brother was stuffed into a trash can. There are so many little punks. When kids have nothing to do, they'll go out and look for trouble."

Because her foster parents are moving away soon, Anne is looking for her own apartment. She's maxed out her credit cards. At nineteen, she's a confessed shopaholic. Recently, her parents brought up the idea of telephone sex because it offers a lot of money for relatively little time. Anne recounts, "They said, 'We're not saying do it or not. We just wanted you to be aware of it.'"

The money is alluring to Anne. "Usually girls go home with a hundred dollars a night for four hours' work," she says. "For doing nothing. That's right up my alley." But she still has ambivalent feelings about working in the sex trade. Every day she weighs the pros and cons. "I've actually gotten into my car, and driven down there. But then I go 'no.' It would be really disturbing. I don't think it would violate me as a person, like rape, but I just don't want to hear stuff like that.

"But I know after a while, I wouldn't even care. It's just actually getting down there. I know if I was trained, I could do the talking. I just get real nervous about it. It's intimidating for me, I guess."

Anne's aware that the "easy money" she might earn doing phone sex would bring a whole new set of problems. "I would know that people calling me are sick," she says. "I'd wonder what they're doing on the other end of the phone. It would be weird and scary. If I got into that industry, I'd change a little bit."

Anne's friends tell her that she's already bitter toward men. She admits she may have problems relating to them—"I already tell guys, 'Don't play around with me.' I set my conditions."

She blames her bitterness on everything but herself. "Sex is just so exploited now. A lot of guys want to screw as many girls as they can before their time is up. And Vegas instills bad ideals into guys. That women are easy and women aren't supposed to be respected. I've known a lot of guys who are players here. They'll say anything to get what they want."

Finally, she concedes she may be part of the problem. "I am bitter towards men, I guess. I hate everybody that I've ever dated. I don't want to even hear about them."

■ ■ ■

Ebony skin golden brown eyes firm plump flesh short dress seductive smile fast fast fast—he's my duty bug.

"'He's my duty bug," says Sasha, a sixteen-year-old single mom about Darrione, her sixteen-month-old son.

"Duty bug. That's what I've called him ever since he was a baby. If I don't wanna be a mother, I still gotta be a mother. I just know that's my son and he's my responsibility." She's in my hotel room, sitting at a round table waiting for lunch from room service. She ordered a strawberry ice-cream sundae.

Overcrowding in the schools has forced the district to dismiss some children at 11 AM and have others start their school day at six. This leaves many children alone with nothing to do during the day, and, some say, contributes to the situation of young girls like Sasha, who became pregnant at fourteen by a sixteen-year-old boy. Some community activists have talked about suing the Clark County School District for running double sessions. If residents refuse to approve sufficient funds through bond elections to return Las Vegas schools to normal hours, concerned parents may have to fight their battle in the courts.

But Sasha refuses to blame her pregnancy on irregular school hours or inadequate supervision. "I was just being fast. 'You just got to have a man,' my granny tells me. I didn't use birth control. I just didn't think it would happen to me. 'Cause I thought I was special," she says, playing with her ice cream and shaking her head.

The epidemic of teen pregnancies in Las Vegas centers on low-income families, says Jean Palmer of the Clark County Public Heath Department. "African American, mostly." Palmer heads up several education and birth-control programs that are trying to make a dent in the conception rate for girls sixteen years of age and under. "Seventeen- and eighteen-year-olds know what they're doing," Palmer says.

Rancho, Horizon, and Cimmaron-Memorial High Schools have child-care facilities on their premises, a program soon to be expanded to most other high schools in the county. Children spend their lunchtime and one class period with their babies. Sasha will transfer to one of these next year, probably Cimmaron, and ride the bus with her baby. "Every school has teen pregnancies, every school," Sasha says. "I only have two or three friends without babies.

"Everybody asks me [what it's like]. It's easy. I don't have a choice. If I don't like being a mother I still gotta be a mother. It doesn't feel any different." For Sasha, that's easier than for many others. She gets a lot of help from the two aunts she lives with in a four-bedroom, four-bath house in North Las Vegas. Her Aunt Catherine has raised several relatives' children (including Sasha) since they were babies. Sasha calls her "Granny."

Afraid of her Aunt Catherine's puritanical attitude toward sex and her volatile temper, Sasha initially tried to keep her pregnancy a secret. "I didn't tell anyone until I was pregnant seven-and-a-half months," she says. "I was scared to death."

Sasha finally confided in her best friend, who told her mother, who then told Aunt Catherine. "It was a big relief, everybody knowing and not just me knowing that secret. But I don't see how they couldn't tell I was pregnant. I wasn't sick, but I was tired. They just thought I was getting fat.

"Granny was so mad at me. She was embarrassed because her other girls didn't do that to her. Every little thing I do now, it rolls up into something big. I still have fun, but not like I used to have. Like going out, staying out late.

"I should have had prenatal care. It was a lot of risk. But I was lucky; Darrione had low iron is all.

"I could have had an abortion, but I was just too scared to tell anybody. If I had, I probably wouldn't have a son now. I don't like abortions, but if you can't take care of a baby financially then you shouldn't have it. The experience I had when I was pregnant, well, I know right now I don't want any more kids."

A sunny afternoon, mild weather, soft sunlight: kids are swinging, running, climbing, laughing. Sasha coaxes Darrione up a slide. Nervously he allows himself to be seated on the top step and pushed gently down. Halfway down he falls back from the unaccustomed force, and finishes on his back. Shaken, he begins to cry, to everyone's soft laughter. Sasha picks him up and walks him to the pond, trying to distract him from his tears with the ducks. He begins to call them, extending his arms, still a little unsteady on his feet.

Sasha started having sex at age thirteen. She says most of her friends started at age twelve, but didn't talk to each other about it for another year or two.

Today Sasha lives on welfare. Although he pays no child support, the baby's father, who lives at home with his parents and operates an amusement ride at Circus Circus, sometimes takes care of Darrione. He and Sasha still date, and she still uses no birth control, except for a condom now and then. "Granny took my birth-control pills away," she says. "She got mad when my [other] aunt found them. She doesn't think young girls should be having sex. But I still see him. They like him, so they let me see him."

"Granny" Catherine, who is childless, is very cautious about Sasha's activities now. "I don't let her go out of my sight. I couldn't stand to have another baby here," she says.

But all the vigilance in the world can't keep the youngsters of Las Vegas away from sex. "Just about everybody's had everybody, except my granny," Sasha says. "Now, I have a baby but I don't have a name. I have to be careful. I like this other guy, but we just hang out. You just don't have sex with a whole lot of people unless you want a name."

What's a lot, I ask? Silence. Seven?

Sasha's eyes open wide in surprise. "That would be bad for you," she whispers. "You'd get a name."

Sasha, who was once a cheerleader, imagines a future in beauty salons. "I like to do hair and nails." In five years, she says, "I'll have my own job, my own place on the other side of Vegas, with my own car, a teal Honda. Darrione will be in grade school."

And when she's thirty, or more? "I can't even see that far. I wanna have a family, a husband and Darrione, and that's it. I wanna be doing hair. I want him to have a good life. That's why I'm trying to get a job and all that. I want him to go through school. I want him to have fun like he's supposed to."

■ ■ ■

Carol Turner, a marriage and family therapist who has been practicing in Las Vegas for three years, says the lack of activities for youngsters, combined with low parental supervision, lies at the heart of the problem. "As a society we should provide things for kids to do. If they go to a park, they may be chased out by the neighbors. They'll go way out in the desert, build a fire and have some drinks. The police chase them off. If they violate curfew, they go to jail. They can't cruise the Strip after nine PM on weekends. Where are they supposed to go?"

The stresses that adults live with in Las Vegas carry over to the whole family. And money problems, the primary source of stress, can lead to an impotent anger toward life that's unleashed on families. "I see lots of domestic violence, women in abusive relationships," Turner says. "Most child-abuse cases arise from overdisciplining out of anger. Sexual abuse is also high here. There's a great lack of communication, which leads to weak marriages. Children grow up in families that don't have the skills to cope. And if parents don't have them, children don't gain them."

■ ■ ■

Hissing expressways muttering alleys rattling valleys vibrating shaking stinking seething—it's my town.

"It's my town," says Eric Weisman, 18. "My parents are real-estate appraisers, they used to take me everywhere with them. Now I know every part. Part of it is really dark around you. Part of it is light and picture-perfect; it's made of huge contrasts. On the rim is where you can be safe."

On the rim is where Eric lives, in a master-planned Green Valley community designed in Southwest Ranch, Hacienda, and Spanish Eclectic styles, near the estates owned by local heroes Wayne Newton and Mike Tyson.

Eric is dressed in baggy jeans hung low on his hips, a large plaid shirt, and a green baseball cap. He was going for a tough but cool streetwise stance near the doorway of a cafe on Berkeley's Northside the afternoon we first met, trying to hold his own among the graduate students, professors, and religious scholars who frequent the area known as Holy Hill.

This bright college freshman, who scored 1380 on his SATs (the Clark County average was about 1010), is, like so many Las Vegans, initially defensive about his hometown. "My friends here [in Berkeley] ask me if I live in a hotel room," he says, without hiding his derision. "They think that's all there is in Las Vegas. But my childhood was never about hanging out on the Strip. It was no big deal until I turned fourteen or fifteen.

"I really do look forward to my twenty-first birthday, though. I'm going to drink and gamble with my dad, then with my friends."

And where would that be? "On the Strip, of course. It's a magnet."

Eric describes the picture-perfect life in Las Vegas. "It's nice to see this stretch of street so bright it blocks out the sky. And I knew I could always drive around and find someone doing something. Bowling alleys, movie theaters, buffets. I used to live in bowling alleys."

But as he sipped his latte and talked further, his attitude toward his city soured. His initial defense gave way to a more thoughtful analysis, as we wound through a verbal journey into some of the darker and more dangerous aspects of Las Vegas.

"There are two parts to the state and this city. There's the Old West, with its morals and values: you shoot a burglar. If he falls inside your home, you're okay; if he falls on your lawn, you're in trouble. The other part is the casinos. Las Vegas is totally about money. The streets are truly paved with gold. They [the usual "they," the people who run things] only want people to know about the Strip. Off the Strip, there's nothing to do. They want people to drop ten thousand dollars and come back later trying to win it back. Casino profits go up and up. They showed us the records at school. There's never a dip. But it's a camouflage. Without casinos, we'd be like Austin, Texas. We'd be lame, but a town, a community. We'd be a little town in the desert. But the Las Vegas mentality is 'We're the whole state.' Clark County became our state, and we let the casinos take care of us.

"What I really don't like about it, is we're not the best at anything. New York has the best delis. Chicago has the best pizza. We don't have the best anything.

"It's a great community because there's a lot of money. Unfortunately, it's not going to the infrastructure, police, or schools. I'd love to know where the money goes. Las Vegas is a place to vacation, to let loose and party it up. But there are two sides to that coin. People forget that people actually live in this town—even people who live here. They think they're on vacation for twenty years. They lose track of priorities here, because everyone comes to let loose their inhibitions. It's not a family town, even for the people who live here."

How is it for young people, then? Eric pauses. The steamy hiss of the latte machine and the whirring of the blender fill the air. He answers, "It's totally not oriented to kids. Nobody goes in there saying 'Let's build a town for families.' No one's talking about the family living next door to the casinos.

"Kids are an abomination there. Our schools are the worst ever, even if the stats don't say it. [In fact, the city's Scholastic Aptitude Test scores are about even with the national average.] We have crummy teachers who don't care. I got lucky with my history and calculus teachers. Higher education is horrible, too. We have three community colleges. I was tutoring calculus at one while even I was in high school. Our educational system doesn't nurture and grow kids to go to Harvard. They grow them to go to UNLV."

What's it like to grow up in Las Vegas? "Among kids it's a turf thing. It's totally territorial. A sense of community? It's not there. I don't feel it. It's every man for himself. People are always trying to outdo each other."

Are there limits, social boundaries for teens? "In Las Vegas there are no restraints on you other than the law. I tried everything that wouldn't get me killed.

"My friends and I, I guess we drank a lot. Not beer, whiskey. And marijuana was huge, but it didn't do anything for me, so I thought, 'Why do it?'

"I used to pull up beside a grandma, an old lady, and make faces at her through my window, like I was trying to kiss her." He demonstrated by pursing his lips and jutting his chin. Then he flattened his features as if he'd run into an invisible car window. "As she inched forward, scared, I would inch up with her," he says with a swift laugh.

"Once I was caught shoplifting. My dad asked me why I did it. 'It's fun,' I said. 'It's wrong,' he said. So I stopped.

"Another night, my friends and I shot the windows out of about a hundred cars with high-powered BB guns," he continues, excited at the memory. "The minivans were the best. Glass shards fell like rain. We got caught that night, but only for speeding. So I've never been in trouble with the police," he concludes.

"Some kids, the environment traps them. Smoking, drugs, drinking, violence, sex—those are Las Vegas things.

"What makes me different is my parents. My mom worked out of our home and was there for me. Both my parents let me be independent, and make my own decisions. And I knew everything I wanted, I could get. I didn't have to steal it. Other kids didn't have all that. Only one or two of my friends don't come from broken homes."

I run into Eric again in Las Vegas, dining with his parents during spring break. He agrees to take me on a whirlwind tour of local hangouts. We make a brief stop in my hotel room so I can change into tennis shoes. Eric spies a full-length mirror. Dashing in front of it, he pulls out his tucked-in white shirt with the hip, banded collar, unbuttons it, and lets it hang loose. He pulls out the white T-shirt underneath and lowers his pants onto his hips.

We drive to the New York New York Hotel, walk onto the Grand Central Station platform overlooking the playing floor, and wander past the tables, slots, and bars, past the arcade, and under a canopy of fake trees into the shopping and food area with street signs indicating Big Apple neighborhoods. Can teens afford to eat at a place like this? "No, they just hang out."

"Those are locals," he says, pointing to three young girls. "They're about sixteen, but they want guys over twenty-one. That's why they wear that makeup and those halter tops. They want to drink and gamble."

Across the street at the MGM Grand, the brightly lit arcade buzzes noisily. "This is a good place for teens to hang out. The lights and noise make it inviting."

Then we take the shuttle to Bally's and walk through its casino, past elegant shops and a small arcade. "They don't want kids here." The arcade is small, dark, and quiet. No noise, no kids.

Exiting through a fluorescent green, blue, and purple tunnel echoing with hit rock songs, we stand in front of our next destination. The Forum Shops at Caesars, lit by a perpetually changing artificial sky on the vaulted ceiling high overhead, is big enough to accommodate huge throngs of walkers, sightseers, and shoppers as well as those who come just to sit. We're just in time for the Roman laser show in the interactive fountain. "I like watching people's faces the first time they see it," Eric says.

"I never noticed there were so many adults here. I guess I was just watching for girls. My friends and I used to come looking, but when we did find some girls to hang with, they were usually locals.

"Those are locals," he says, picking out of the swarms of tourists a rough group of six tall boys dressed in long shorts and big T-shirts walking purposefully past the fountain. Other locals are hanging out in groups of four, five, or six, usually male. The teenage girls I had been talking to were either working, had plans, or hadn't been allowed out.

Eric and I walk out into the warm breezy night. A shapely young couple cruises the Strip, arm in arm. She is dressed in a wedding-white dress and pumps, he in jeans, a dress shirt, and a string tie.

The newlyweds lead Eric's thoughts in a different direction. "One summer, I hung out with a group of guys, all they wanted was sex. We went around to several girls' houses, round and round. I had more sex that summer than I probably ever will in my life again."

Is that usual?

"A lot of guys don't really respect girls very much here. But my mom won't let me get away with that.

"I had a girlfriend once who said she'd strip. If I was a girl and I had a body, I totally see the mentality. Fifty grand a year and no talent required.

"Sex in high school is carefree. Not in that you think you'll live forever, but there was no one who wanted it that couldn't get it."

It's past midnight now; I've been interviewing since 7 AM. Can we go back to the car now?

"You'd never make it as a teen here," he tells me shaking his head in mock disappointment.

We stop at a 7-11 and buy sodas. Slots line the walls, and smoke clings to the air. Late night patrons are buying liquor. "Teens gamble here," Eric says. "There's slot machines all over. No one can really stop you. If casinos catch you, they let you go. They get in more trouble than we do. I have friends with fake I.D.'s who play blackjack. And at my high school, you couldn't get caught with cards or dice or you'd be expelled.

"Smoking and gambling are inseparable. The smoke just follows you around."

He directs me to a darkened shopping mall, past some local pool halls, into TownCenter as the last movies finish and stragglers head toward their cars. We drive past grand houses, mostly dark now, in Green Valley. Out on the rim, you can look down from the soft darkness into the city's bowl of lights and quickly make out the Strip, the brightest stripe of all. I drop Eric off at home, where the safety is palpable.

On the way back to my hotel, I puzzle over something Eric said. "Some friends were doing heroin. I stopped hanging out with them because they started to change. And commit crimes. But once I went to see an ex-friend of mine and another guy was there. There had been a drive-by shooting the week before. My friend told me, 'This is the guy who killed so-and-so last week.' I thought, 'Oh, and here we are sitting together.' It was kind of weird.

"Everyone I know has contemplated suicide. It's a teenager thing, not just a Las Vegas thing. All these troubles and no experience. One guy I know slit his wrists. I understand why. I respected him. I thought, 'The only reason I don't do it is I don't have the balls.' It's something we all go through. I'd start to think, maybe there's a reason why I should do it too. But it's way too scary. And I hate the sight of blood. So slitting my wrists was out."

■ ■ ■

Dorothy Bryant, who runs the Las Vegas Suicide Prevention Hotline, has known a lot of people who have killed themselves in her more than twenty years of service. For as long as records have been kept (about sixty years), Bryant says, Las Vegas suicides in the fifteen- to twenty-five-year-old range have been consistently twice the national average.

The reasons young people commit suicide, she believes, are self-image problems, and relationships gone wrong. Problems with self-image can lead to diminished self-esteem; the result can be self-loathing, and can end in self-destruction. Relationship problems, as Bryant defines them, include connections with parents, lovers, and friends as well as the deaths of loved ones.

"When you can't establish quality relationships," she says, "you have more problems. Children of transients have no roots, no extended family close by. Suicides increase when social problems increase." Throw in easy access to alcohol or drugs in an age group already at high risk, and the mixture can be highly volatile. Family therapist Volmar Franz says, "If you see suicides going on around you, it becomes more acceptable. People think, 'Well he did it, she did it....'

"This town assimilates its own. A twenty-one-year-old client of mine was thinking of getting out. But his mother, who is high up in a casino here, got him a job as a valet parking cars. He's making sixty thousand dollars a year—to park cars! I don't see him leaving. Las Vegas kids will grow up and become part of the industry, and they'll continue to perpetuate generations of Las Vegas kids who grow up and assimilate back into the structure. They'll continue to perpetuate the things this town needs to support its economic base.

"My own son spends all weekend hanging out with his friends in a casino. In an arcade, okay, but an arcade in a casino. They see all this crap going on around them. They think nothing of it. Gambling becomes a way of life. It certainly affects the view they develop of the world. But in what ways, other than a gambling addiction, I'm not sure.

"Gambling is not a big problem with teens. They gamble, but it takes years for it to become an addiction. Most parents wouldn't call their kids' behavior in the arcades gambling. But most of the so-called family-oriented activities in Las Vegas are casino-sponsored, so a gambling perversion persists everywhere.

"Keep in mind that this is a tough town. You're told that you can finally have all your dreams of wealth fulfilled; but in the meantime this town will eat you up. It's a mean town. Understand one thing: this town was built on one concept and one concept only: taking other people's money.

"People come here with a dream. Fairly low-functioning people, with a hope of being able to get over, do something, based vaguely around the idea of getting something for nothing, something they don't have to earn. This town is their last stop—their last shot.

"This town is a lot tougher than they think it is. It kicks the living shit out of them, three, four, five times over six months and they've just played their trump card. It didn't pay off.

"Teens see it. They live in it every day."

El Pueblo de Las Vegas

Bill Dauber

"I love Las Vegas. I love the people, the weather. But mainly it's the job."

—Fernando Moya, 26, who earns $35,000 a year as a bellboy at the MGM Grand

"I'll find a job. They tell me construction will start picking up in the summer and I'll find something."

—Luis Ramon Ramirez, 32, a laborer who earns about twenty-five dollars a day when he's working

For nine years, John Soltelo fixed flats and inspected brakes at Goldstar Tires in Pico Rivera, California. He worked weekends, holidays, and overtime, but was never able to earn more than $6.50 an hour. Cleaning soiled sheets, dirty towels, and bedpans, his wife, Bernice, earned a maximum of $7 an hour at a convalescent hospital.

The Soltelos didn't mind the work as much as they did the economic bind that an income of $28,000 a year placed on a family of four living in Southern California. As their family grew, they moved from West Covina to Montebello to Pico Rivera. Each move meant squeezing into a smaller space for a break on the rent. They cut back on clothes for the children. Bernice mastered the art of customizing hand-me-downs with a needle and thread.

Eager for a new start, the Soltelos followed the path from California to Las Vegas worn by many other Mexican-born workers and their families. John found a job as a steward in a casino; his starting pay was lower than what he had earned at Goldstar, but at least there was room for advancement. Bernice began waiting tables at a Mexican restaurant in North Las Vegas.

Two years after they arrived, John was promoted to senior steward, at a salary of $24,000 a year; with tips, Bernice now earns $300 a week. This adds up to an $11,000 increase in their yearly income, with no deductions for state income tax. The couple now owns a new three-bedroom home in Las Vegas and a new Ford Aerostar, luxuries they could never have afforded in California. They can pay for day care for their children and an occasional night out. Bernice feels better about both their own lives and the chances of success they have given their children. "It just proves that if you work hard here you can make it." On $28,000 a year, the Soltelos felt they were barely making it in southern California; in Las Vegas, without any further training or education, they are now earning $39,000 a year. "We are definitely a success story," Bernice Soltelo says. "You won't believe the things we can afford now."

Fernando Moya loves to go hiking on Mt. Charleston and takes an occasional trip to Lake Mead. He has his own apartment and recently bought a new car. This new life is made possible by his job as a bellboy at the MGM Grand Hotel on the Las Vegas Strip, in 1996 the largest hotel in the world, where he is one of 8,000 employees. "There just wasn't a job in Texas that was going to pay me thirty-two thousand dollars a year without a college education," says Moya, 26, who moved to Las Vegas with his mother and sister. All three of them work at casinos; his sister now holds an executive position at the MGM Grand. "As long as you have a job in a casino and benefits to go with it, you should be happy," he says.

After eighteen years in the same job in California, Elena Burdett found herself unemployed, and she too set out for Las Vegas. She was first hired as a maid at the Frontier Hotel, where she earned $6.50 an hour. Two months later she was supervising other maids at Days Inn; two years later, she found herself in the same position at the Luxor with a salary of $24,000 a year. But inspecting 260 rooms a day, six days a week, ten hours a day came to seem too much work, so Burdett moved to another hotel with the same position, but less responsibility. Most recently, she took a job at Columbia Sunrise Hospital, where she plans to start a new career. She doesn't really like Las Vegas, she says, but can't complain about the local economy.

"I wish I never had to move from California, because I left so many good friends behind there," says Burdett, who is originally from Peru. "But the good thing about Las Vegas is that if you don't like one job, you can easily find another."

■ ■ ■

Stories like these are one reason southern Nevada had a population of more than 1.3 million in 1997, almost a 300-percent increase since 1980. Even more dramatically, they help explain why the region's Hispanic population has swollen from 20,400 in 1980 to more than 180,000 in 1999, an increase of more than 900 percent. In increasing numbers, Hispanics are moving from their traditional U.S. homes in the border states of New Mexico, Texas, California, and Arizona to look for jobs in Las Vegas. Although predominately Mexican, the Hispanic population in Las Vegas also includes people from Cuba, El Salvador, Puerto Rico, Peru, and the Dominican Republic. It includes businessmen, lawyers, and politicians, as well as owners of radio stations, newspapers and magazines. "I came to Las Vegas at the right time," says Luis Ramirez, who is living comfortably on the profits of the three Mexican restaurants he has opened since 1991. "I left California when the economy was on its way down and came to Las Vegas when it was just starting to go up." Ramirez, 71, sold a restaurant and other properties in southern California and was ready to retire to his native Guadalajara, Mexico, when his son convinced him to move to Las Vegas. He said there used to be some resentment from other businessmen in Las Vegas when a Mexican came to open a restaurant, but that most of those attitudes had disappeared in the last six years. "I am happy here," Ramirez says. "We are living in the right spot, and I do like going to the casinos. I like playing poker. I have a system."

Susana Reyes says she makes "lots and lots of money" as an attorney in Las Vegas. Her father moved here from the Texas-Mexico border in the 1960s, when Susana was eight, and took a job at Caesars Palace as a busboy. Susana, who began her education in Mexico, attended UNLV and McGeorge Law School in Sacramento. She has been practicing law in Las Vegas for the past ten years. She complains about the lack of Latino culture and political solidarity in Las Vegas; most Latinos, she feels, are just "out to get theirs." But she still decided to move back here after law school. "I had to come back because this is home," says Reyes, a personal-injury specialist. "This is were a lot of cases are." (More than two hundred attorneys specializing in personal-injury cases advertise in the Las Vegas phone book, many with full-page ads announcing, "Se habla español.")

But well-to-do lawyers and restaurateurs are not the Las Vegas Latino norm. According to a 1994 report, 37 percent of southern Nevada's Hispanic population works in the service industry. These people include waitresses, cooks, maids, laundry workers, machine operators, and stewards. They are predominately young: forty percent of them are under twenty-one, and only five percent are sixty-five or older—a statistical anomaly in a region heavily populated with retirees. Their children make up 21 percent of the students in southern Nevada's elementary schools, 19 percent of those in the middle schools, and 16.6 percent of those in the high schools.

Despite success stories like the Soltelos', Moyas' and Burdetts'—let alone those of Susana Reyes and Luis Ramirez—Hispanics remain the poorest ethnic group in Greater Las Vegas, as they do in the nation as a whole. According to Census Bureau statistics, the median household income rose between 1992 and 1995 for every American ethnic group *except* the nation's 27 million Hispanics. Their incomes dropped 5.1 percent, to an average annual income in 1995 of $22,860 per household. And most undocumented (and usually uncounted) Hispanics in southern Nevada must make do with considerably less than that.

Unlike the relatively secure Hispanic workers (male and female) who find jobs in the casino-hotel industry, the low end of the wage scale is filled with young Mexican (occasionally Salvadoran) men—most of them undocumented—with very limited or no knowledge of English. They flock to Las Vegas in the hope of earning from $3 to $8 an hour as day laborers on road projects and construction sites. When hired by the day, the most these men can hope for is $25 for six, eight, or ten hours of work—on the days when work is available. They sometimes live eight to an apartment, or three families to a house.

The Nevada state demographer's office estimated that southern Nevada would number 188,000 Hispanics in 1999, 16 percent of the population. According to 1990 Census Bureau projections, Hispanics could account for as much as 21 percent of southern Nevada's population by the year 2000.

Some argue that if you add the undocumented, these numbers are already there. "Hispanics are already twenty-one percent of the population in southern Nevada," declares Frank Corro, editor of *El Mundo*, southern Nevada's largest Spanish newspaper. Eighty percent of these, he says, are Mexican. "The problem is that Hispanics, especially in North Las Vegas, won't allow themselves to be counted," says Brian Bonnefant, a spokesman from the demographer's office. "But they [represent] at least twenty-one percent of the population in Clark County alone, if not more." Some Hispanic businessmen put the number of their fellow countrymen in southern Nevada at 250,000, including 60,000 to 70,000 undocumented, or "illegals."

Whatever their current numbers, the uncounted Hispanics are coming to southern Nevada for the same reasons as the Moyas, Burdetts, and Soltelos: jobs. "They come here looking for something better," says Josephina Natera, a social worker with the Nevada Association of Latin Americans, Inc. "They live in horrible and unsanitary conditions, and come looking for a better life that's not often there."

■ ■ ■

At 3 PM on a Friday afternoon the Cambio de Cheques at the back of the indoor swapmeet on Eastern Avenue is buzzing. It's payday for the men who are helping to build the thousands of new homes in Las Vegas. Three women behind a large glass window are counting out twenty-dollar bills. "Viente, cuarenta, sesenta, ochenta, cien. Viente, cuarenta, sesenta, ochenta, doscientos. Viente, cuarenta, sesenta, ochenta, trescientos." The men stand in three lines of seven or more, holding onto envelopes and identification cards. "Gracias por cambiar sus cheques con nosotros, mantenemos nuestras tarifas bajos," the sign says. "Si al cambiar su cheque usted trae su identificacion ayudara a protejerse y nosotros" ("Thank you for cashing your checks with us, we keep our fees low. If you offer an I.D. as you cash your check, it helps protect both you and us"). The center charges the standard 1.5 percent commission, or $1.80 for a $300 check. In less than ten minutes, forty-five dusty men in shorts, construction boots, and T-shirts have cashed their checks. After a week's work, it's time to enjoy the weekend; some men have brought their families to the swapmeet, and treat their wives to a gift and their children to an orange soda. "A lot of the illegals come here to cash their checks," a man sitting next to me says. "They get here at three PM. You can set your watch by it."

Luis Ramirez (no relation to the restaurant owner) wasn't cashing a check or buying his sons sodas. He had come to North Las Vegas three months ago, leaving Guadalajara to look for a better life. He left behind his wife, Rosalva, and their two sons, Pedro, 6, and Emilio, 5. "As soon as I get myself a full-time job, I will send for them," he says. Ramirez, 32, left Mexico because he was tired of working in a pipe factory for $4 a day. He now lives with his cousin Jaime and three other men in a two-bedroom apartment near the swapmeet.

It was Jaime who convinced him that Las Vegas might be the place. Luis took his cousin's old job on a small construction crew that remodels kitchens. But as the fourth man on a three-man crew, he doesn't get much work. The four men live together to save money. "We've become like brothers," he says, "We help each other when we need it."

Luis' story is a familiar one in North Las Vegas. Relatives from Mexico follow each other here, living together until they find a job. He says he knows of several men sharing one-bedroom apartments, or several families sharing one home. "Americans don't understand that," he says. "Once we [Mexicans] live together for a while we all become like family."

Ramirez is five feet eight inches tall, with a wiry frame and narrow shoulders. His black T-shirt highlights a mahogany skin that's been in the sun much too long. His eyes are light brown, beady, and slightly sunken. When he takes off his red bandana his face looks friendlier, and he reveals a slightly receding hairline. He's a skilled craftsman and calls himself a good concrete-finisher. "But I can also frame and lathe," he says. Concrete finishing and rough house framing are, in fact, among the most popular jobs open to Mexican newcomers, who make it possible for Clark County builders to put up more than twenty thousand new houses a year.

Luis's last check, two weeks ago, was for $150, most of which he sent home to his wife. "I send the money in American dollars and they get it in pesos," he says. "Family is the most important thing to a Mexican man. We make sacrifices for our families." Luis is still searching for a full-time job. "The best way is to know somebody who can get you a job," he says. "If not, you have to ask around and wait your turn." Luis's cousin Jaime worked on the same small crew he now works for, but Jaime was able to turn a three-day job into a permanent place—which is what Luis is hoping for now.

■ ■ ■

In the sports book at Arizona Charlie's, a popular neighborhood casino-hotel in West Las Vegas, you can find men standing around any night of the week in standard construction-worker gear—shorts, heavy tan boots, sweatshirts, and bandanas— watching (and placing bets on) games on the big-screen TVs. It was there that I met Carlos Martinez and started talking with him about the Monday Night Football game, just an hour away. "The Chiefs own the Raiders," he said. "And they are giving us three points."

Martinez proved to be wrong about the football game, but he knew a lot about construction. He has spent fourteen years in the business, including stints in California and Arizona before the jobs dried up. He moved to Las Vegas five years ago. "Vegas has about ten more years of building and that's it," he says. "Then it will be just like Arizona, nothing but additions and repairs." On the twenty thousand new homes being built each year in southern Nevada, he said, 90 percent of the work is done by Hispanics—specifically, by Mexicans. Driving through the county you can see young Mexican men laying tile in Summerlin, pouring concrete in West Las Vegas, framing in Green Valley, and lathing in North Las Vegas.

Martinez explained the casual, inequitable wage system for construction workers in Las Vegas. "The border brothers are the guys that get screwed," Martinez says, using the common term for Mexican day laborers without papers. "They hang out on D Street waiting for a job. If they are lucky, they get picked up and paid thirty dollars a day."

■ ■ ■

The search for work on D Street begins before 5 AM. Dozens of anxious men gather on Bonanza Road between North Las Vegas Boulevard and Rancho Drive. The more experienced men stay away from Las Vegas Boulevard and the 7-11 convenience store on its corner, knowing that the owner will often alert police and Immigration Service agents. The clerk in the 7-11 on the corner of Rancho, however, on the west end of Bonanza, doesn't mind the day workers, because many of them come into the shop to buy their day's supplies. "They start getting here at five AM, buying drinks, sandwiches, and ice," the clerk says. "They don't bother me." The more experienced men gather on the corner of Bonanza and D or Bonanza and F. These streets are race-divided; the blacks, who often blame the Mexicans for low wages, gather on D Street.

"We'll never get along with the Mexicans," one black fellow says. "They come to our corner and work for pennies. They aren't going to get away with paying me that. They can pay a Mexican twenty-five dollars for a day's work, but not me." The Mexicans huddle on F Street, or closer to Pacific Supply, where contractors come to purchase tile, drywall, and other materials. This largely black neighborhood, with its dirt lots, run-down apartments, and the long shuttered Moulin Rouge Casino, is bleak and depressing. As each car or truck passes, the men hold out a finger, as if to ask, "Do you need one?"

"You have to be aggressive," one man tells me. "If you aren't, you might as well go home." He says that the best time to look for a job on D Street is in the summer, when warm, dry weather means that work picks up. To impress prospective employers, most men wear standard construction gear and carry their lunch in a plastic bag; some even bring their own hard hats, tool belts, and tools. The level of anxiety rises each time a construction truck passes by, making hungry men hungrier and more aggressive. They knock on the truck's door, or try to open it. "I feel sorry for those poor bastards," says one man who pulled his truck into Pacific Supply.

Other men gathering on the street corners don't look all that interested in finding a job. Some are already drunk, with half-empty bottles of liquor at their sides. Some are strung out on drugs. Others look as if they haven't slept for days, and couldn't make it through a two-hour work shift. Other men seem to be there just for the company, and spend more time reading the newspaper or talking than they do looking for work.

When Luis Ramirez found his first job, he and two other men were hauled in the bed of a pickup to a private home. His employer for the day simply needed a few tons of dirt wheelbarrowed from the front yard to the back. It took Luis and his coworkers six hours to move and flatten the dirt; for this, they received $75, $25 each. Luis was thankful for the work, but disappointed that he wasn't able to send money to his wife and kids, or show his talent and hard work to a construction crew—not that a real construction job would have guaranteed him much more.

■ ■ ■

"You can bring in a Mexican who's a skilled craftsman and pay him three dollars an hour and he's perfectly happy," says Peter Nelson, a construction supervisor with National Heritage Industries. This is part of the reason, Nelson explained, that 90 percent of the company's employees are Mexican. "Shit, if it were up to me, they'd all be Mexican." On this particular day, he had two crews finishing lathing and laying foundations for a Sunbeam Homes development in North Las Vegas. Nelson sat in his trailer, inspecting a water pipe that had been broken by one of the men on the lathing crew and hadn't been reported. "I tell them, if there's a problem you can come to me. There's no reason to be afraid, I'm 'Paydro,'" he says. "I have to know these things. If I put together homes with broken pipes, it's my ass." Over the sounds of beeping trucks, shovels, hammers, and conversations in Spanish, Nelson doesn't seem to have any communication problems; this is partly because the Mexican foremen speak English well enough to communicate with him. The foremen are the highest-paid men on the job, earning sixteen dollars an hour.

Nelson has nothing but praise for Mexican workers. But he also has plenty to choose from, and he knows it. "If they don't bust ass for fifteen hours without sniveling, then they're out of here," he says. "There're plenty of other guys that can do the job." Nelson says he can be hard on the Mexican workers, and will berate them for a job poorly done. "You bring in any other race and cuss him out for doing a poor job and they'll get up and leave," he says. "But the Mexicans will get it right." Nelson explains why he thinks Mexican workers are the best. "One, you don't have to tell them what to do. Two, they work fifteen hours a day without bitching. Three, they stay until the job is done. Four, they can take the Vegas heat."

Nelson stares out of his trailer and points to a home foundation that's waiting for the cement to be poured. "Look at that quality of work," he says. "It looks like a machine smoothed that stuff out, but it was all done by hand."

The work was done by Angel's crew. The crew went home by noon, but Angel, the foreman, has come back to inspect the work. He meticulously explains the different layers of rock and plastic that had to be laid before the cement could be poured. Angel snaps a line to show how the frame matches precisely to the foundation and declares, "Perfecto." He is proud of his crew, and brags that they finished the foundations for six houses in one day. His ten-man crew is made up entirely of friends and relatives. "All my guys are skilled craftsmen that have been with me for five years," he says. "We all learned our skills in Mexico and are paid for them here."

His crews need more than building skills, Nelson explains. They also have to work fast to keep up with southern Nevada's building demands. "My job is to make my boss rich," Nelson says. "If that means having five guys on the payroll and five guys off the payroll, then that's what I'll do." For a company like Nelson's, that means almost half his men are paid under the table, and it's those guys, he says, who will make three to four dollars an hour. But even if they make it onto the payroll, wages are still not safe, because there are often kickbacks to be paid to foremen or others. "If a guy's on the payroll for eight dollars an hour, then he has to kick back four dollars an hour," Nelson says. "That's just the way it is. I had to do it. Everybody has to pay kickbacks."

■ ■ ■

Luis Ramirez knows all this. He knows that three to four dollars an hour amounts to only six thousand to eight thousand dollars a year. With his wife working too, maybe they can earn sixteen thousand dollars. But for all the stress and uncertainty, men like Ramirez continue to come to Las Vegas. They talk about the four dollar a day wage in Mexico, the better education their children will get here, and their dreams of becoming American entrepreneurs. At the very least, they might learn enough English to run their own construction crew and earn sixteen dollars an hour.

Ramirez does miss the ease of life in Guadalajara, but he's lived in U.S. neighborhoods far less friendly than North Las Vegas. As he tells his wife, everything they need is within walking distance: Tacos Amarillos, Tacos Mexico, Tacos Latinos. In Stewart Square on Eastern Avenue, the heart of North Las Vegas, there's a *carniceria*, Video Jalisco, Botas Cowboys, and Costa Azul Travel. At the indoor swapmeet where he cashes his checks, he can buy baby clothes, jeans, T-shirts, luggage, car stereos, toys, auto supplies, and basic groceries and pharmaceuticals; apply for a sheriff's I.D. card, birth certificate, or driver's license; and take out a mortgage. What makes North Las Vegas most comforting to so many Hispanics is that so many of the signs are in Spanish. Most of the clerks, restaurant owners, and waitresses speak Spanish. The Korean grocer at the swapmeet sells pigs' feet, tripas, and Jarritos (a soda made in Mexico), and can even quote the goods' prices in Spanish. There are big Cinco de Mayo celebrations at Freedom park, and Mexican soccer leagues. St. Christopher's (or San Cristóbal) and two other Catholic churches hold services in Spanish, and Mexican bands that come to Las Vegas play for large crowds.

"It's not horrible here," Ramirez says. "But the main thing is that I have a better chance to improve myself and my family in the United States than I do in Mexico."

■ ■ ■

Southern Nevada's Hispanic population is obviously going to keep growing, probably at an increasing rate. The prospect of new home construction continuing at a breakneck pace for at least another decade will attract tens of thousands more Mexicans and Salvadorans like Ramirez. Thousands more documented Hispanics like the Soltelos and the Moyas have moved to Las Vegas from other states to fill jobs at the new Bellagio (3,025 rooms), the Paris (2,916), the Venetian on the former Sands site (3,300 in its first phase), and the Mandalay Bay (3,700) as well as major expansions built or planned at the Aladdin, Caesars Palace, Harrah's, the Luxor, the MGM Grand, the Sahara, and the Tropicana. It has been estimated that every new hotel room in Las Vegas creates two and a half new jobs: one and a half at the hotel itself, and one in the ancillary industries that help service it. Hispanics without English-language skills will overwhelmingly take the nonunion service jobs—as maids, cooks, laundry workers, machine operators, stewards—that pay between $5.50 and $7.50 an hour. Indeed, according to the U.S. Census Bureau, Nevada, with its immense casino-hotel industry, employs more Hispanics in service jobs than any other state. A 1997 *Newsweek* article projected that Hispanics in Nevada will number 583,000 by the year 2025—the fourth-highest concentration in the U.S., after California, Texas, and New Mexico. A few of them will master the English language and make their way up the ladder of American success as businessmen, professionals, and politicians. But when they first arrive, Las Vegas will be waiting for them with vacuum cleaners, lawn mowers, shovels, and hammers.

A View from West Las Vegas

Nefretiti Makenta

When the sun goes down and the lights go on, the glittering thirty-story towers of the Las Vegas hotels can seem alien colossi from a neighborhood only a mile away, where shabby, single-story bungalows, storefront churches, and empty lots dominate the terrain. A clear-cut boundary—marked today by two elevated freeways, as well as the old Union Pacific railroad tracks and a vast tract of unused railway land alongside them—separates this neighborhood from the Las Vegas known to millions of tourists and moviegoers. The pulse and flicker of the visible hotel signs—"Lady Luck," "Golden Nugget," "Stardust," "Stratosphere," "Mirage"—seem to mock the people scratching out a living in the 3.5 square miles north of Bonanza Road and south of Lake Mead Boulevard, between I-15 and Rancho Drive.

West Las Vegas, as it is respectfully called nowadays (the historic label "Westside" has taken on a pejorative taint, which leads some residents, planners, and journalists to avoid it) is actually northwest of Downtown, adjacent to the original city center. The name makes it sound like an independent city, but unlike North Las Vegas, which adjoins it but is in fact autonomous, West Las Vegas is very much a part of Las Vegas itself.

Though open-housing laws have helped disperse black families to other regions of Clark County, West Las Vegas remained (as of the 1990 census) home to 41 percent of African Americans in the city of Las Vegas itself, and

17 percent of those in the county. At the time, its residents were 78 percent black, by far the highest concentration in any part of the city or county.

West Las Vegas flings funk into the fantasyland image of Las Vegas, reminding residents that its notorious "boom" has not spread evenly over the city. In 1990, West Las Vegas had an unemployment rate three times that of the Las Vegas metropolitan area, and a percentage of welfare recipients six times that of the city at large. Almost one-third of its area was empty space; vacant land represented the number-one "land use" in the neighborhood. Reaching out north, west, and south into the desert, new housing tracts now encircle West Las Vegas, a predominately no- to low-income district whose population has remained stagnant at about fifteen thousand since 1960, while that of Clark County has grown by more than 400 percent.

The nineties have been a decade of change in West Las Vegas. Beginning in 1991, the area witnessed the ascension (and sometimes the fall) of black leaders, elected or appointed to positions never before filled by African Americans. The area received tens of millions of dollars in economic and community-development projects. West Las Vegas received its first middle school in 1997, thirty-nine years after the first middle school in the city opened its doors.

Even so, driving in from the east, such signs of progress are overshadowed by the preponderance of vacant lots and storefront churches. Small beauty salons, hair-supply stores, and liquor stores are the dominant commercial presence.

Unlike Clark County's prosperous new master-planned communities, West Las Vegas received very little attention of any sort from planners before April 1992. "There's no rhyme or reason to land use in West Las Vegas," says Richard Blue, former head of Economic Development for the city. "You could have a house, and next to your house could be an auto-repair place, and on the other side could be a church." From the start, the few zoning laws in place in the area have been unenforced in West Las Vegas, where city planners' traditional approach has been "hands off."

■ ■ ■

The broad, empty dust lots that dot the West Las Vegas landscape perform multiple roles, as neighborhood depositories, concourses, playgrounds, and rendezvous points. Beside Jimmy's Market, on Lake Mead Boulevard, green and brown shards of broken beer bottles are layered deeper into the ground by the feet of little boys crossing an expanse of dirt and refuse on their way to "Grandma's house." On D Street, an open-air living room carpeted by concrete is the centerpiece of a dirt tract and a home to transient wanderers on their way to and from the corner liquor store. In a field at the edge of Martin Luther King Boulevard, a multitude of white plastic shopping bags catches sagebrush limbs and flags in the wind, creating a surrealistically ornamental effect.

At the westernmost corner of Coran Lane, a three-year-old and her baby brother await the 210 bus, resting their bottoms on thick, jagged-edged cement chips. Their mother stands behind them. An unflagging gust of wind agitates the litter behind them, and lifts loose dirt from the lot on the left into their eyes.

Each of the children peeks out now and then from behind tiny elbows as cars and trucks roar past. Further down, on the opposite side of the road, two cinder blocks planted in dirt serve as seats for those awaiting the next westbound bus. A city plan for West Las Vegas, completed in 1994, states that "Bus shelters are provided by a private company and are paid for with advertising in the shelter. Currently, there are no bus shelters and none are planned." (The neighborhood has received several shelters since then.) In front of elementary schools, parks, and churches, tobacco companies promote the glamour of smoking on large, seductive bus-shelter billboards—the closest West Las Vegas gets to the flashing, two-hundred-foot-tall lightboards of the Strip.

On Coran Lane, I pass the Bread of Life Ministries. Maroon shingles run around the top of the building; flat-roofed, without a steeple or a cross, it could pass for an old-fashioned hamburger joint. "You can stand on the corner of Jackson and D and literally see ten churches," said one resident. "If you stand on Jackson and H, you can see nine."

Three crosses. Two crosses. Paradise Apostolic Church. Pilgrim Church. On a mid-afternoon Sunday drive down Madison Avenue, a medley of gospel hymns bursts out of the churches onto the streets in stereo sound.

Two steeples. Twenty-six chandeliers. True Vine Baptist Church. Moments of Miracles. New Revelation Baptist Church. Padded pews or couches.

"There's a church on every corner," one local journalist had told me of West Las Vegas, and it seemed almost literally true: there are more than forty-five churches within just over a square mile here. In fact, the churches of West Las Vegas are the only draw for the thousands of blacks who have moved out to the suburbs.

Almost every Sunday, Jerry Leigh and her husband, Thomas, back their white Chrysler New Yorker out of the driveway in Green Valley, click on KCEP radio for gospel tunes, and take the D Street exit off I-15 to Second Baptist Church. One of the largest churches in West Las Vegas, Second Baptist has approximately two thousand members and twenty-one assistant preachers. (Black civic leaders often become ministers of local churches.)

The ride to church in West Las Vegas is a sad one for this retired couple, both in their seventies. "Look at it," says Jerry Leigh, gazing out the car's window at wooden makeshift shacks, relics from the fifties and sixties standing no higher than six feet, with "swamp coolers"—primitive air-conditioning devices—perched on their roofs.

"People see all the glamour outside. I wish they would come and see what the city fathers have done here, it's so depressing." Leigh has been an executive committee member of various local NAACP branches for the past eleven years. "It's deplorable, with all the glitter in this town. We've moved sixteen times and this is the damnedest place. They don't need us out in Green Valley. They need us over here."

■ ■ ■

After work one day in 1985, Deborah Jackson, recently arrived in Las Vegas from Detroit, walked up and down Fremont Street laden with groceries, trying to catch a cab to get home and prepare dinner for her two children. She stopped at a taxi stand in front of a hotel. When the driver in the first cab rolled down his window, she told him her address—a place less than three miles away.

"Is that the Westside?" he asked.

"I guess so," she answered.

"I'm not going there."

"Why not?"

"We don't have to. I don't have to take you there." he said. "That's just the way it is."

She tried the next cab, and the next, and the next, until she was weeping with frustration. After two hours, a black woman walking a picket line in front of a casino stepped off in mid-protest and approached Jackson. "I've seen you walking up and down all this time. You're not from Vegas, are you?" said the woman. "These cabs are not going to take you to West Las Vegas." The woman left the picket line, went and got her own car, and drove Jackson across the tracks to her new home in the Sierra Nevada Arms apartments.

"I'll never forget that," says Jackson. "When I first came here from Detroit, it was like I had stepped into a time warp."

Twelve years after Jackson's Fremont Street experience, I find myself standing in the same place. Along with hundreds of happy-go-lucky tourists, I ogle the three-block-long canopy of electronically simulated birds, planes, fireworks and Rockette-like females captured on a row of fluorescent pixels swimming above our heads. Arching high over what is now a pedestrian strip, this fifteen-minute extravaganza, shown once an hour after sunset, is the centerpiece of a $70-million-dollar downtown redevelopment project called the Fremont Street Experience, which opened in 1996. After the show, I repeat Deborah Jackson's quest with a couple of cab drivers parked less than a block away, giving a West Las Vegas address to the first driver in line.

"I can't take you to West Las Vegas, because I can't go there from here. It's against the rules." I try the second cab.

"How much to West Las Vegas?"

"What did *he* say?"

"He says it's against the rules for a Henderson cab to go there from here."

The driver jerks his head back and lets out a puff of breath. "Where in West Las Vegas?" he snaps.

"D and Jackson Streets." The driver finally agrees to take me, but only if I pay in advance. "It's going to be four to six dollars, so give me six. That's a bad neighborhood."

Residents maintain a different perspective. "West Las Vegas is a low-crime area, but the stigma is out there about the Westside. You ask a cab driver and even, in some cases, other black people about the Westside, and they'll tell you 'Don't go over there, you're going to be kidnapped, mauled, raped, murdered.' But," says John Edmond, owner of the largest shopping center in West Las Vegas, "you never hear any of that stuff going on over here."

But the bars on the windows and doors of the neighborhood's businesses, homes, and storefront churches back up the outsiders' perception.

■ ■ ■

Before I first came here, I telephoned a number of civic officials to set up interviews and ask preliminary questions.

"Have you ever seen West Las Vegas?" one city planner asked me. "From the time we left slavery to now, a lot of things haven't been done. But in West Las Vegas it sticks out like a sore thumb." The very appearance of the area, he said, "lets you know that something normal has not transpired here. And the conditions that created West Las Vegas continue to exist today."

"What conditions?"

"The redlining, the...Wait a minute. Are you going to quote me?"

"I was planning to, yes."

"No. No. No. No. You can't quote me. This is a very racist town. I gotta live. I gotta work in this town."

■ ■ ■

In the 1920s, Las Vegas's fifty-eight black residents could patronize any and all of its businesses, with the exception of the downtown, white-only whorehouses. During the next ten years, the black population grew to 178, or 2 percent of the population. This small increase disturbed the white men employed on the Boulder Dam project, as well as the merchants and casino owners.

With the legalization of gambling in Nevada in 1931, the repeal of Prohibition in 1933, and the completion of the Boulder (now Hoover) Dam in 1935, southern Nevada became a popular tourist destination. Partly because of the city's newfound success with tourism, a pattern of Jim Crow segregation was established. White casino owners decided that African Americans, the first of whom arrived in town as early as 1905, did not fit into the image they wanted to offer white tourists and newcomers to the area.

Blacks could work as entertainers in hotel showrooms and lounges for all-white audiences; but when the show was over, they had to leave by the back door and make their way across the tracks.

In 1939, the local NAACP made the first of three unsuccessful attempts to bar discrimination against blacks with a "Race and Color Bill." The city refused to issue or renew business licenses to blacks in the Downtown area. Downtown merchants (as well as hotels) began denying them service. White landlords refused to rent lodging to them elsewhere. In effect, African Americans were systematically evicted from Downtown, and directed across the railroad tracks to the derelict streets of West Las Vegas.

"My uncle owned property on Fremont Street," said Elijah Green, co-owner of the dilapidated New Town and Tavern lounge on Jackson Street. "I learned to swim over there, as a kid. But they flip flopped us from Downtown to over here."

For years, "Westside" had been the neglected part of town. It was left without paved streets, power lines, sewers, or even running water much longer than neighborhoods east of the tracks. Barred from renting or buying housing anywhere else, old-time black residents, along with thousands of black newcomers, were forced to form a ghetto.

Drawn by the World War II economic boom, and the promise of jobs at the Basic Magnesium (BMI) plant south of town, thousands of blacks headed for Las Vegas. The majority of newcomers were recruited from the cotton fields and timber mills of places like Talullah, Louisiana, and Fordyce, Arkansas; by 1950, blacks represented 11 percent of the population. (They now total about 9 percent.) Thanks to the war, these migrants from the South experienced a newfound prosperity.

"We had never experienced that kind of money," said George Kline, a building contractor who came from Louisiana on one of three trucks that transported his family and friends. "They needed people at wartime. Defense plants. That was one of the ways God promoted black people."

Officially barred from living in North Las Vegas and Boulder City, many of the black factory workers crowded into a government-built, segregated village called Carver Park on the Boulder Highway north of the Henderson plant—their only alternative to West Las Vegas. As this new dormitory and apartment complex was built with only 324 units, more than 1,000 blacks were left to their own devices. "We had plenty of money," says Sarann Knight Preddy, former co-owner of the Moulin Rouge hotel. "We just didn't have anywhere to live."

If black people wanted houses in West Las Vegas, they had to build them themselves. Knight Preddy's father was one of several migrants who did just that. During the war years, many set up tents, built lean-to shacks, or slept on cots on the sand. The city refused to create adequate housing in West Las Vegas, expecting a mass exodus of both black and white workers after the war.

When Nevada's first open-housing law was finally passed in 1971, Bonanza Village—formerly an all-white subdivision across Highland Avenue now Martin Luther King Boulevard—became the first middle-class area in West Las Vegas to allow blacks to move in. With its ranch-style houses and lots considerably larger than those elsewhere in the area, Bonanza Village remains the most desirable residential neighborhood in West Las Vegas, with average resale prices higher than those for the city at large. In 1978, Sarann Knight Preddy says, she signed the deed to a Bonanza Village house which contained an old (and, of course, no longer valid) clause stipulating, "No niggers, no Chinese, and no goats."

"West Las Vegas is very depressing to me," says Knight Preddy. "Having been here all these years, the whole city has grown up everywhere, but that one little spot over there is almost the same as it was when I came fifty-four years ago."

Not allowed to patronize casinos and other businesses outside of West Las Vegas until 1960, blacks sustained their own island of prosperity. "Jackson Street used to be like a little heaven for blacks," says George Kline, 55.

In the late forties and fifties, at least five black-owned casinos on Jackson Street helped provide Las Vegas's blacks with a thriving nightlife and the beginnings of economic self-sufficiency. The New Town and Tavern, the Cotton Club, the Brown Derby, the El Morocco, and the Ebony Club were "after-hours" clubs, playing host to entertainers like Harry Belafonte and Sarah Vaughn after they had performed on the Strip. "West Las Vegas used to be the black Strip," says State Senator Joe Neal. Longtime resident Roxie Newton agrees, though she was too young to participate in the festivities. "Blacks would dress up, just like they did on the Strip, walk on the rocks, and go out and party."

But then came the ironic victory of integration. As the Strip casino-hotels were forced to admit all races, black entertainers and residents stopped supporting the Jackson Street casinos. Meanwhile, says Neal, "There was a concerted effort to get blacks out of gaming, to deny them licenses after the civil-rights movement."

In 1997, Jackson Street was a desolate eyesore. One gambling lounge, the New Town and Tavern, remained open—barely. Several bulbs on the sign above its doorway needed replacing. The only thing bursting with life inside were the electric-pink, green, and blue tropical flowers on its carpet. A note tacked onto a video game read, "Play at your own risk."

Elijah Green, co-owner of the family-run, one-story lounge, had turned down offers to buy the property. "We're not in the market to sell," he said. "We're trying to save." In debt for taxes and without a nonrestricted gaming license, the owners were allowed to house no more than fourteen slot machines.

■ ■ ■

I hang a right off Martin Luther King Boulevard onto Owens.

It's a trailer. It's an instant-photo booth, a hot-dog stand. No, it's a bank. I walk in and stand on the welcome mat. With my back against the door and one person before me, I am in line. At the left wall, two customers stand shoulder to shoulder filling out deposit slips at the miniature information table. At 1,200 square feet, this is one of the smallest Bank of America branches in the West. "What happens when there are more people here?" I ask. "We pack them in any way we can," says a bank officer.

"I call it a bucket," jokes Senator Neal. But before 1992, there were no banks at all in West Las Vegas. Now there are three, and one loan center—in part the result of a devastating study, publicized by Neal, of redlining practices in this community. "The report shows that Las Vegas banks have cordoned off the Westside and imposed a financial curfew on its largely African American residents," Senator Neal told *American Banker* in 1992. In 1990, only 59 of more than 10,000 home loans in Clark County were made in West Las Vegas.

"Black people have always put their money in financial institutions. And those institutions would not respond in kind with commercial loans, or even loans to remodel their homes," says Neal, a state senator since 1973. "In an average year banks were taking in more than sixty million dollars from the Westside, but they had only loaned two hundred fifty thousand. We needed some documentation to get at what banks were receiving from the community and what they were able to put back." The report was released less than two months after West Las Vegas was rocked by its own version of the Rodney King riots of April-May 1992.

Since those three weeks of confrontation and violence, West Las Vegas has received an unprecedented amount of financial investment. Following the uprising, city officials cleared hundreds of tons of rotting cars and old furniture out of residents' yards and dumped them in a landfill. "If we hadn't got all that crap out of there," says city planner Frank Reynolds, "people wouldn't have dreamed of investing there."

But according to black businessman John Edmond, owner of the largest shopping center in the area, people had not dreamed of investing in West Las Vegas because the majority of its residents were black. Less than two blocks from the minibank on Owens Street is Nucleus Business Plaza, half of which was looted and burned down in the 1992 riots. For years after that Edmond tried unsuccessfully to entice private investors to help fill his property, he says. After major retailers continually refused his offers, he took a different approach.

At first glance, the plaza looks like any one of the dozens of strip malls all over Las Vegas. At Nucleus Plaza, however, you won't find The Gap, McDonald's, or even a 7-11. With public tenants such as Juvenile Court Services, Clark County Social Services, the Nevada State Welfare Department, and a community health center, Nucleus Plaza has become a one-stop civic-services mart. The only retail storefronts are Dee Dees Original Beauty Salon, a barber shop, a hair-supply store, and the Heritage Lounge.

The food court at the center of the plaza was built to house five eateries, but a donut shop and The Fish Place are the sole occupants of this cavernous hall.

■ ■ ■

The violence began on the evening of April 29, 1992, the same day that twelve white jurors in Simi Valley, California, acquitted four white Los Angeles police officers of the beating of black motorist Rodney King a year before.

John Edmond says he saw it all, watching from the parking lot of the plaza. A fight broke out in a check-cashing store at the plaza's east end. A white man servicing the air-conditioning unit was beaten up behind the building. Edmond saw the Sparkletts water-delivery man sprint away from his truck with blood smeared across his shirt. Employees at the Big 8 Market advised its Korean owner to go home. Five police cars pulled into the parking lot; the officers scanned the area, then left.

Suddenly, a trash can flew through the front window of the Big 8. Las Vegas police drove past Edmond's property, up and down Owens Street, while looting proceeded apace. Then, a fire truck arrived. Firemen lifted the hose from the truck and attached it to the hydrant. "My building is going up in flames," Edmond remembers thinking at the time. But the firemen got back on the truck and drove away, leaving the hose hooked to the hydrant. Firemen say they left when a bullet hit the truck, but Edmond insists, five years later, "I'm right there. I don't see or hear gunfire."

"Why did the police leave?" I ask him.

"I guess they said, 'Y'all might as well go on over there and burn Nucleus Plaza, 'cause y'all are not coming downtown.'"

Today, in the food court at Nucleus Plaza, Carl Johnson, now 29, drinks a super-size Coke, munches a fried catfish sandwich, and recalls the events of 1992. "I lived with the Crips and went to school with the Bloods. The majority of the guys that were together [during the riots] didn't like each other," he says. "Gangs that wouldn't go into other people's neighborhood for years came together." Metro police agree that the riots marked at least a temporary truce between the two warring Los Angeles-based gangs.

Later that evening, two to three hundred teenagers and young adults started off in the direction of the Las Vegas City Hall and the Downtown casinos, but were stopped by a police barricade at Main Street and Bonanza Road that sent them back into West Las Vegas. Reverend Jesse Scott, head of the local NAACP, told the *Las Vegas Sun*, "[The rioters'] plans covered more than just West Las Vegas." "Riots Were Headed Downtown," read the newspaper's front-page headline on May 6.

During much of the twenty-two nights of "civil unrest" that followed (the riots in Los Angeles, though far more widespread and damaging, were contained within three days), West Las Vegas was effectively sealed off and shut down, largely to protect the casino hotels of Downtown and the Strip from both physical damage and the even greater damage that might be caused by the image of rioters and protesters in their vicinity. Gas and power to the area were cut off for days. Huge semi trucks were used to block traffic from entering or leaving the neighborhood.

"It would have been total, total disaster if they had gotten downtown," Sergeant Dennis Thomson told the *Las Vegas Sun*. Another police officer was quoted as saying, "One major hotel fire would have tied up the entire police department, and that was their intention. Then they could have gone and had the rest of the city."

When the first day's rioting was over, three dozen people were wounded, and one eighteen-year-old high-school student was found dead in the rubble of the Big 8 Market in Nucleus Plaza. Every business in Nucleus Plaza that was not black-owned was destroyed, presumably on purpose; several other spaces were burned out as well, including the local NAACP headquarters, a welfare office, and an AIDS clinic.

Meanwhile, heavily armed police patrolled the area in armored vehicles borrowed from Nellis Air Force Base, and gatherings of more than six people were forbidden. Three white drivers were reported as having been pulled from their cars and beaten; police and firemen were attacked by missiles and gunfire. Four hundred National Guardsmen were mobilized, although never deployed. Thirteen schools in Las Vegas Valley were closed on May 1, and no school buses were sent into West Las Vegas. By the time the uprising had ended, West Las Vegas suffered $6 million in damage, $3.5 million of it to Nucleus Plaza. (The Los Angeles riots caused at least $800 million in property damage, and fifty-two deaths.) In the end, sixty-five people were arrested in West Las Vegas.

Police blamed the rioting on some of the five thousand young gang members from southern California who had moved into West Las Vegas some time earlier and were simply taking advantage of the Simi Valley verdict to show their muscle and defy authority. Black city officials and West Las Vegas residents I spoke to said the rioting was the result of decades of neglect by the city and unwarranted police harassment.

At mid-afternoon in the Heritage Lounge, a bar in Nucleus Plaza that was spared during the riots, Thomas Sanders sips a Miller Lite. "It's worse here than the South. Excuse my French, but it's fucked up," said Sanders, who was born in Tallulah, Louisiana. "In 1992, I was driving through West Las Vegas and a policeman pulled me over," he says. Sanders, an engineer, was driving a black Cadillac. "He asked me if I had ever been to jail. When I told him no, he said, 'I can't believe you've never been to jail.' I guess I was in the wrong place in a nice car," says Sanders, 38.

"We've all been jacked up by the cops." says Carl Johnson. "Las Vegas is really a little hick town. That's all it is." At a special meeting of the Las Vegas City Council held in West Las Vegas in July 1992, several residents made similar claims of persistent police harassment.

Today, city officials prefer to categorize the riots as "civil unrest," a phrase that reveals the city's desire for a sanitized self-image and belies the level of anxiety and fear that spread quickly throughout the county, particularly in its dominant industry. Two weeks after the riots, the Las Vegas Convention and Visitors Authority rushed the production of a video to calm down nervous travel agents in Asia. A Canadian tour company considered offering refunds to customers who had booked trips to Las Vegas, as they had already done for customers heading for Los Angeles. Mayor Jan Laverty Jones went to a travel agents' convention in San Francisco a few weeks later in the hope of exercising damage control.

Suddenly, having languished for decades, the neighborhood on the wrong side of the tracks became a focal point of civic activism and largess.

On the sixth floor of the luxurious, new, redrock-sheathed Clark County Office Building, I meet with Yvonne Atkinson Gates, the forty-year-old black woman who chairs the Clark County Board of Commissioners—the most powerful elected political group in Las Vegas. "Here you have a picture on national news of burning and looting in Las Vegas. Las Vegas!" says Commissioner Gates. "I mean, here we are the gaming mecca of the world, and you have this occurring. You think they want that kind of image? NO WAY."

Gates, who had lived in West Las Vegas all her life, was running for her county commissioner's seat in May 1992. At the time, she denounced the looters and burners as juvenile thugs who were ruining their own community. "They really don't understand the significance of the Rodney King verdict, they don't even care," she declared on National Public Radio. She denounced neither the Metro Police nor the city, but "the people that are terrorizing the community right now—a community that people have worked very, very hard to try and build. Although it's not great in terms of services, it took us a long time to build what we have, and now you turn around and you look and it's all gone."

Today, her take on the situation is slightly different, her perspective more nuanced. "The riots were a perfect opportunity. It was an unfortunate situation that occurred, but it brought about positive change. Lots of it."

"How is it that community has been there for fifty years," I ask, "and nothing had been done to bring it on line with the growth of the rest of the valley?"

"Elected officials just didn't care." says the two-term commissioner. "They just didn't care."

Like Gates, Frank Hawkins Jr., the city's first black city council member, was born in West Las Vegas. In a widely quoted remark on NPR at the time of the riots, he said, "If this happens again, you won't see the burning of West Last Vegas, you'll see the burning of downtown—the burning of the Strip, the burning of the airport." The remark drew down Las Vegans' anger. *Las Vegas Sun* columnist Jeff German described Hawkins' comment as "costly rhetoric." "His remark," German wrote, "is likely to cause fear among the traveling public."

In a city controlled by tourists' perceptions, the strongest catalyst for change may be a threat to its international image. "They will use whatever means necessary to protect the industry," says the NAACP's Chester Richardson. "Rioting scared the gaming interests so bad. We didn't get redevelopment money by accident."

The riots did scare everyone, agrees Mike Leonard, then vice-president for marketing at Harrah's Casino-Hotel. Before the riots, he said, he barely knew West Las Vegas existed. Today Harrah's sponsors a program at a church in West Las Vegas, serving dinner to about a hundred kids. "It was an opportunity to bring big business to the table," says Hawkins, "to say, 'This is not an isolated incident, but we can make sure that this is a one-time incident because there is enough to go around and everybody needs to do their part.' And for the most part, no one said no."

Von's, the first full-service supermarket in West Las Vegas, opened its doors in 1994. Meanwhile, John Edmond, who had been unable to get building loans before the riots, has rebuilt and extended Nucleus Plaza. "Less than two months before the riots, banks weren't interested in loaning me a penny," says Edmond. "'We don't loan money over there. We don't do that.' Because this area was seriously redlined in 1992."

The neighborhood received private funds for a million-dollar expansion of its Boys and Girls Club, which opened in early 1997. Public housing was upgraded, an art center and theater were built in 1995, and construction began on a $7-million community center. Hundreds of welfare recipients from West Las Vegas were employed, at least temporarily, by the casinos.

A month after the uprising, Mayor Jan Laverty Jones and Councilman Frank Hawkins created a twenty-six-member Multi-jurisdictional Community Empowerment Commission with the goal of improving community-police relations, employment opportunities, affordable housing, economic development, and youth activities. The commission included some of the most powerful people in Nevada, including Steve Wynn,

president of Mirage Resorts; Brian Cram, the county school superintendent; and Senator Neal.

"Frank was the motivating force," says Neal. "The riots spoke of a
need. When you have an explosion, that tells you you've got to move
much quicker. Frank was there and could understand what needed to be
done.

"He had friends among the people who were rioting. He made deals
with people to keep the peace. He had the authority in the city to direct
the resources to meet the need."

■ ■ ■

The cream-colored security gate opens. Past the Mercedes-Benz and the
Jeep Cherokee parked in the horseshoe driveway, Frank Hawkins's
mother awaits me at the double doors in her housecoat. In the living
room, a bronze head of Martin Luther King, Jr. adorns the coffee table.
Anchored on the wall behind the couch, an Earnie Barnes portrait cap-
tures a kid doing a backflip in midair.

Hawkins, a star athlete at the University of Nevada at Reno, was born
in 1960, and named to the College Football Hall of Fame in 1997. After
graduation, he played professional football for the Los Angeles Raiders
(including a trip to Super Bowl XVIII in 1984), before retiring in 1988 with
a torn tricep. A life-size portrait of him in his black and silver uniform
hangs on another wall.

"When I retired from the L.A. Raiders in nineteen eighty-eight and
began working for the city," he says, "I learned that nothing had been done
in West Las Vegas for thirty years. There were no major grocery stores and
no buses when the sun went down."

While growing up in West Las Vegas, he had only a vague sense of the
extent of the neighborhood's desperate conditions. "I remember spending
one to two-and-a-half hours every day for eleven years on the school bus
and realizing that the closer I got to other communities, the better it
looked," says Hawkins, who opened the first gas station in his old neighborhood in 1986. Later, he opened a sports bar, two convenience stores,
and a car wash there as well, in an attempt to help "build a community."

Wasn't it a community already?

"A community is having everything everybody else has. Well, what does
everybody else have? They have schools, so they can walk their kids to
school," says Hawkins. "Communities have grocery stores. They have
businesses and banks. They have jobs. They have Dairy Queens and auto-

parts shops. West Las Vegas had none of that. They have public-housing units and a great unemployment rate and teenage pregnancy rate."

Many West Las Vegas residents protested the inundation of public-housing units, begun in 1949. In June of 1994, Frank Hawkins was appointed to chair the Las Vegas Housing Authority, with a $25 million budget; he was the first African American to hold this position. Since then, the Housing Authority has spent more than $40 million in HUD funds on upgrading public-housing projects in West Las Vegas, almost half those allotted to the city.

In 1989-90, Hawkins chaired the human resources committee of a city-wide, 300-person planning group called "Las Vegas 2000 and Beyond," which recommended (among many other things) a shift to neighbor-hood-based planning, so that residents could have more of a voice in determining their future.

City planner Frank Reynolds insists that the "Las Vegas 2000" report spurred plans for the revitalization of West Las Vegas before the riots ever took place. The first neighborhood meeting had been held in August 1991, and a neighborhood advisory board (appointed by Hawkins), whose input largely determined the scope of the plan, had held its first meeting just a week before the uprising broke out.

As a city councilman, Hawkins represented more than 61,000 people in Ward One, an area that encompassed far more constituents and terri-tory than West Las Vegas alone. But the former athlete seemed to hold a particular fondness for his old stomping ground, and many residents and civic leaders attribute most of the positive changes that took place in West Las Vegas after 1992 to his presence on the city council. "Frank was the first black politician to be elected without a significant black base," says Senator Neal. "You could feel his presence in city government. He began to move things, and knew how to move things. You could see the changes."

Once Hawkins realized that he only needed three votes to pass resolu-tions through the five-person council, his power seemed to equal if not exceed the mayor's. Political columnist Jon Ralston, of the *Las Vegas Review Journal*, once dubbed the body "Frank Hawkins' City Council."

Planner Reynolds, from his own cramped office in Nucleus Plaza, agreed. (He has since moved back to City Hall.) "He was young—only about thirty-three—but he worked very hard for his people. If it hadn't been for him pushing, I believe it sincerely, nothing would have happened. People came from West Las Vegas and asked the city for storm-door repair; nobody came. Over all those years, nothing had ever happened here. Look at all those vacant parcels on the map, the mixed-use zoning, zero population growth: thirty years of neglect! Hawkins said, 'We'll do this,' and it was adopted."

Under Hawkins, blacks were appointed to top positions in the city government. "When I got there, there were no minorities making any decisions in any departments," says Hawkins. "I had blacks and women appointed to positions that had never been filled by minorities before." Hawkins secured the appointments of Richard Blue as director of Economic Development, and Barbara Jackson as director of Parks and Recreation. Dozens of other African Americans were appointed to positions in top and middle management. In 1992, when one city council member left office in mid-term, Hawkins fought for the appointment of banker Ken Brass, who became the second black person on the Las Vegas City Council.

Hawkins wanted to change the dominant perception of the area by persuading a major institution to locate there. He believed that the perception of West Las Vegas as a dangerous, high-crime area had helped to cripple investment and large-scale development. When the Veterans Administration closed their Charleston Street hospital, he says, they searched high and low for a new site—off I-95, for example, and near Nellis Air Force Base—everywhere except Ward One. Hawkins took a map of his five-year plan for West Las Vegas to Washington, D.C., to lobby the Veterans Administration to locate its facility there.

In the spring of 1997, at the corner of MLK Boulevard and Vegas, eighteen-wheel trucks loaded with large, white plastic piping were parked in a fenced-off lot. Slender palm trees, bagged at the head with burlap, had yet to burst into fronds. The new V.A. Hospital was being erected as the centerpiece of an eighty-acre Enterprise Business Park. Chester Richardson had accompanied Hawkins on his lobbying trip to the nation's capital. "The V.A. Hospital," Richardson says simply: "that's Frank."

No one denies that Hawkins was the catalyst in negotiating the deals that began to bring significant development to West Las Vegas. But even he admits that the riots of 1992 helped to sensitize the movers and shakers. "The riots made power brokers think," says Hawkins today. "We used the riots to accomplish a lot of things we wanted to do."

During his council term, Hawkins helped commission a study which concluded that a disproportionate share of contracting dollars from fourteen government agencies was going to companies owned by whites. He then led the charge to ensure that businesses owned by minorities would receive 25 percent of the city's redevelopment dollars.

But although his accomplishments for Las Vegas blacks have become a part of local folklore, Hawkins was not immune to the harsh realities of political life. His failure to disclose a business loan he had received from a company for his sports bar prior to the 1991 election brought him before the city's Ethics Review Board in 1994, after he had voted on actions involving the lender.

In early 1994, he staged a profit-making golf tournament, charging $1,000 per participant. He invited several casino owners and staff members and various high profile athletes. Many viewed this event as another breach of political ethics, since several of those who attended the tournament regularly appeared before the city council with planning and zoning requests. Yet, because his seat on the city council (which pays $35,000 a year) was a part-time position, Hawkins insists even today that the tournament was simply a marketing endeavor.

When the *Las Vegas Review-Journal* learned that the city's Ethics Review Board was powerless to initiate its own investigation of the tournament, the paper undertook an investigation of its own: it printed a coupon on its editorial page and asked readers to mail it in if they wanted Frank Hawkins's dealings examined by the ethics board. Five hundred readers did.

After the various charges were leveled against Hawkins, support from his constituents waned. Hawkins was found guilty of violating Nevada's ethics code by the State Ethics Commission in April 1995. In June, he lost his bid for reelection. Although he carried West Las Vegas overwhelmingly, he only won 39 percent of the overall vote in Ward One.

Sam Smith, with a beer-barrel belly and bright-eyed stare, doles out advice and information as a kind of neighborhood sage from his small Native Son bookstore on a corner in West Las Vegas. "He had too much concern for his brothers and sisters," Smith says of Hawkins. "He was young, learning fast, and understood his power. He played politics just like he played football. He tossed a lot of people out of power. The money people said, 'This man is dangerous.'"

With West Las Vegas's most successful advocate out of office, the mobilization of human resources and capital required to transform the neighborhood into a "community" seems to have lapsed. The Multi-jurisdictional Empowerment Commission has virtually collapsed. "Since Frank left," says Neal, "everything is dormant." Chester Richardson, local NAACP spokesman and longtime civil rights activist, says, "He's done more in his four years than anyone had in twenty-five years in West Las Vegas. Since he's been gone, ain't shit happening."

Planner Frank Reynolds disputes this, pointing at new infill development in all four precincts of the neighborhood, a plan for new commercial development along Jackson Street, the $17-million ambulatory health-care center scheduled to open in 1998 ("the biggest single thing that's ever been done on the Westside"), and negotiations for a large general-purpose store on city-owned land across the street from Von's. But he agrees that it was Hawkins who started and kept the ball rolling.

After policeman Mike McDonald defeated Hawkins as Ward One's representative on the city council, the council redefined Las Vegas's electoral boundaries, effectively shifting West Las Vegas into Ward Three. What this move has done is to lump together the city's two largest concentrations of minorities, African Americans and Hispanics—and its two poorest neighborhoods—into one ward. Leaders of both communities protested the change, seeing it as an attempt to limit their political power. An attempt (supported by Senator Neal and the NAACP) is currently being made to enlarge the council from four to six members, in the hope of giving greater voice to the residents of these districts.

Several people Hawkins appointed have been either removed or shifted to lower positions in the city hierarchy, although Clark County appointed the first black fire chief in Nevada's history in 1996, two months after black firefighters won a $600,000 settlement for claims of racial discrimination. "We have never in the history of Clark County had a black department head," says Yvonne Atkinson Gates, chair of the county board of commissioners. "I waited six months [after my election] and now we have three." The directors of two county social-service agencies, Family and Youth Services and Clark County Social Services, are also African American. Atkinson Gates remains the area's most visible and powerful elected black politician, along with Senator Neal. Like Hawkins, both of them have been constant targets of criticism in the local press.

Frank Hawkins, meanwhile, has moved on. "Just like football, when it was over, it was over," he says.

"When you redistribute the wealth, which is what I did, changing the structure of the power base, the people used to the wealth don't want that to happen. That's why people invest in the political system—those who understand. When you go against the grain, or you threaten what they have, those people who do not agree want you removed. Those who do, they side with you and work with you. I didn't want to be a lifetime politician. I went to the city council with a mission."

Today, in addition to owning a marketing company, Hawkins directs the non-profit Community Development Program Center of Nevada. In collaboration with U.S. Bank, the center disbursed more than $16 million dollars in home and minority-owned small-business loans in 1996. In 1998, the Center was given the right to develop Gerson Park, a derelict, 40-acre housing project in West Las Vegas, by the U.S. Department of Housing and Urban Development. CDPC demolished the old buildings in 1998, and (in collaboration with local builders), plans to erect 365 units of new, affordable housing on the site.

■ ■ ■

Coming in on Vegas Drive, the western extension of Owens, I roll toward Martin Luther King Boulevard. Flags of change now flank Vegas Drive. RICHMOND AMERICAN GATED COMMUNITY. HILLCREST PRICES FROM THE 60S. SINGLE STORY HOMES NOW AVAILABLE. FREE MINI-BLINDS. APPLIANCES. POOL SIZE LOTS.

While the populations of both the city of Las Vegas and Clark County have more than doubled since 1970, the population of West Las Vegas has decreased. "Who moving to Las Vegas wants to live in a thirty- to forty-year-old house?" asks Hawkins. Though more than three hundred houses were built in West Las Vegas in the 1970s, only a handful went up in the 1980s. But the pace has picked up since then; private developers have begun new subdivisions west of Tonopah Drive. More than 900 new houses are in construction along this corridor in West Las Vegas.

As I pull into the parking lot of the school on Vegas Drive, five Latino workmen methodically spread mortar between varied heights of concrete blocks across from Advanced Technologies Academy. With 650 computers for 750 students, two nineteen-inch TV monitors in each classroom, and students whose reading and math scores lead those of all eighteen Clark County high schools, "A-Tech" definitely stands out in West Las Vegas.

It stands out because (1) it was the first and only high school built in this neighborhood; (2) it is the only high school in the county visited by Vice President Gore; and (3) many local residents still regard this science-and-technology "magnet school," which draws students from all over the district, as an unacceptable alternative to a comprehensive public school built for youths who live in the community. At the end of each school day, at least seven bright-yellow buses line up outside A-Tech and leave West Las Vegas via Martin Luther King Boulevard taking students home to neighborhoods as far away as McCarran Airport.

Admission to this elite school at the edge of the " 'hood," funded in part by the federal government for its first two years, is highly competitive, drawing four applicants for each available spot. Advanced Technologies is supposed to create a representative racial balance, meaning that the ratio of white students to nonwhite students is to reflect the total student population in the county, plus or minus 5 percent. When the school first opened, in 1994, more than 17 percent of the students were African American; by 1997, that proportion had decreased to less than 14 percent, and was then representative of the population of black students in Clark County. However, in the 1997-98 school year the population of white students at A-Tech was 65 percent, or 9 percent higher than their representation in the county. Fewer than thirty five students at the school live in West Las Vegas.

According to Clark County School District spokesman Ray Willis, "There are no seats reserved for West Las Vegas kids" at Advanced Tech.

Though West Las Vegas has more school-age children per capita than any other region in the county, there was no middle school within its perimeter until 1998. Before then, middle-school students were bused to ten different schools outside the neighborhood. High-school students denied admission to Advanced Tech are still bused to seven different schools. Until 1994, all West Las Vegas youth were bused outside their neighborhood for eleven of their twelve public-school years. (The area now has five elementary schools.) "We've lost two generations of kids," says Marzette Lewis, an uncompromising fighter for West Las Vegas schoolchildren.

Some residents criticize Lewis's approach as "rough around the edges." But this fiery woman with big hair and a perennially hoarse voice seems to get results despite (or perhaps because of) her pit-bull style. In 1994, Marzette Lewis and her organization, "Westside Action Alliance Korp-Uplifting People" (so named in order to yield the acronym "WAAK UP"), protested a $300-million bond issue for Clark County school development because neighborhood schools had not been scheduled for West Las Vegas. "They had passed bonds before, but we didn't get anything from it," says Lewis, 56.

Indeed, the bond issue did not pass, although most observers attributed its failure to an implied rise in property taxes, which Clark County voters abhor, rather than to any injustice done to West Las Vegas. (Another $605-million school bond issue, with no tax implications, was passed at the same time, as was a $643-million school bond vote in 1996. In 1998, voters approved a ten-year extension of these earlier tax increases, which should yield another $2.5 billion for Clark County Schools.)

"In my view," says spokesman Willis, "Marzette Lewis is talking reparations. She's talking about getting our forty acres and a mule. But that's a luxury," he says. "We're chasing growth."

If reparations are Lewis's goal, her appeal for federal intervention affirms the intensity of her quest. Lewis filed a complaint with the Civil Rights Division of the U.S. Department of Justice for what her organization deemed abuse of bond funding by the Clark County School District, and the department supported her claim. Lewis is largely credited with the conversion of West Las Vegas's sixth-grade centers into elementary and magnet schools, and the allotment of $17 million for a new middle school in West Las Vegas.

But, says Lewis, this is not enough. She and the twenty active members of WAAK UP want a neighborhood high school as well. In 1996, Lewis led an appeal to the county school board to expand A-Tech into a comprehensive school for at least 2,000 students, but the board voted 4-2 against it.

Across the country, blacks are questioning the social costs of the cross-town busing that civil-rights leaders once supported; questioning the idea that their children need to sit beside white children in order to learn; realizing that in the name of racial balance, magnet schools often exclude the very students desegregation was intended to help; and deciding that their new focus should be improving the schools in their own neighborhoods.

Roxie Newton, a West Las Vegas cosmetologist, is among them. "I'm not trying to say we shouldn't have had the freedom to do and go where we want to, but integration in this city was bad because it took away more than it gave back—our businesses, our kids. That's where we lost our kids," she says. "When those school districts integrated."

Newton peers through the Venetian blinds at Dee Dee's Beauty Salon in Nucleus Plaza, towards the big new Von's supermarket in Westland Plaza—a project funded in part by basketball star Magic Johnson, whose development group owns the lot. Von's, the anchor tenant, with thirty thousand square feet, made the decision to erect the metal fence by which the entire new plaza is surrounded.

While the walls surrounding other Las Vegas communities signify exclusivity and privilege, the black-painted iron fence around Von's took on another connotation. "It looked like a prison," says the NAACP's Richardson.

"Strange," murmurs Newton. "If the gate is going to stay open, why did it need to be fenced off, anyway?" Like many stores and eating places in Las Vegas, the market is open 24 hours a day, every day of the year. "You have no other grocery store in town with a fence around it. So why this one?" Her granddaughter Mahoganny runs around the salon as Newton massages acetone on a customer's nails.

According to Von's spokesman, Brian Dowling, the fence is there to protect the business and present an "aura of security" to employees and customers. This particular Von's, one of sixteen in Clark County, is the only one enclosed by a fence.

After community protests, the fence was painted beige to blend in with the rest of the center. But the symbolic barrier remains.

■ ■ ■

The Moulin Rouge Casino opened in West Las Vegas in 1955 as the first integrated casino-hotel in the country. At 88,900 square feet, the casino rivaled those on the Strip in reputation, size, and splendor. Its official host, heavyweight champion Joe Louis, greeted celebrated entertainers such as Harry Belafonte, Sammy Davis Jr., Pearl Bailey, and George Burns. At the height of its popularity, the Moulin Rouge instituted a "third show" at 2:30 AM, a move that led Strip hotels to add late performances of their own, since the club drew high rollers away from the Strip and was packed for every performance. But in less than five months, the club closed its doors.

The official story is that the owner went bankrupt because of mismanagement. Some believe, however, that Strip operators urged creditors of the Moulin Rouge to sue for payment of overdue bills. Following the club's closure, Strip casinos began to ease their racial restrictions for black entertainers.

The club was reopened in 1957. In 1960, under Leo Frye's ownership, the Moulin Rouge became a part of local history when a series of meetings between Las Vegas civil-rights leaders and public officials culminated in the official end to racial discrimination in public accommodations in Nevada, with legislation signed at the Moulin Rouge.

The property has been in the hands of a number of leaseholders since. Sarann Knight Preddy made an attempt to restore the Moulin Rouge when she and her family leased the property in 1985. Preddy's father was a construction worker who helped build the resort; some members of her family were the first blacks to own a casino-resort.

But despite its historic landmark designation, and all the attempts to salvage it, the Moulin Rouge has stood as a defunct relic of the past, a black hole in Las Vegas for decades.

On a spring day in 1997, abandoned vehicles without hubcaps, tires, or signal lights lie in the landmark's parking lot, which is shared by the Religious Emporium, the Beauty Bar, and the Lipstick and Nail Center. Large cracks run along the front and sides of the mauve building. The swimming pool has been empty since 1992.

Inside, the scent of mildew fills the air. A long piece of silver duct tape runs down the carpet. The gaming tables are blotched with numerous shapes and hues of brown. Glitter and water spots cling to the ceiling, from the middle of which dangle three little red puffed stars. The showroom has been closed for more than forty years.

In the vacant restaurant and bar, more puffed novelties hang from the ceiling. A three-tiered display case offers costume jewelry and T-shirts with "Historic Moulin Rouge" written across the front. A large, black-and-white photograph of Joe Louis hangs next to the door, where once upon a time he greeted visitors. Beyond the picture, a large crack runs down the wall in the foyer, allowing natural light to shine into the dark hall. A sign on the wall reads, "No drugs, firearms, outside food, drink. We support our police."

A study initiated by Hawkins and commissioned by the city determined that the Moulin Rouge would have a good chance of financial success if it could be renovated. So the city agreed that if the Preddy family could raise $3 million for its restoration, they would submit a proposal to HUD to match that amount, and contribute a grant of one million dollars on top of it.

But the Preddys were unable to come up with the money. After investing almost a million dollars in the property (plus thousands more in their unsuccessful applications for a permanent gaming license), Sarann Knight Preddy says she is broke, and her family's entreaties to investors have all failed.

Over the last twelve years, Preddy has sold her home and other property to keep the Moulin Rouge open. "My whole life went into the Moulin Rouge," she says. "It really hasn't gotten out my system, but as far as my family is concerned we've had enough of it." Although Preddy received $250,000 in state funds for renovation, she says the amount was only enough to replace the roof, so she gave it back. Soon afterwards, she voluntarily handed the keys back to longtime property owner Leo Frye.

In October 1996, the club's doors were closed once more. Since the Moulin Rouge was declared a historic site but not a historic building, Frye planned to demolish the building, divide the land, and lease it out in separate parcels.

But in the spring of 1997, Frye sold the Moulin Rouge for $3 million. Bart Maybie, who owns six hundred apartment units in West Las Vegas, has purchased and gated all the apartment buildings in close proximity to the club, and he expects his full-service casino to be renovated, restored, and brought up to code before the year 2000. His prescription for success includes a transformation of the surrounding dilapidated neighborhood. But without a nonrestricted gaming license (which John Edmond hopes to obtain in order to lease the restored casino), the fate of the only casino in West Las Vegas remains unclear.

"For it to sit right there in the black neighborhood, so bleak and run-down, is really like a sore thumb," says Preddy. It makes the whole area feel isolated—like it's the end of the world."

Water for the Desert Miracle

Jenna Ward

From the window of an airplane, the city of Las Vegas appears like a vast oasis in the middle of the drab Mojave desert. The emerald green of golf courses contrasts with the flashes of aqua from thousands of backyard pools and the deeper blue of scattered artificial lakes and ponds.

On almost any day in the streets below, you can see water flowing along the curbs and into the gutters, runoff from sprinkled lawns of Kentucky bluegrass and dusty driveways being hosed clean. Fountains and waterfalls adorn not only the city's casinos, but also its strip malls, business parks, and apartment complexes, which bear names such as "Lakewood Cove," "Flamingo Bay," and "Harbor Island."

In an average year, only four inches of rain fall here, yet Las Vegans use more water per person than residents of any other major city in the country. They pour most of it on the ground around their homes, trying to force greenery out of the alkaline desert soil.

In this city of illusions, the sense of abundant water is perhaps the biggest mirage of all. Barring a major drought, Las Vegas's existing water supply will carry it through the year 2007. A series of interim measures should provide enough water for continued growth through the year 2025, when the population is projected to reach 2.3 million.

And after 2025? No one knows exactly, but Las Vegans are fond of reciting the maxim "In the West, water runs uphill toward power and money."

In keeping with the city's reputation for free-flowing cash and overnight fortunes, its inhabitants display a serene confidence that if all else fails, they will simply *buy* the water they need to maintain their desert miracle.

But there is another old saying in the West: "You can take my wife, but you can't take my water." In the arid and rapidly growing southwestern United States, water rights are precious, and not always for sale. Any major change in interstate water allocations would not only concern the buyer and seller, but would also be scrutinized by seven quarrelsome, litigation-prone western states as well as the Mexican and United States governments. To strike a deal, Las Vegas may find that, in addition to money, it will need a good helping of the city's second-most-prized civic value: luck.

Meanwhile, an estimated thousand or more new residents move to Greater Las Vegas each week. This metropolitan area is growing faster than any other in the country, and water officials are determined not to be the ones to spoil the party by calling a halt to expansion.

Still, the basic question remains: what will happen in 2025, when the children of these transplants need more water than the city can supply? David Donnelly, deputy general manager of the Southern Nevada Water Authority, says (with a smile), "I don't care. I won't be here."

■ ■ ■

Despite appearances to the contrary, Las Vegas was not built in the middle of nowhere. The city exists where it does for one simple reason: water. The history of water in Las Vegas is in many ways indistinguishable from the history of the city itself, and the tensions between the alternating availability and scarcity of this life-giving resource form a discernible pattern.

"Las Vegas" is Spanish for The Meadows. Once upon a time, the Las Vegas Valley was filled with mesquite trees, willows, cottonwoods, and saltgrass, all irrigated by three artesian springs, the Big, the Little, and the Middle.

Before settlers arrived, Paiute Indians spent their winters by these warm, clear waters. No one knows who was the first outsider to stumble across the valley, but by the 1830s, it had become a vital rest stop on an otherwise waterless leg of the Old Spanish Trail that led from Santa Fe to Los Angeles.

In 1855, Brigham Young sent thirty Mormon missionaries to settle Las Vegas. Although the early Mormons were masters of irrigation farming, the missionaries had to struggle to eke crops out of the poor desert soil, and were recalled to Salt Lake City two years later. A handful of other settlers followed; but it was the San Pedro, Los Angeles and Salt Lake Railroad that put Las Vegas on the map.

In 1905, William Clark (as in "Clark County"), a railroad magnate and U.S. senator from Montana, chose Las Vegas as a division point on the railroad line because it offered water for the steam trains and passengers, and was located at an ideal distance to change crews and refuel. A scruffy little company town was formed.

The railroad-owned Las Vegas Land and Water Company controlled the water from the three artesian springs. But new residents soon discovered that if they drilled down about 300 feet, they too could strike water.

From its earliest days, Las Vegas was a city of water gluttons. Homeowners drilled hundreds of private wells throughout the valley, some of which "spewed forth thousands of gallons of water per minute, which flowed into ponds or gullies, with no use whatever being made of the water," as Florence Jones and John Cahlan wrote in their book *Water: A History of Las Vegas* (1975). In the decades to come, "It was common practice for families going to Mt. Charleston for a weekend, to escape the blazing heat of the Valley, to leave sprinklers running in their front and back yards until they returned."

No one saw anything wrong with this, the authors say: "It was the generally accepted theory that Las Vegas was sitting on top of a vast lake of underground water which could be tapped with impunity for years with no danger of diminishing the supply."

In an indirect way, water was responsible for transforming the sleepy railroad town into a world-famous location. In 1928, President Calvin Coolidge signed legislation authorizing the building of the Boulder (now Hoover) Dam, and the construction of this spectacular structure, which spans the Colorado River forty miles from Las Vegas, captivated the nation in the midst of the Great Depression. In 1935, more than 250,000 visitors passed through Las Vegas en route to the dam and Lake Mead, the vast reservoir created by the project. The town of Boulder City was built to house the dam workers, and Las Vegas joined in the boom.

Preceding construction of the dam, a fateful agreement called the Colorado River Compact divided up the river's water among seven states and Mexico. The United States' share of the water was split among four upper-basin states, Colorado, Wyoming, New Mexico, and Utah; and three lower-basin states, Arizona, Nevada, and California. Each basin is entitled to 7.5 million acre-feet of river water annually; an acre-foot, or 326,000 gallons, is generally regarded as enough water to supply two families for a year.

Nevada was the first state to approve the compact, ratifying the agreement in 1922. At the time, it was thought quite a coup that the negotiators had secured 300,000 acre feet for the state, which then had a population of less than 100,000. By contrast, California, which had 3.4 million people in 1920, was allocated 4.4 million acre feet, and Arizona 2.85 million.

The division of water was based on agricultural potential rather than population, and not even the Mormons could farm Nevada. Three hundred thousand acre feet seemed more than adequate. Who, in 1922, could have predicted air-conditioning, freeways, and golf courses, let alone the gambling and resort empires created by men like Howard Hughes, Kirk Kerkorian, Bill Bennett, and Steve Wynn? Today, the state's allocation is a noose, for the numbers are still binding.

For years, Nevada used none of its Colorado River allocation; Las Vegas relied on its springs and wells. In 1944, however, the state engineer warned the Las Vegas Chamber of Commerce that the city was running out of water, and that unless they found a new source, growth would have to stop—a warning the city is hearing again, more than half a century later.

■ ■ ■

"This site was originally the major source of water for the valley. This is where it started," said hydrologist Erin Cole, gesturing toward a desolate well field now bordered by Interstate 15 and Highway 95. "There were three major springs in this area. Some flowed three to four thousand gallons a minute. They used to flow, but we pumped them too much." Now the ground is powder-dry, and the old creek bed still littered with trunks and branches of trees that died once the water was gone.

Since the town was formed, in 1904, the underground water table has dropped a total of two hundred feet. With so much water pumped out, the earth itself has subsided, as if deflated. Near the former creek bed, old well heads that were once at ground level now jut five feet into the air. On the north side of town, foundations of houses have cracked and split as the ground has sunk around them. Water that took centuries to accumulate would have disappeared in a handful of years if Las Vegas had not turned to a new source just over the horizon: the Colorado River.

Las Vegas first began to get water from Lake Mead in 1955, using pipelines that belonged to BMI (Basic Materials Inc., originally Basic Magnesium), a major World War II defense contractor based in Henderson, eleven miles south of Las Vegas. The city's own plant, the A. M. Smith Water Treatment Facility, began delivering water from Lake

Mead to the city in June of 1971. Water in Las Vegas was once again plentiful.

Today, 85 percent of Las Vegas's water comes from the Colorado River. In the summer months, when demand soars, the town uses ground water to augment the supply. Water is still being pumped out of the aquifer faster than it can be replenished, but the rate of the overdraft has slowed.

The location of the city's treatment plant was controversial at the time it was built, and it still is: the city's drinking water is drawn just six-and-a-half miles downstream from the place where its treated sewage is dumped into Lake Mead.

One of the plant's first critics, Howard Hughes, the reclusive land baron and hotel owner, found this arrangement unpalatable, and he begged Nevada Governor Paul Laxalt to stop the project. In an undated memo to his aide Robert Maheu, Hughes wrote, "This water system will comprise the only water system in the world where the outlet of the sewage disposal plant, plus tons of raw sewage, will flow into a small, stagnant pool of water and then pour right back out again with a screen to remove the turds.

"It is not so much the technical purity or impurity, it is the revolting vomitus, unattractiveness of the whole thing. It is sort of like serving an expensive cut of New York cut steak in one of our showrooms on a beautiful plate. Instead of a slice of parsley and lemon and trimmings, instead of this there is a small pile of shit. Now maybe technically the shit doesn't touch the steak, but how much will the patron enjoy eating that steak?"

Although a noted germ freak, Hughes did have a point. The issue has become more pressing, for as the city has grown, the volume of wastewater discharged into the lake has reached Niagara proportions.

"As the flow to the lake increases, it gets harder for the lake to absorb," said Phil Sanders, the senior wastewater treatment plant operator at the Clark County Sanitation District. The plant discharges an average of 68 to 69 million gallons of treated sewage a day—and even more on weekends, when tens, sometimes hundreds of thousands of tourists are in town and an extraordinary number of toilets are flushed. When the wastewater leaves the plant, it is "pretty clear-looking," said Sanders, with no more than five or six parts per million of suspended solids, and only trace amounts of ammonia, phosphates, and nitrates—all well within federal guidelines.

But in Lake Mead, a plume of pollution is often visible, spreading out from the point where the Las Vegas Wash, as the river of the city's waste is called, enters Las Vegas Bay. The plume is made of potentially toxic blue-green algae, which thrives on nutrients found in sewage, although water officials say no one has proven that the discharge creates the plume.

To date, the plume has not caused any scientifically documented problems, says Dr. Richard French, a hydrologic engineer with the Desert Research Institute in Las Vegas. "However," he added, "There have been rumors in the community, of scuba divers getting ear infections and things like that out of the water; so there is a problem."

In the water business, there is a slogan: the solution to pollution is dilution. Yet despite Lake Mead's enormous size, the concept is not quite applicable here. "If there was some way to put the wastewater back in Boulder Basin (in the middle of the lake), it would be insignificant compared to the volume," said Dr. French. "The real problem is that we put the water back in this limited body, [Las Vegas Bay]."

The path of the wastewater as it flows down toward Saddle Island, where the drinking water is taken in, remains unexamined. "Nobody has ever really wanted to take a look at it," said Dr. French. "I think they are afraid of what the answers might be."

David Donnelly of the Southern Nevada Water Authority (SNWA) finds such concerns unnecessarily alarmist. "People are making a whole lot more of the plume issue than they should be, I think," he said. "The plume is two-and-a-half miles north of the intake.

"The people who want to put a scare into other people are always saying things like 'Las Vegas has thirty million visitors a year, and in their bowels are every parasite and disease known to man, and it's all getting flushed down into the water supply.' But that's exactly what happens in the Ohio River, the Mississippi River, every river system in the United States."

By early 1997, nagging concerns about water quality had become strong enough for the Environmental Protection Agency to establish a Lake Mead Water Quality Forum, bringing together for the first time high-level water and sewage officials, their counterparts from Parks and Recreation and Fish and Game, and representatives from the city, county, and state governments. The impetus was a 1996 U.S. Geological Survey study of endocrine disruption of carp in Lake Mead: for some reason, the male carp were turning into females. A two-year-long, federally-funded, half-million-dollar study begun in 1999 is trying to figure out why.

"If the water is feminizing the fish," said Dr. James Deacon, a professor of environmental studies at the University of Nevada at Las Vegas, "there is the possibility that it could be feminizing other creatures that drink the water...including Guess Who?"

The Colorado is a large and very heavily used river, both upstream and downstream from Las Vegas, so determining the effect of the city's discharge on the system is not a simple task. But the most devastating blow to Las Vegas's water supply today would be to halt or even scale back the amount of wastewater the city is allowed to discharge.

The reason is that Las Vegas has found a surprising loophole in the Colorado River Compact, which allows the city to get more water from the river by swapping wastewater for fresh water. Under an arrangement known as "return-flow credits," for every gallon of treated sewage the city dumps back in the lake, it is allowed to take out an additional gallon of fresh water.

In 1996, Las Vegas pumped out 356,000 acre-feet from the Colorado, said Susan Selby, a SNWA resource analyst; obviously, this exceeded their mandated limit of 300,000. But the city also returned 131,000 acre-feet of wastewater to Lake Mead. Under the return-flow arrangement, this reduced its official draw of Colorado River water to 225,000 acre-feet.

Because Las Vegas is returning water (albeit wastewater) back to the river, it is not reducing the overall quantity of the flow; only the quality is affected. This arrangement is not popular with downstream user Los Angeles, which gets one-third of *its* fresh water from the Colorado.

Return-flow credits create a powerful incentive for Las Vegas to dump as much wastewater back into the lake as possible. Other desert communities, like Phoenix and Tucson, often use wastewater for irrigation, especially on golf courses, but Las Vegas has shown only minimal interest in following their example. In its 1997 general plan, the SNWA decreed that no more than 21,800 acre-feet of wastewater should ever be withheld for irrigation in the valley. In the year 2000, a small waste-treatment plant is slated to open on West Cheyenne Boulevard; the plant is being paid for entirely by local golf course owners, who have agreed to finance the $45 million project in return for the one million gallons of wastewater it will generate daily.

But for now, almost all the water used in the valley is potable, and officials say this is one reason per-capita use among residents appears so high. In 1996, Las Vegas citizens used an average of 319 gallons per day. In Tucson, the average citizen used 155, in Santa Fe, 160, and in Phoenix 250. The city's well-publicized golf course boom cannot alone explain the disparity: in 1997, Greater Las Vegas had thirty-plus courses; metropolitan Phoenix had six times as many.

■ ■ ■

People involved with water in Las Vegas, whether as officials or concerned citizens, display a remarkably similar attitude when discussing the town's number-one industry: they consistently blame tourists for skewing the per-capita consumption figures while praising the casinos as responsible users. The apparent contradiction never seems to register.

"The per-capita use is slanted because of the recreation base we have," says Sue Baker, president of the citizens' group AquaVision, which promotes conservation. But, she added, "People blast the casino industry as the ones using up all the water, and they're not getting a fair shake."

Judy Laws, a Clark County water-quality and natural-resource planner, complains that the per-capita numbers reflect a lack of "understanding of our local community. Tourism is our number-one industry here.... We have two hundred fifty or three hundred thousand people coming for a weekend. That's not something that a lot of communities face." Yet she also had nothing but praise for Steve Wynn, creator of the Mirage and Treasure Island casino-hotels. "He's very proactive. What looks like a real waste of water actually is not."

Wynn built his own treatment plant to reclaim his casinos' wastewater, and thus deflects all criticism of his lavish water displays. Both the water volcano at the Mirage and the mock pirate-ship battle on the miniature lake at Treasure Island use gray water, not potable.

According to the SNWA's breakdown of water usage, hotels account for only 8 percent of the city's consumption. Furthermore, when tourists use water, virtually all of it runs down the sink, the bathtub, and the toilet and back into Lake Mead as a return-flow credit. From the water district's point of view, it's almost as if this water was never used at all.

But when residents use water to sprinkle their lawns or wash their cars, it soaks into the ground and never makes it back to the river. Residents consume 64 percent of the water in Las Vegas, and in the blazing summers, 80 percent of that water is used outdoors. From the district's point of view, this water is almost a total loss; by its estimate, at least half the water used outdoors is wasted.

"The amount of water that goes toward watering thousands of lawns, that's a lot more water than the casinos use," said environmental consultant Kurt Gobel.

Although Las Vegans no longer leave their sprinklers running for the weekend, the populace is still guilty of chronic overwatering. If there is blame to be laid for Las Vegas's bloated water consumption, it belongs at the feet of residents, not tourists. The most common explanation for the high residential use is that homesick new residents transplanted from other, less arid regions are trying to recreate the lush surroundings they left behind. "We're attracting people here from other places, i.e., the Midwest and the East," said Mary Manning, who writes about water for the

Las Vegas Sun. "They want it green here." But Tucson and Phoenix also attract people from the Midwest and the East, and newcomers there do not feel compelled to impose the aesthetic of a wetter clime. Something is different about Las Vegas.

"This is a city of excess, it really is," said Carol Jansen, who moved to Las Vegas from Albuquerque and now teaches a class on water at UNLV. "Nothing is done in moderation here."

Some residents speak as if the hedonism of the Strip has pervaded the entire town. "Las Vegas is such a material place. It's all about pleasure. Water conservation doesn't seem important here," said consultant Gobel, who has lived in Las Vegas for twelve years. "The mentality is that the desert is the abnormal, and a temperate, humid, rainy climate is the norm."

Another word for this mentality might be denial, a mass reluctance to acknowledge that the Las Vegas Valley is one of most arid spots on the planet. "We live in a desert, and the desert is not going to adapt to us," said Allie Smith, the UNLV Campus Green coordinator. "We're going to have to adapt to the desert."

Still, there is something viscerally satisfying about trying to turn the desert green, especially a desert as dusty and barren as the Mojave. A monochrome dirty beige, it lacks the subtle elegance and striking plant life of the high Sonoran Desert that surrounds water-conservation role model Tucson. In Tucson, a lush rainforest-style front yard looks tacky; in Las Vegas, it is a relief from the starkness of the Mojave.

Persuading residents to surround their houses with "xeriscapes"—yards composed of native plants that need little water—has been a tough sell in Las Vegas. Not so long ago, there were even ordinances on the books requiring people to plant lawns in their front and back yards, says Sue Baker of AquaVision.

The SNWA has the formidable task of trying to change habits that date back to the very inception of Las Vegas, and their extensive campaign promoting conservation is gradually producing some results: since 1990, per-capita water consumption has dropped 11 percent. The goal is to reduce it an additional 14 percent by the year 2000.

"We are trying to instill this conservation ethic into our customers, and it's beginning to really show," said the SNWA's Donnelly. "We got into it late and we should apologize for that, but really don't have a whole lot to apologize for anymore because we are doing everything everyone else is doing and more."

Between May and October, it is illegal to water lawns and gardens between noon and 7 PM, and residents can be fined up to $1,000 for wasting water. Low-flow shower heads are available free of charge, and the SNWA offers a cash-for-grass rebate to homeowners who convert lawns into xeriscapes. The water district also funds the Desert Demonstration Gardens, which feature model yards of water-efficient plants and a staff of landscape experts to help residents design their own xeriscapes. "Ten years ago, fifteen years ago, you would not have bought a house that had desert landscape," said Donnelly. "Now people are saying, 'I don't want grass. I love the desert look.'"

But despite all the good intentions and reminders to "Be Water Smart," the water district has not implemented the single biggest incentive to get people to conserve: cost. Water rates in Las Vegas are among the lowest in the West.

"Why is the water bill so unconscionably low?" asked Beneth Morrow, who moved to Las Vegas from Ohio in 1996. "We've never lived anywhere where it was so low." In Ohio, she said, she and her husband paid five times as much for water. Other transplants expressed similar feelings. "It seems to me our cost of water is about one-tenth of what it should be," said T. L. Wallace, a retired airline pilot from Wisconsin who moved to Las Vegas in 1988.

Las Vegas has a four-tier rate structure. People who use the least water are rewarded by the lowest rate—98 cents per 1,000 gallons. The biggest users are charged more—$2.27 per 1,000 gallons, still a bargain compared to many other cities.

"Frankly, the community is wasteful because the water is cheap," said Dr. French of the Desert Research Institute. "There ought to be a reasonable price on a certain amount of water so everybody can meet their basic needs. But you know, I have a fifty-foot-long swimming pool and…I have some grass in the front. If I want those things, I ought to pay for them."

Donnelly acknowledged that higher rates would probably reduce consumption. But, as he pointed out, "We can only charge our costs as a public agency. We can't make money." In the future, rates will rise, in part to pay for the district's "second straw" now under construction, a system of pipes and pumps designed to draw additional water from Lake Mead. Much of the cost of this and other water supply improvements, however, is scheduled to be paid from a quarter-cent increase in the sales tax designed to raise $2.3 billion, approved by Clark County voters in 1998.

The second straw represents a gamble by the water district that they will eventually be able to draw more water from the Colorado River. Although the water district needs the additional straw to use 100 percent of its current river allocation, the system has been designed with the capacity to process more water than Nevada is currently allowed to take under the 1922 compact. In building the straw, "we're betting we'll be able to renegotiate the river compact," said Jeff Harris, head of long-range planning for Clark County.

But the image of Las Vegans as water wasters presents a considerable obstacle to securing more water. "None of the other states is going to feel sorry for Nevada, specifically Las Vegas, and our shortage of water, if we aren't showing an effort to conserve with the resources we have," says Baker of AquaVision. "Until we show that we are as lean and mean and efficient as we possibly can, who is going to want to help us try to secure new water rights?"

In all fairness, it must be said that, despite Las Vegans' predilection for water-intensive landscaping, the amount of water they waste is minuscule compared to what California does with its vastly larger share of Colorado River water.

"This is something that has always kind of irritated me about people and the way they view water," said Donnelly. "People will drives miles and miles, past thousands of acres of cotton and Savannah grass in the family car coming to Las Vegas for a vacation, chit-chat and never think anything about it. Then they pull up in front of the Mirage Hotel, they see the fountain, and they say 'Oh lord, what a huge waste of water.'

"All those cotton fields use a million times more water than the Mirage ever uses…it's just an outrageous, wasteful abuse of water to grow cotton in the middle of the desert. It's just mind-boggling."

But California has a fifty-two-member Congressional delegation and fifty-four electoral votes. Whether or not farmers should be growing rice and cotton, the state has no incentive to transfer water from them to Las Vegas, and Nevada lacks the political leverage to force the issue.

For decades, California has consistently exceeded its 4.4-million-acre-feet allocation of river water, mainly because Nevada and Arizona have traditionally not used their full allotments; California has claimed their leftovers. But this is changing. Nevada is now determined to hold on to its entire 300,000-acre-feet allocation and store the unused portion underground, in an arrangement known as water banking. Emptied by the groundwater mining system of the past, water is injected back into the aquifer to be extracted as needed in the future. "That's why the program was started, so we could take advantage of the water and save for the future," said SNWA hydrologist Cole. "Otherwise it'll just run downriver and California will use it."

Water officials estimate they can store between 800,000 to 1,000,000 acre-feet in the Las Vegas Basin, and have already injected 120,000. They will start tapping into this water in the year 2007, at which point they expect the river will no longer cover their needs. In addition, both Las Vegas and Los Angeles have made deals with Arizona to bank water underground near Phoenix. In December 1997, U.S. Interior Secretary Bruce Babbitt approved the principle of interstate water banking; Nevada now plans to store at least 100,000 acre-feet of its surplus each year in Arizona, to draw on (at an estimated cost of $300 per acre-foot) in times of need—a scheme that should see them through the year 2030. The new national water policies are also aimed at forcing California to live within its allotment.

As long as Arizona does not use all of its 2.8 million acre-feet, Las Vegas has the right to force California to share the lower-basin surplus. The big problem will begin when there is no surplus to share. According to Marc Reisner, author of *Cadillac Desert*, the original surveyors behind the 1922 compact overestimated the total flow of the Colorado: although the compact apportions 17.5 million acre-feet, the actual flow is nowhere near that amount.

As the lower basin, led by Las Vegas, begins to demand its full allocation, the stage is being set for a full-scale water war. Upper-basin states are fearful that the lower basin will start to come after their water, and the antagonism is already starting to show.

Las Vegas has been talking to Utah about leasing surplus-water rights, but Colorado has threatened to file suit over any proposed transfer. The last time two states (Arizona and California) disputed the river compact, the suit took thirty-years to settle and wound up in the U.S. Supreme Court. But now Nevada has joined forces with five other states—Arizona, Colorado, New Mexico, Utah, and Wyoming—in the hope of counterbalancing the arrogant political power of California, the most profligate water waster of them all.

In its 1997 annual plan, the SNWA describes another scheme for a future water supply, one that is also likely to end up in court. The city has water rights to 113,000 acre-feet of the Virgin River, which originates in Utah and flows through the northwestern corner of Arizona into Nevada, where it joins the Colorado River. If Las Vegas were to dam the river before it reaches the Colorado and build a 70-mile pipeline across the desert, it could use the Virgin's water.

The project would cost about a billion dollars, destroy part of a breathtakingly scenic river, threaten several endangered species, and provide water so salty that its value would be marginal. "Environmentally, it's the craziest thing ever to do," admitted Donnelly, who described the Virgin River pipeline and dam as a low-priority option.

Instead, the SNWA is hoping to convince the other states that since the Virgin River flows into the Colorado River anyway, why not avoid the destruction and expense of building a pipeline, which would only take the water where it goes naturally? Las Vegas wants to use the Colorado as a sort of pretend pipeline, and is asking the other states to let it have the 113,000 acre-feet of Virgin water in addition to its 300,000-acre-feet allocation. The concept is called "wheeling," and while it has a certain logic— the water is theirs if they take it upstream, so why not downstream?—some of the other states involved will almost certainly challenge the proposal.

But if Las Vegas continues to grow at anything like its present rate, there are not many other options. The last resort, said Donnelly, would be to suck the ground water out of the adjacent rural counties of Lincoln, Nye, and White Pine. When the SNWA filed preliminary claims to do precisely this in the early 1990s, such a shriek of outrage arose from ranchers and environmentalists across the state that the Authority backed down. All Las Vegas really wants, say bureaucrats, advocates, and citizens, is to have water treated as a commodity, something that can be bought and sold like anything else. On those terms, Las Vegas—whose major product, after all, is money—would be able to compete with any city or farmer in the West, and would never have to worry about water supply.

It seems almost inevitable that such a shift will eventually occur. "When you get an agricultural enterprise paying five to ten dollars an acre-foot for water, when a city is willing to pay fifteen hundred to two thousand dollars an acre-foot, there is a disparity there that won't last," said Deacon of UNLV.

The key question is, will the city be able to sustain itself on its existing resources until the day when it can buy its way out of the predicament? In true Las Vegas spirit, the developers who are driving the economy and the residents who have made the city their home are betting that somehow, some way, the water will always be there to sustain their desert miracle.

For Sale

THIRTY THOUSAND HOMES A YEAR
Lisa Moskowitz

"Poverty Sucks."

The silver-foil adage is pasted across a framed photograph in Barbara Reed's real-estate office. The picture shows Barbara standing by a swimming pool with her hands in the pockets of a black denim skirt. She's wearing a ruffled red blouse and matching red-leather cowboy boots, western-style. The wind ripples her long blonde hair, apparently at twilight. At the front of her waist is a heart-shaped sterling-silver belt buckle. She smiles slightly without parting her lips. She looks rich.

"I don't need to work. I do it because I like it." Since she became a real-estate agent nine years ago, Barbara has sold an average of eighty homes each year for an average of $3,000 in commission. In 1995, she was ranked fourth in sales and production among 45,000 agents affiliated with the nationwide RE/MAX chain; that year she sold more than one hundred homes and netted $500,000. She is a Multi-Million Dollar Producer, a Platinum Club member, a Hall of Famer. She has earned $2.3 million of the $3 million required to make her a Life Time Achiever. She is in the top 1 percent of the almost 8,200 licensed real-estate agents operating in southern Nevada.

There is no date on the photograph in her leased office on West Sahara Avenue. But when Barbara, known as Barbie, returns from lunch wearing an oversized pink cotton T-shirt and stretch pants, with a gold pony-tailed

Barbie Doll head pendant swinging from her neck and her red-polished toenails spread in a wide arc across her black patent-leather thongs, it's evident that it was snapped several years (and several pounds) ago. A similar glamour shot graces Barbara's business cards, FOR SALE signs, and stationery, as well as the pages of local real-estate booklets, wipe boards, magnets, and other marketing giveaways scattered around the office. That picture, oozing sweet perfume, with Barbara's eyes heavy with blue eyeliner and her glossy lips in a slight pout, has been good for Barbara Reed and good for her business. She is in the right town at the right time.

For this is Las Vegas, the never-ending boomtown where the American Dream lives large: in particular, the dream of holding a job and owning your own home. Hundreds of people flood this desert town daily to park cars, scrub toilet bowls, deal cards, and build houses on foundations of fantasy. Most of them make their homes well beyond the central (yet non-urban) span of bright, blinking hotel towers that defines Las Vegas in the world's imagination. When they can afford to, they migrate to stucco houses painted seashell pink and desert ecru, topped off with Spanish-tile roofs, on roads named Sweetwater Place, Shorecrest Drive, and Snorkel Circle. Huddled around newly paved cul-de-sacs, these homes form master-planned communities (MPCs) that seem to rise and expand across the desert overnight. Others live on horse ranches or around exclusive golf courses and synthetic lakes, surrounded by guarded gates. They live in row after row after row of identical three-bedroom adobe homes, or in mobile-home parks for retirees, or in pastel apartment complexes overlooking blue swimming pools full of well-tanned singles working the night shift. Those who cannot afford homes like these live in public housing. Those who can't get into public housing live on the streets.

Laid between the housing tracts are retail strips of gas stations and movie theaters, 7-11s and Circle Ks, Savon drugstores and Albertson's groceries. In these sun-baked malls, hair salons adjoin law offices next to U.S. Marine recruiting stations across from car dealerships. Traditional Main Streets don't exist; the familiar corner store and post office, police station and middle school of a small town are nowhere in sight. There is no business-district bustle, and few of the street-front boutiques or quality restaurants one expects in a city of a million people. There is no traditional downtown. Each strip mall is fronted by its own parking lot, and each parking lot is fronted by a boulevard that eventually meets the desert, trailing off into a cluster of road-building equipment and truncated blacktop.

Las Vegas may look like any other suburban sprawl; but here there was never even a memory of anything urban. The city began life in 1905, with the sale of lots of railroad-owned land surrounding what is now called

Downtown; but this area has not been a city center for decades, and betrays no sign of its origin today. Transplanted architects impose on Las Vegas Valley the same patterns of fast-growth subdivisions they learned in southern California and Arizona. Real-estate investors slot retail centers into the pockets of space between housing developments and scatter post offices, banks, grocery stores, drugstores, and churches inside the malls; the result is a hundred or more nondescript streetscapes emerging from the desert in the same unplanned, entrepreneurial way that the Strip took shape. The major difference is that the people who live here don't check out of their rooms when their vacations are over.

Welcome to Barbara Country.

■ ■ ■

The latest housing boom in Las Vegas was kicked off in the late 1980s, fueled by a steady migration of Texans, Arizonans, and midwesterners, but above all southern Californians. The pilgrimage across state lines began with retirees and others moving to escape crime, pollution, and ever-increasing traffic jams. When real-estate prices in southern California hit all-time highs, many people sold their homes there for major capital gains, and moved to Las Vegas with money to spare.

Richard Lee, president of First American Title in Las Vegas, says that approximately 62 percent of all new homes sold in 1989 and 1990 were purchased by former California residents. "A person who bought a house years ago for $30,000 could sell it for $200,000, move to Las Vegas, buy a new house with half the money, and put the rest in the bank," says Lee. "Then the California market changed, and people couldn't sell."

With the beginning of a nationwide recession in 1991, the flood of California residents slowed down to a steady stream; but, according to Lee, they still accounted for about 35 percent of new-home buyers in Las Vegas between 1991 and 1996.

■ ■ ■

Steve and Lisa Weisman, both real-estate appraisers, moved to Las Vegas from southern California in 1980, before the rush, to escape the pollution and overcrowding. They were also part of the large group of housing professionals attracted to the apparently limitless residential-construction boom in Las Vegas. Appraisers, architects, builders, real-estate lawyers, inspectors, surveyors: all were pouring in. In these years, Las Vegas was still a small city (or a large town) with few urban woes. "There was no traffic at eight AM or five-thirty PM," says Steve. "We could get a new three-bedroom apartment for four hundred dollars a month." At the time, a comparable apartment in Los Angeles went for twice that or more.

By 1997, the median monthly mortgage payment in Las Vegas was $926, the average apartment rental, about $647—but the urban cost-of-living index had more than doubled in those seventeen years. Taking inflation into account, rents in Las Vegas have remained fairly steady even as the city continues to grow. The current vacancy rate is under 3 percent.

■ ■ ■

By 1989, home builders couldn't keep pace with demand. "People lined up for hours to get a number just to talk to a real-estate agent," says Lisa Weisman. In the early nineties, resales were selling faster and at higher prices than new homes; buyers had become too impatient to wait the six months or more it took for a new home to be built. Broad swaths of red-tile roofs soon cut through the valley in every direction. Subdivisions were laid out on squares like those of a patchwork quilt on any acre of available land. In between, pockets of privately held land and Bureau of Land Management (BLM) holdings remained clear; now, much of that land is also developed.

By 1993, as the effects of the recession wore off, construction surged once again. By the end of 1994, gaming revenues surpassed the $5 billion mark and the number of residential building permits issued had risen to 25,000. The rapid building pace alarmed some industry analysts, who feared a fall-off in growth or even a regional recession. At this pace, they said, supply would soon exceed demand, and a surfeit of unsold new houses would stand empty in the middle of the desert, as they had in Phoenix in the eighties. At the very least, the water supply would run dry, or the land would run out. The Las Vegas market was going to crash.

"Nobody gave credit to the Las Vegas economy. Las Vegas has a mystique about it and a lot of controversy surrounding it," says Lee. "Institutional investors all said it was a flash in the pan and didn't take it seriously because it was Las Vegas."

To some degree, the analysts were right: the number of people moving to Las Vegas did slack off in 1995, but not nearly enough to cause alarm. As they had for years, millions of people continued to visit Las Vegas to bet on the slot machines, marvel at the magicians, and feed on cheap but filling buffet meals. Casino-hotel and residential developers continued building, if at a slower rate than in 1989-90; a little more than $4 billion a year was still being invested in construction, and construction and service jobs multiplied. The water has not yet run out, and the federal government, which still owns 85 percent of Clark County, continues to swap and sell land to big developers like the Howard Hughes Corporation, Del Webb, and American Nevada Corporation.

■ ■ ■

Today, more than one million people call Las Vegas Valley home. That number is expected to reach two million by 2007, according to state demographer Dean Judson. Several housing-market researchers believe the city will reach the two-million mark even sooner. In 1995, Stephen Bottfield estimated that one in six people shopping for a home in Las Vegas don't even live in the area yet.

In 1996, permits were issued for 32,381 new units of residential housing. The permit for figures 1997 and 1998 were 30,876 and 32,173 respectively; the median sales price of single-family homes, $126,000 in 1996, had risen to about $135,000 in 1998—still considerably cheaper than in California's major urban and suburban areas. Traditionally, single-family housing has accounted for most new construction, but in recent years the number of multifamily units—duplexes, condominiums, and apartments—has increased to one-third of the total. Clark County reported an all-time high in multifamily housing construction in 1996, when building permits issued for apartments reached their highest level since 1989.

In metropolitan Las Vegas in 1996, there were almost 200 licensed building contractors, 450 new-home projects or subdivisions under development, and more than 1,500 model homes on the market from which to choose. But today competition among builders, an increase in land prices, and additional building fees are pushing the market up. There's relatively little land left to buy—certainly not of the scale needed for another city-size master-planned community. But those already under development, like Summerlin to the northwest and Seven Hills in Green Valley to the southeast, have at least seven to ten years of building left in them—which is just as well, considering the two million people who are expected to need housing somewhere in the valley by 2007.

■ ■ ■

It's 8:30 AM on Friday and Barbara is already in a mild frenzy. The printer won't print fast enough for her, the Multiple Listing System (a metropolitan database of properties for sale) keeps kicking her out, and she's due downtown in fifteen minutes.

"I can't connect or disconnect. I can't even work!" Barbara presses forcefully on the command keys that should let her exit the program. Nothing happens. She taps her freshly painted neon-pink nails on the desk, then tries again. Frozen in cyberspace, she yells for Tom Lawson, her sales associate and marketing manager. "Tommy? I can't get out of MLS. Tommy?!" She walks over to the white-wicker love seat in her office and fidgets with the edges of a Barbie Doll pillow. She doesn't like to wait.

Tom strides in, his hair still wet from his morning shower, the smells of cologne and stale cigarette smoke hovering around him. He takes a look at the static screen and presses the power button. Barbara rolls her eyes. "I could have done that," she says. "Now the printer. It's way too slow. I need something that can spit 'em out as fast as I can go." Her eyelids drop seductively. If she weren't already married for the third time, she might be flirting. Tom looks out into the middle distance, somewhere beyond the room's pink vertical blinds, and scratches his new goatee. "Well, we just need a new printer. A faster, new printer," he says in a lispy southern drawl.

Tom, 31, was born in Tennessee. After serving in the Air Force at Nellis, he decided to stay in Las Vegas and try his hand at real estate. His first year out, 1990, he earned $125,000. Three years later, he quit to design and build custom log-cabin homes, but after barely breaking even, he went back to real estate. He still sells an occasional cabin, but nowadays he mostly sells Las Vegas homes—and Barbara Reed.

Barbara squints her eyes and watches the computer reboot, her hand ready on the mouse. Time is running out. She's due at the Palace Station Hotel on East Sahara in a few minutes to meet Faye Chi, a weekend gambler and Las Vegas property owner from Hawaii. Faye wants to unload a rental property she bought years ago in Los Prados, a gated golf community; Barbara says it's the only affordable golf community left in Las Vegas, with home prices from $99,000 to $300,000. (Painted Desert, in contrast, is in the medium price range, with houses for $150,000 and up; Spanish Trail and Canyon Gate, $200,000 and up, are considered expensive.) As Barbara grabs a sheaf of printouts listing the recent selling prices of Los Prados homes, the phone rings. It's Larry, her advertising rep at *Las Vegas Homes Illustrated*. The magazine was supposed to go to the printer an hour ago. As usual, Barbara is late with her order insert, but she is one of Larry's best customers, and she knows he'll wait for her to give him the layouts he needs.

"Larry, back off!" she screeches into the receiver. "You have two of my listings duplicated in the last issue.... I want the last eleven pages and the back cover! You make me very stressed out!" Barbara slams down the phone. It rings again right away.

"Barbara Reed's office," she answers sweetly. This time it's a prospective buyer. He noticed her number on a house-shaped magnet stuck to his refrigerator. "I think my ex-wife put it there. It's been around a while," he says. They set up an appointment and Barbara heads out the door to her custom black Hummer, an army-issue sport-utility vehicle that spans the entire width of its parking space. Riveted to the front-door panels are pink-scripted signs: Barbara Reed Sells the Lifestyles of Las Vegas. People turn to stare at the high-riding Hummer as it rumbles along I-15.

Faye is waiting outside the hotel in a prism of reflected light. Chunky Christian Dior sunglasses protect her eyes from the desert sun that bounces blindingly off brass and glass. Even the pavement seems to sparkle. It's quite a step up into the Hummer's passenger seat, and Faye makes it with some effort. She has a gift: a box of chocolate-covered macadamia nuts. Barbara's eyes widen in anticipatory ecstasy. "Oh cool, oh cool, oh cool," she says, and opens the box immediately.

"That means you gotta sell my house fast now," says Faye. She smiles, but she is entirely serious. Faye wears gold hoop earrings, a diamond-studded Cartier watch, and a ruby and diamond ring. This is all the jewelry she ever wears in Las Vegas, she says; too much more might attract thieves, and she prefers to part with her money betting at the blackjack tables or shopping in at the Fashion Show Mall on the Strip. In Hawaii, she lives in a home worth $500,000, and she used to own a Rolls-Royce. She still owns a few rental properties on the islands, but she's thinking of unloading those, too. The real-estate market in Hawaii, inflated by Japanese investors in the eighties, is now depressed, and Faye no longer wants her investments scattered, nor does she want to pay a property-management company in Las Vegas. "We really want to sell as fast as we can," Faye says again. She knows this is a buyers' market and is willing to bring down her asking price. "Just price the house to move. Fast."

A surplus of new homes built at the end of 1996 forced both new-home and resale prices down. Other Los Prados homes near Faye's are priced competitively, and in order to sell quickly, her asking price will have to be only marginally more than the original selling price, seven years ago, of $115,760. A brand-new house in a similar northwest Las Vegas community starts at around $117,000. At that price there might not be a golf course, but amenities like state-of-the-art kitchens, sunken bathtubs, and intercom systems are now standard.

If Faye weren't in such a hurry to sell, she might see her property appreciate in the next few months. Tim McKenna, president of Prudential Southwest Realty, the third-largest real estate company in Las Vegas, says resales are on the upswing. "I think it's just that resellers haven't started asking for more money. Building restrictions are increasing new-home prices, and buyers can get more for their money with a resale," he says. According to city and county Planning and Development offices, permit, plan-check, and water fees have increased in the last five years, and there's now also a desert-tortoise fee, charged to builders to help relocate the endangered species their developments are displacing. "People from out of state will look at a new home, then realize that resales are only three years old and the upgrades are already in. There's a pool, the landscape's done, and they can get it for a better price." Most new homes are sold to Las Vegas residents upgrading to bigger houses or into a better neighborhood, McKenna says. In 1996, an estimated 52 percent of the homes sold in metropolitan Las Vegas were new, down from 84 percent in 1995 and 90 percent in 1994.

At the entrance to Los Prados, the guards recognize Barbara's Hummer and wave it through. Weekday golfers, many past retirement age, park their carts by the clubhouse. As they push through the doorway, a wave of cool air rushes out and is quickly dissipated by the sun. Inside, too-tan men settle in to drink a beer together before returning to the course and the last nine holes. Women in pink shorts and visors play bridge on the patio out back. Birds chirp and flowers bloom. Ducks flap their wings in the fountain of the man-made pond. All is safe within the guarded gates.

Begun in 1989, construction at Los Prados is still going on, despite the many FOR SALE signs scattered about the thousand-home development. On some streets, it looks as though half the community is selling. "People are moving up; there's a lot of turnaround here. They're building three hundred more homes," Barbara explains.

Faye's house is vacant. She takes off her shoes before walking through the linoleum-floored entranceway. The decor is bland, rental-house beige: the walls, the freshly vacuumed carpets, the kitchen countertops. Fake ivy plants trail along the windowsills. Yellowing back copies of *Northwest View*, still in their plastic bags, lay in a pile by the garage door. Barbara quickly inspects the ground floor. One of the sliding doors from the dining room is off its track, and a few blinds are broken in the living room. "We want it to look as big and airy as we can. You want enough to show, but just the right stuff." The windows need washing in the living room, so she closes the blinds just enough to cover them. In the dining room, she pulls the blinds open to show the distance between houses. The next house is about fifty feet away, and in Las Vegas every inch of green grass is a luxury.

The upstairs rooms are painted the same innocuous beige. The three bedrooms are modestly sized, and the master bathroom is small compared to those in the homes being built a few streets away: grandiose master bedrooms are currently in vogue. Barbara peers out a bedroom window. The house backs up to the main street and the cinderblock wall that protects the development from outsiders—not a selling point. "You never notice these things when you buy it," mumbles Faye. "It was strictly an investment." Back in the kitchen, Barbara produces a six-month contract and assures Faye that she'll sell the house sooner than that; the trick is to price it a little lower than those listed around it, and to stay firm on that price during negotiations. Faye knows the house has not appreciated, and agrees to list it for $119,900. "In Hawaii, if you hold onto a property for seven years, you'll make a lot of money," she says pouting.

"You really haven't taken a loss, you just haven't made any money," says Barbara. "You're going to make up the difference at the tables." Faye reads the contract carefully and signs her name. Meanwhile, Barbara has composed a caption for her next advertising spread: "Motivated out-of-state seller wants sold yesterday! New paint, clean. Ready for immediate possession." Faye gives a small smile, then a sigh. Jaunty blurbs like this one make up Barbara's bimonthly advertising section in free magazines like *Las Vegas Homes Illustrated* and *The Real Estate Book*. The few sentences are usually printed next to a picture of the home and include phrases like "Drop Dead Gorgeous!", "Stop! You've Just Found It!" and "Divorce! Seller's Loss Is Your Gain!" Booklet advertising makes up only a fraction of the $12,000 to $15,000 a month that goes into marketing Barbara Reed, but, as Tom says, "You have to spend money to make money"—a Las Vegas slogan if there ever was one.

Barbara's less-traditional marketing techniques require big bucks. In addition to the $60,000 Hummer, she also drives around in a full-size, fully furnished recreational vehicle that's custom-painted with murals of wild horses splashing through crystal-clear rivers. "Don't Let Wild Horses Keep You Away From Barbara Country," reads the script across the sides of the Barbie Mobile. For a few months, Barbara tried advertising on posters around town, like hotshot Las Vegas lawyers: her bouncy blonde mane, hazel eyes, and pink, cotton-candy lips beckoned life-size from behind the Plexiglas of twenty-seven bus shelters around town. After he had been working in Barbara's office for three months, Tom had the posters taken down. "They cost seventeen hundred dollars a month. They just weren't effective. They were all about ego, not business," he says.

Barbara says the posters came down because people were defacing them, drawing mustaches and black eyes on her face. One poster even depicted her with a dripping bullet wound right between the eyes. "It hurts my feelings that someone would do that," she says. Barbara attributes the vandalism to the jealousy of other real-estate agents. Meanwhile, Tom and Barbara have a few other marketing strategies to keep the 8,000-plus other real-estate agents active in Clark County chasing Barbie from one dream house to another.

On the way back into town, Faye asks Barbara to drop her off at the Fashion Show Mall, across the street from Circus Circus on the Strip. She's going to celebrate the listing with a few new purchases. "I want to thank you for choosing me," says Barbara solemnly. "No problem," says Faye, eager to begin her shopping. "I liked your ads."

"If you go into Macy's, ask for Sue, she's my personal shopper. Just mention my name. She'll be glad to help you." After Faye steps down and says her goodbyes, Barbara starts up the Hummer's rumbling engine. "Now that's personal service," she says. "I'm very aggressive, but the bottom line is customer satisfaction. If the customer isn't happy, there must be something wrong with them."

■ ■ ■

As you drive west from the city center, towards Spring Mountain and Red Rock Canyon, the congestion of I-95 quickly gives way to wide lanes of fast traffic. In less than ten minutes, the tight knit of downtown buildings disappears. Low cinderblock walls line the roadway. An occasional abandoned shopping cart lays overturned along the shoulder. Exit signs (Rainbow Boulevard, Summerlin Parkway) signal the arrival of Las Vegas's instant new suburbs. The highway rises slightly above the valley, but the ascent is so gradual it goes unnoticed. Acres of terra-cotta tile unroll beneath you as the Spanish-style roofs of newly built homes undulate for miles, almost to the base of the barren brown mountains. The fiberboard coverings of soon-to-be stuccoed houses make them look like skinned animals next to the finished and already occupied models. Each house is a duplicate of the one next door. Down the line, the simple wooden skeletons of houses at a still earlier state of construction look like pencil sketches. Black plastic tarps flap from the roofs. Mounds of chalky desert soil pile high in the barren yards. This is the Las Vegas housing market at its most basic: a giant army camp of subdivisions made up of mass-built model homes.

The first Las Vegas subdivision was built in 1940-41, south of town on part of a four-thousand-acre tract once owned by Leigh Hunt, a pioneering Las Vegas speculator. Called the Huntridge Addition, it offered homebuyers land and house in the same package. Other developers followed the Huntridge model, building homes and installing their own utility services. Grid-patterned subdivisions sprang up overnight as developers scurried to buy land, going as far as a mile out of town to find vacant tracts. A lack of planning, a multitude of zoning variances, and speculators who simply sat on undeveloped acres created a leapfrog effect that is still the rule. Expensive gas- and water-line extensions and insufficient road improvements pushed housing prices upward. But people kept moving to Clark County, mostly for jobs at the Basic Magnesium plant southeast of town and, in the 1950s, at the Nevada Test Site. In the mid-1940s, Howard Hughes purchased 40,000 acres of land from the Bureau of Land Management and became the largest private landowner in Clark County. (His never-realized hope was to attract major aircraft industry to southern Nevada.) Although his successor, the Howard Hughes Corporation, has sold off much of his estate, it remains the county's largest private landowner today. A 22,500-acre portion of Hughes's purchase, named "Summerlin" after Hughes's grandmother's maiden name, has become the best-selling master-planned community in America. Building there began in 1990, after the Hughes Corporation had built—at its own expense—a 3.5-mile, $22.5-million parkway to connect Summerlin with Las Vegas's existing freeway system.

■ ■ ■

The exit for Summerlin Parkway is about eight miles from the Las Vegas Strip, but it still falls within the city limits, which were enlarged to accommodate the new town. The curving parkway is a sort of Yellow Brick Road leading to the center of a "total community," complete with its own schools, a library, theater, several houses of worship, and retail shopping centers. Six sculpted championship golf courses, biking trails, parks, and playgrounds are placed to blend in artfully with the natural wonders of Red Rock Canyon, to the west. The recreation facilities closest to completed subdivisions are open, but others exist only in the model of Summerlin, located in the Visitor's Center. Wide, unmarked streets, sometimes four lanes across, connect the separate "villages." Bulldozers and flatbed trucks loaded with construction equipment cruise around the labyrinth of curving avenues without the inconvenience of traffic signals to slow them down.

At the end of one cul-de-sac lined with bright-white houses, finished dwellings stand next to fiberboard-sheathed frames crawling with construction workers. A salsa tune blares from a portable radio, reverberating in the empty street. Footsteps echo. No cars are parked out front, no children play in the yards. Inside the model homes, the music of Michael Bolton and Celine Dion is piped into every room through ceiling speakers. Plastic plants and silk flowers repose in corners and on tabletops. Vanilla-, apricot-, and rose-scented potpourri floats in the air, attempting to mask the smell of drywall and fresh paint. "Upgrades" (i.e., added-cost extras) like Formica kitchen counters, walk-in pantries, and top-of-the-line appliances are installed to entice homemakers with their luxury. Almost every model is set up to suggest family life in progress: a pile of gourmet pasta and pickled artichoke hearts rests by the stove, colorful Pottery Barn plates are set on the table, a little boy's football helmet and shoulder pads are spread across one bed, and a dollhouse in another bedroom waits for its owner to come home from school.

Next door, a middle-aged couple stands admiring their newly laid lawn. Although people are starting to realize that Las Vegas is a desert, lush green strips of grass are coveted, says landscaper Jack Zunino. "People are starting to do the mini-oasis concept using water-thrifty materials in the front and around patios and laying turf in the backyard," says Zunino. "But most are not willing to give up their petunias and pansies"—thirsty annuals that need frequent watering and replacing. Indigenous plants like native yucca, bottle brush, and desert marigold, Zunigo adds, are gaining popularity, as are other desert flora imported from Texas and Mexico. But in these newer developments, greenery is rare, and mature trees or landscaping are unheard-of.

Within the boundaries of Summerlin live 24,000 people, more than 13,000 of them residents of Sun City, an upscale, age-restricted retirement community. Approximately eighteen different home builders construct houses, condominiums, and townhouses ranging in price from $50,000 to $500,000 and up. Young families, roommates, and retired couples are welcome. In 2005, when Summerlin is scheduled to be completed, an estimated 180,000 people will call this master-planned community home. Summerlin collects a Special Improvement District fee from all residents based on the size of their lot, and uses some of the money to install sewers and sidewalks and to pay for the Summerlin Parkway, Nevada's first trilevel interchange. All of Clark County's nineteen master-planned communities levy improvement fees, although the amount varies. Another fee is typically collected by the community association all homeowners are obliged to join, which enforces the "Covenants, Conditions and Restrictions" that bind them all.

These regulations, which can dictate everything from exterior paint colors, noise levels, and what kind of vehicles can be parked in the driveway to the size of plants, fences, antennas, and garbage cans, are ostensibly intended to preserve real-estate values by preventing eyesores and penalizing bad neighbors. Association fees range from seven dollars a month, in the Legacy Collection community (built by America West Homes), to $255 a month, in The Islands community at Spanish Trail. Not everyone who lives in a planned community in Las Vegas is happy with these restrictions, or with the way they are enforced by fussy neighbors.

Southeast of Las Vegas, in the city of Henderson, are Summerlin's most powerful rivals, the large Green Valley and Green Valley Ranch MPCs developed by the American Nevada Corporation. More than twenty years old, Green Valley encompasses 8,400 acres and is home to approximately 42,000 people. Hank Greenspun, founder and publisher of the *Las Vegas Sun*, purchased this land in 1957, when it was in the middle of nowhere and going cheap. In the 1960s, Henderson was still a blue-collar town, housing workers from Basic Magnesium and neighboring chemical-processing plants. Over 50 percent of the town's housing was low-income or substandard, much of it temporary housing built during World War II. The city was redlined as a low-income area. None of the executives who worked in the city's chemical plants lived there, and not until 1978 did the Greenspun family start building on the land they had bought.

Today Henderson is best known for Green Valley and Green Valley Ranch, whose residents account for almost half of the city's population; in 1997, it was the fastest-growing city in the U.S. (Henderson, like the incorporated cities of North Las Vegas and Boulder City, is generally considered a part of Greater Las Vegas.) In addition to these two popular and established tracts, American Nevada is also developing Seven Hills, on the other side of Lake Mead Drive.

The difference between these two dominant MPCs is one of image. People who live in relatively conservative Summerlin tend to look down on those who live in Green Valley, says Roger Kidneigh, an instructor at the Southern Nevada School of Real Estate. Local luminaries like Mike Tyson and Wayne Newton live in or near Green Valley, making it seem a flashy, new-money kind of place. "It has a reputation for being full of yuppies, snobby and elitist." But Kidneigh and his wife, Carol, live there, and they love it. In their opinion, Summerlin is too far away from the city and the airport, and lacks the established infrastructure of Green Valley.

Summerlin residents cite the benefits of their higher elevation, which means cooler temperatures in the summer and less smog year-round. But

Green Valley is an older, more established neighborhood, with mature palm trees lining the paseo, a pedestrian and bicycle path that winds around the community. Several life-size bronze statues (sometimes mistaken for real people) populate the landscape; a bronze mother bends to tie her daughter's shoelace, and bronze children splash through real water in a fountain.

Carol Kidneigh, who moved to Las Vegas from Denver in 1991, insists, "We have plenty of things to do here. We have Shakespeare in the Park. We have our flea markets like everybody else, and a farmer's market. Gambling is secondary. It's Anywhere, USA."

■ ■ ■

What Clark County's nineteen master-planned communities have in common is a sense that they somehow provide a better—and safer—lifestyle than the ones beyond their gates and walls. "Buyers look for neighborhood safety first, then school quality, then the house itself," says Tim McKenna, who sells homes in both Green Valley and Summerlin. The walls, guards, and elaborate security systems that are now a standard feature in most new Las Vegas subdivisions help persuade newcomers not only that they are safer inside an MPC, but also that it's dangerous to be on the other side.

In addition to the all-important sense of security, MPCs offer ready-made, pop-up communities for those who have left old neighborhoods behind. Since Las Vegas has no urban center to focus on or build out from, places like Green Valley and Summerlin have created their own town centers within exclusive boundaries. "There's a feeling that people want to recapture from the fifties and sixties of belonging to a neighborhood, of having block parties," says McKenna, who lives in Green Valley. "Within Green Valley and Summerlin, there are a whole bunch of small communities. They range from eighty-five to a hundred homes within a subdivision. That becomes a small little community within itself. People who live there feel like they belong somewhere. That's something people are reaching for."

Creating that neighborhood feeling may be easy in a master-planned community, but for those who live outside the walls, it's more challenging. "To get to know your neighbor is very difficult, so what we'll do is go inside, close the door, and put the TV on. We might have a few friends over for a barbecue, and then the neighbors will walk by with their noses stuck in the air," says Tom Lawson. "I think as a whole, everybody feels kind of empty because it's kind of new."

Las Vegas residents Bruce and Kathy Pringle have been looking for a new house for the last six months. After seeing almost fifty homes, most of them resales, the one thing they know for sure is that they want to live in Green Valley. "We're concerned about the neighborhood and security," says Kathy as she inspects one of the three bathrooms at 525 Lariat Lane. "I want a newer house with a family room and a view." The house is at the end of a street that looks out over a bluff. In the distance lies Sunrise Mountain and, beyond that, Lake Mead. In between, bulldozers level the ground in preparation for new tracts of houses. Kathy and Bruce poke around in the kitchen and notice that the cabinets need some work; they'll also need a new oven. Built in 1989, the house contains 1,981 square feet and is listed at $164,900, a little more than the Pringles want to pay for a used four-bedroom. "We'll just keep mulling," says Bruce, heading for the station wagon parked in the driveway. Their twelve-year-old son, Keith, is waiting impatiently in the back seat, almost late for soccer practice.

The rapid expansion of MPCs like Green Valley and Summerlin is often cited as an example of what ails Las Vegas growth management. Geoff Schumacher, city editor of the *Las Vegas Sun*, has written that at the same time city officials are wondering how to deal with traffic congestion, pollution, and overcrowded schools, they are approving additional construction at Summerlin without batting an eye.

But city and county officials say they cannot stop growth; that would mean putting a halt to new casino-hotel construction and expansion and thereby slowing job creation, the single most powerful attraction for newcomers moving to Las Vegas. How can a city ask its heart to stop beating? Right now, it's not even an option. All city and county planners are allowed to do is to try to cope with growth as it comes.

"The planning is market-driven. It hasn't been advanced planning for years," says Jeff Harris, head of long-range planning for Clark County. "We have a different philosophy and process here. We're typically asked to find ways to *accommodate* growth."

The easiest way to accommodate residential and commercial building is to rezone areas formerly designated no-growth and rural zones. The lack of infrastructure in those areas, however, increases builder's fees and is reflected in the price of homes. Eventually developers will run into what Harris calls the Ultimate Growth Boundary: topographical and geological barriers like Nellis Air Force Base, Lake Mead, and the steep slopes leading up to the mountains. But for now, finding land is not a problem. According to Schumacher, there's an estimated 121,000 acres of undeveloped land between privately owned lots and swappable Bureau of Land

Management holdings; at 8.5 people per acre, the current maximum residential density, that's enough land to house 1.03 million people.

■ ■ ■

When she's not keeping tabs on her ex-husband, a Hollywood actor who played Talia Shire's husband in *The Godfather*, Barbara is tracking the activities of the other agents in town. With Tom's help, Barbara usually knows what properties are listed with which agents. As her own broker, Barbara both sells and lists homes, which means she gets to keep the entire 6 percent commission. Buyers are relatively easy to come by, either because Barbara's widespread marketing catches their eye or because they're referred by other RE/MAX agents across the country; it's the listings she has to compete for. So when Tom announces that a certain property in Spanish Trail has been listed with another agent, Barbara grimaces. "That seller is ignorant, unsophisticated, and stupid. I told her where to price that house so she took our advice and went with someone else. Those agents aren't going to do what I would do as far as marketing. Eventually they'll come to me." Driving through Las Vegas neighborhoods from The Lakes to Desert Shores, she can name the agent a home is listed with, his or her reputation, and in most cases the asking price. She watches those properties very closely. If they aren't selling, she rings the doorbell. Any property is fair game, but Barbara feels the area she lives in, southwest of the city where half-acre horse ranches and estates are still available for sale, is her prime farming area. This is the heart of Barbara Country.

A farming expedition usually entails a trip in the Barbie Mobile. Barbara cruises different sections of town, referring to her MLS printout. When she finds an address that's been taken off the market, or is "For Sale By Owner," she sends Tom to the door with his latest marketing hook in hand: Barbara Reed's Ultimate Real Estate Marketing Plan, a thin, spiral-bound, plastic-covered booklet touting the talents of his boss.

In his warm southern accent, Tom will explain to the seller how Barbara receives referrals from agents across the country whose clients are moving to Las Vegas, and how a home is entered into the Multiple Listing System and exposed to thousands of real-estate professionals in the Las Vegas area. Finally, Barbara lists a property using a comparative marketing analysis of the pending and sold homes in the area. At any one time, Barbara will have between twenty and sixty listings to her name.

The latest annexation to Barbara Country is the Mount Charleston market. Less than an hour from the Strip, Mount Charleston is southern

Nevada's ski resort, and even Las Vegans who don't ski like to point to it as an example of the diversity of their recreation options. When Barbara gets a call from a potential buyer from Illinois who wants to look at cabins on the mountain, she quickly rearranges her schedule. She is eager to sell one particular cabin on her sheet as soon as possible; it's a property Barbara recently "farmed" from another real-estate agent after it had been on the market for some time. Barbara is determined to turn this "just looking" into a "just sold," and anchor her reputation as a can-do Mount Charleston agent.

As Barbara heads north up I-95, the landscape changes quickly from tiled roofs and corner quickie-marts to desolate desert brush planted with oversized "For Sale" signs. Barbara exits the highway to a two-lane road that fades into the flats leading to the base of Spring Mountain. Snow still streaks the higher peaks and bluffs in late March. On the valley floor, the sun beats down on shaggy cacti that look like something out of a Dr. Seuss book. Hand-painted signs indicate P.O. boxes for a few scattered ranch homes, barely visible from the road. There is so much vacant land just a few miles from Las Vegas that the idea of a land shortage is hardly credible; but, as Tom points out, there are no hookups to the city's facilities out here. Generators and wells provide power and water. In a few more miles, a beat-up road sign warns, there will be no gas stations. As the Barbie Mobile bumps along the road, bottles of Evian water roll back and forth on the carpeted floorboards. For a few minutes, the only sound is that of the RV's powerful engine. Then all hell breaks lose.

"Oh, shit!" Barbara slams the steering wheel with both hands. "The keys to the cabin are in the Hummer!" She reaches frantically for her cell phone, tucked away in the purse by her feet, trying to keep her eyes on the road. "This is beyond normal for us. I don't believe it! We could lose the client over this."

"That's a bummer," says Tom calmly from his perch on the sofa. She phones the office, but there is no answer, and no way to get the keys up to the mountain in time. "I could break in," Tom suggests. Barbara is silent for a moment, then shakes her head. "Unless a window's open or something, that probably isn't a good idea. We'll just have to tell him the truth."

Jack Anderson is waiting in his rented Mercury Cougar in the parking lot of the Mount Charleston Hotel. He doesn't have much time, he tells Barbara, who is a good thirty minutes late; he has to catch a plane back to Chicago in two hours. Barbara leans into the open passenger-side window, apologizes, then sheepishly admits that she doesn't have the keys to the cabin.

"The truth of the matter is, we have egg all over our face," she says. Jack doesn't say anything at first, he just chews his gum and looks straight ahead over the top of the steering wheel. He seems a quiet man by nature, a couple of years from retirement, a burly white beard curling around his face. But right now, Jack's steady silence suggests he's not pleased. "Well, it's all right," he finally says. Barbara gives Tom a nervous look, then gets into the passenger seat. Tom hops in back and starts the sell.

"There's a nine-hole golf course here at the hotel, and they're putting in a convenience store this year," he says. "I'd say of the about four hundred fifty properties up here, only five or six lots are left. For a quarter-acre in Rainbow Canyon, it's going to run a hundred twenty-five to a hundred thirty thousand with the power and water hookups." Jack listens quietly. After a few minutes of negotiating narrow, twisting roads, Tom pulls alongside the locked, two-story cabin on the side of a hill. The trip up to the house is steep, and Barbara is soon out of breath. "It's the elevation up here," she says. Tom looks for a way into the cabin. After failing to find an extra key in all the obvious places—above the door frames, under welcome mats—he starts pulling at window screens. Everything is locked tight. Jack will have to be satisfied with simply peering through the windows. His job done, Tom lights up a cigarette and wanders off to take a piss in the woods behind the house.

The owners just reduced the asking price to $289,000 from $295,000, says Barbara. "I told them to reduce the price because the carpeting needs replacing." When Jack is out of earshot, Barbara adds, "It may be good he couldn't see the inside, because it really needs some work." Since she cannot sell the inside of the cabin, she sells the scenery. "This is probably the greatest view up here, and this property is unique because it has a front lawn." The "lawn" is somewhere beneath several fallen tree limbs, decaying garden hoses, and a couple of plastic milk crates. An old doghouse and a children's play kitchen lie under the porch on a criss-cross of discarded wood. Jack walks around the cabin, asking about sewer and water fees. "I think I'd have to get me a hammock up here," he says. The unfinished look of the property actually appeals to Jack, who says he's interested in working on a fixer-upper anyway.

Before heading back to the Barbie Mobile, Barbara takes Jack for a quick tour of the other homes on the mountain. She spouts off the listing and selling prices of most of them; her FOR SALE signs are planted at the edge of several properties. Jack is impressed. At the end of an hour, he assures Barbara that he'll be in touch soon. "As far as my level of interest, I predict I'll probably buy something in the next six months," he says.

"All I can say is buy sooner," says Barbara. "The demand is high. Right now there's not really a lot of people looking up here, but another month from now you might get fifty cars driving past us."

"I'm sorry you didn't have your keys. Shame on you. But it happens."

"Actually, it never happens. That's why I'm so upset at myself for letting it happen. Please, give us an A for effort."

"I'll give you more, but not much more," says Jack smiling. Tom and Barbara wave as he pulls out onto the main road.

Barbara can't believe her luck. "Talk about backpedaling into a sale!" she says. "If you can't dazzle them with brilliance, you baffle them with bullshit."

■ ■ ■

Despite downturns in the national housing market, the metropolitan Las Vegas area has enjoyed strong construction and home sales for nearly a decade. As long as hotel and casino construction continues, jobs will be plentiful, and both job-seekers and retirees will keep moving here. R. Keith Schwer, director of the Center for Business and Economic Research at the UNLV, estimates that two and a half jobs are created for every room added on the Strip. In 1996, $1.9 billion was poured into hotel building and expansion, adding almost 10,000 rooms; in 1997, $600 million in new construction created another 4,000 rooms. Three major new hotels opened in 1998, the number of rooms grew by 17,000, and the number of jobs accordingly. Of course, not every new hotel maid or dishwasher—not even every new construction worker—is going to be in the market for a house. But all these workers will need somewhere to live; and the economic multiplier effect of so much new building, so much more tourist spending and servicing, is likely to increase both the job and the housing markets for people in a great many fields unrelated to gambling.

"I don't really see it slowing down," says Richard Lee, of First American Title. "Including what opened in 1996 and what was under construction and what will be under construction through 1998, it's an investment of eight billion dollars. You find me another city on planet earth that's currently investing eight billion dollars in new job growth and construction." If job growth is the number one factor bolstering the housing market, then developers and builders have nothing to worry about.

But this is not the Las Vegas of twenty or even ten years ago. The terrific influx of people has brought new considerations to bear on the housing market. Increased pollution from traffic and construction has decreased air quality; people who once moved to the area to escape such problems find that Las Vegas is not the haven it once was. Although land is still abundant, rapid development keeps pushing prices up, and the Bureau of Land Management is talking of getting out of the game. Essentials like new schools and roads and new water and sewer lines need to be paid for, at a price tag now estimated in the billions. Recently, the county has turned to prosperous homebuilders to help supply those funds, and that cost will be added to the price of each new home. Permit, planning-commission, and sewer fees have been steadily rising over the past few years; water-hookup fees are now as high as $3,000 per home. Slowly, the price of a new home in Las Vegas has been edging up, even as California prices have declined; between 1995 and 1998, the median price of a home crept up more than 20 percent. To keep prices down, builders have become more competitive, offering buyers reduced closing costs, special financing packages, and "free" upgrades.

"One of the challenges facing home builders is that profits are decreasing. It's a very competitive marketplace and it's very price-sensitive, so profit margins are difficult to maintain," says Dennis Smith, president of Home Builders Research. Up to a point, builders will swallow increases in fees and land prices, so that their homes sell as quickly as possible. The longer a new home stands empty, the longer the builder has to pay interest on his construction loan, decreasing the chance for a profit.

Since casino and hotel construction seem unlikely to slow down soon, the neighborhoods and highways, schools, and parks of Clark County will become more and more crowded; lot sizes will shrink, and home prices will climb. In some ways, Las Vegas is going through the same growing pains as any other burgeoning metropolitan area, like Albuquerque or West Palm Beach, only at a more rapid pace. But its reliance on a single industry makes its problems unique.

"People think the streets in this town are paved in gold as far as real estate goes," says Roger Kidneigh. He tells the thousands of students who take his course at the Southern Nevada School of Real Estate each year that seven out of ten current real-estate agents won't be in the business a few years from now. "I think the market will continue like this for another three to five years, but no longer. Nothing lasts forever.

"Of course, I said that five years ago."

Houses of the Holy

Lori Leibovich

It's Saturday night in Las Vegas.

A charismatic host welcomes one thousand spectators to a night of singing, sharing, and live entertainment. Lite rock wafts from a dimly lit stage as ushers hand out programs and escort older women to their seats. The crowd sits on folding chairs, eyes gazing at the large movie screen unfurled before them. A catchy TV tune begins playing over the sound system; whispers hiss through the audience as it recognizes the theme song from *The Andy Griffith Show*. Anxiously, the crowd waits for the main event.

This performance is one of many jam-packed extravaganzas taking place around the city tonight—but this one is miles from the sparkle and spectacle of Downtown and the Strip. It will not showcase master magicians, country-western singers, or the Girls of Glitter Gulch. Tonight's show will be fronted by a new breed of Las Vegas celebrity, one who makes use of many of the same gimmicks that have always drawn people to this city—dazzling sights, captivating music, and the promise of great entertainment.

It's Saturday night in Las Vegas, and the headliner is working for God.

The crowd at Central Christian, one of a handful of so-called megachurches that have sprung up in the last decade, taps its feet to the whistle of the *Andy Griffith Show* theme. Along with clips from this 1960s

TV show, tonight's service will include a theatrical performance, live Christian rock, and a sermon, all based on the theme "How to Make the Most of Time."

Looking more like a rodeo fan than a traditional clergyman, Gene Appel, Central Christian's boyish-looking pastor, takes center stage dressed in blue jeans, a denim shirt, and a bolo tie. "Friends," he begins, in a squeaky, nasal voice, "one of the biggest time-wasters is sin."

Appel ticks off a few prime examples of time-squandering: drinking, looking at pornography, committing adultery, gossiping. He speaks earnestly, his eyes half-closed, his head slightly bowed.

"For me, the most important thing is to love and serve God with all my heart, to love my wife, Barbara, as Christ loved the church and to nurture and discipline my children," Appel says. By identifying what is important, he explains, one can live a more productive, godly life. More than half of the crowd is made up of working parents, who presumably understand what it is like to juggle obligations to work, family, and the Lord.

"The road to hell is paved with good intentions, friends." Appel stops abruptly, his eyes searching the faces before him. "Remember friends, Satan likes to steal time."

Before the weekend is through, the same words, performances, and rituals will be repeated three times, to nearly four thousand people. Kevin Odor, pastor of Canyon Ridge, another Las Vegas megachurch, sums up the appeal of these mammoth, new-style, nondenominational churches: "The scene is better."

Unlike traditional Protestant churches, where members worship together on Sundays and, save for the occasional bazaar or funeral, rarely return until the following week, megachurches encourage frequent visits by offering several high-quality, in-demand "products" under one roof.

"We are not trying to steal sheep from other flocks," Odor insists. "We are going after the 'unchurched,' those who found the church they grew up in boring or irrelevant or damaging. We try to show them something different."

If the bulletin board in front of Central hadn't a cross attached, this drab, sprawling one-story building could be taken for another Las Vegas office complex. The holy campus of Central Christian includes a dozen classrooms, a gym, a library, an eight-hundred-seat chapel, a kitchen, a courtyard (complete with espresso cart), the Infantree (a state-of-the-art child-care facility for infants to two-year-olds), and a parking lot that can accommodate three thousand cars—more than the parking lots of most casino-hotels. Across the street, the Central Christian Preschool occupies another low, nondescript building.

■ ■ ■

Like its hometown, Central Christian is experiencing serious growth pains. In November 1998, the congregation moved to a new, $23-million, 56-acre facility in the southern suburb of Henderson, which offers sanctuary seating for 3,200—more than any hotel showroom on the Strip.

The church was founded in 1962 by twenty-five families; now there are more than 700 families, and two thousand members. If Las Vegas's rapid growth patterns continue, Central could be serving close to ten thousand people each weekend by the turn of the century.

Megachurches like Central Christian and Canyon Ridge are helping to usher in a new age of American religion. Avoiding traditional liturgy and music, most megachurches hope to entice unchurched Baby Boomers and their families with goods and services, instant community, and a accessible, techno-saavy God.

"The megachurch is a mixture of old-time tent revival and a rock concert," said Gordon Melton, founder of the Santa Barbara-based Institute for the Study of American Religion. "Traditional churches are offended by the notion of church as entertainment."

But in Las Vegas, where entertainment itself is a sacrament, the megachurch fits. So, surprisingly, do more-traditional houses of worship. While the image of Las Vegas as a modern-day Gomorrah may be culturally indissoluble in the rest of the country, beyond the Strip and Downtown the city is a sea of religious faith. In 1996, Las Vegas was home to 590 churches, synagogues, and mosques representing 63 denominations.

The moral climate of the city was established by the Mormons in 1855-57, when they became the first non-Indian settlers of Las Vegas Valley. While they represent only 6 to 10 percent of the city's population today, the Latter-day Saints continue to wield enormous political and financial influence. Mormons own substantial tracts of real estate in the Valley and hold influential public offices.

"The Mormons set the standard for what church should be in Las Vegas," said Yvonne Jacoby, a Las Vegas native who now ministers to teens at the Greater Las Vegas Church of Christ. "The Mormons are very family-oriented. Without their powerful voice a lot of people might think that topless dancing was an acceptable occupation."

Jewish and Catholic communities have also flourished in Las Vegas. Twenty years ago there was only one synagogue in town; today there are eleven, representing every tendency in Judaism from the liberal Reconstructionists to the ultra-orthodox Chabad movement. Catholics, who make up the largest religious group in the city (28 percent), are outgrowing their parishes and parochial schools.

"If I had the priests I could fill three more parishes, easy," said Bishop Daniel Walsh of the Catholic Diocese of Las Vegas, a former auxiliary bishop of San Francisco. "This is the most devoted religious community I have ever been in."

Locals like to boast that while the rest of the world considers their hometown Sin City, there are actually more churches per capita in Las Vegas than any other place in America. Unfortunately, this oft-cited statistic—if it was ever true—is certainly not true today, given Las Vegas's population boom. "If you compare Las Vegas with a city its size, like Memphis, you can see there is no truth to the most-churches-per-capita statistic," said Bruce Brown, author of a sourcebook of facts and figures about the city.

As the fastest-growing city in America—which it truly is—a geographical magnet for the luckless and forlorn as well as the entrepreneurial and ambitious, Las Vegas teems with rootless migrants hoping to make it big. They arrive in this desert boomtown searching for community and strength—and often find it in a house of God.

"In Las Vegas, people are hungering for church, not because they are searching for God, but because they are disconnected," says Mark Whelchel, the director of adult ministries at Central Christian. "This is a boomtown. People are new to the area, they have left their families and their roots. There is no tradition here. We want to help create some."

The tradition he and his colleagues have created does not require typical religious accoutrements such as steeples, pews, hymns, and vestments. Las Vegas's new churches are perhaps not as "mega" as the movement's most famous congregations; Willow Creek in suburban Chicago and the Crystal Cathedral in Garden Grove, California, both serve up to 15,000 people each weekend. They are not even "mega" compared with some of Las Vegas's largest traditional congregations; Baptist, Lutheran, and Catholic churches serve thousands of parishioners each Sunday as well. The prefix *mega* (a commonly overused form of Vegas hype meaning, literally, a million) has come to refer not to numbers but to a kind of theology. Whatever the size of their congregations, megachurches nationwide share a few basic ingredients: charismatic leaders, an evangelical mission, vast children's programs, small discussion groups and ministries, lively music, and a casual atmosphere. Yvonne Jacoby of the Greater Las Vegas Church of Christ said that her congregation of five hundred is considered "mega" not because of its size but because it is nondenominational, growing rapidly, and equipped with these essential ingredients.

■ ■ ■

Joe Boyd is a stocky, corn-fed Ohio kid. His large frame is topped by a freckled face and reddish, straw-straight hair. Tonight, though, Joe Boyd looks small as he stands alone on a large stage at the Seventh-Day Adventist Church in northeast Las Vegas.

This is not Boyd's church. Boyd, a twenty-three-year old youth minister, works at Canyon Ridge, but he can't preach there yet. (Even though the Canyon Ridge congregation boasts more than five thousand loyal members, its new quarters only opened in April 1998. Until then, high-school auditoriums and borrowed churches had to suffice.)

"Sometimes I look out over all the lights of this city and I think about all the lost people out there. This city—it is growing so fast—I drive by building after building, and again, all I can think about is all of the lost people," he tells the crowd. With so many rootless souls, Las Vegas is fertile ground for conversions—good news for these new, evangelical churches.

"Do people ever ask you, 'Why are you so happy? Why is your family life so good? Why do you smile?' And you think, 'Gee, if I tell them it's because I'm a Christian, they're going to think I'm nuts!'" Boyd says. The Canyon Ridge crowd laughs.

Without the least shred of clerical garb, Boyd looks remarkably secular. Tonight he is wearing blue jeans, a plaid shirt, and work boots.

"We must be culturally engaged," Boyd says. "If we can talk about music, movies, current events, then we can start conversations with people that may lead to friendship. And then when we know a person better, we can tell them about church."

A few days later, at the Canyon Ridge administrative offices in a Summerlin strip mall, Boyd reflects on the challenges of ministering in Las Vegas.

"If you have an addiction, whether it's alcohol, gambling, or pornography, and you move to Las Vegas, you're stupid. Those people get chewed up." The good news, he explains, is that the megachurch can help put broken lives back together, not only by filling a spiritual gap through Sunday service, but also through small recovery groups that meet frequently at the church.

"So many people we see are simply screwed up, and it is difficult to know whether that's because of the city we live in, or because our church encourages people to be real. We are on the front lines of sin in this town. This makes the victories sweeter and the defeats harder."

Boyd recalls a recent defeat. A young couple in one of the small groups he ministers decided to divorce. "The husband freaked out, left the group, and started gambling, and he won't return my calls," Boyd said, shaking his head. "It breaks my heart."

Most megachurch leaders (like most casino owners) view gambling, in moderation, as nothing more than a harmless form of entertainment. "Some of the pastors here gamble recreationally," said Kerry O'Bryant of Central Christian, who personally avoids the casinos because of his own addictive tendencies. "In Las Vegas, it's like going to a movie." But gambling isn't encouraged.

"There is an ability to get into trouble here," says Central's Mark Whelchel. "There's a lot of alcoholism, drug abuse, suicide. It's one of the least healthy cities to live in." Whelchel, who leads a support group called "Solid Ground" for Central members in dire financial straights, says people are lured to Las Vegas because of the many relatively high-paying jobs, like cocktail waitressing or valet parking, that are available to anyone who looks good in a miniskirt or can park a rental car.

"When people arrive in Las Vegas they often feel overwhelmed," Whelchel said. So many head for the roulette wheel or the dollar slots. "I see some people with large gambling debts in the small group. But," he added, "I see ten times more people with credit-card debt."

The ubiquity and power of the gaming industry make it impossible for religious leaders to condemn it without offending someone in their congregation. Moreover, relationships between religious groups and the casinos are mutually beneficial. The casinos get good press, and the churches and synagogues get things *they* need: the Catholic diocese holds administrative meetings in Strip-hotel function rooms. Jewish congregations hold Rosh Hashana services in casino ballrooms. Steve Wynn, the current patron saint of Las Vegas's gambling industry, has donated money and land to synagogues, Mormon stakes, and several churches.

Only one Las Vegas religious group, in fact, the Mormons, officially forbids gambling (along with alcohol and tobacco). But the church makes concessions for its Las Vegas members: Latter-day Saints in Clark County are permitted to work in the administrative, managerial, or executive branches of the casino industry, though they're discouraged from working at the tables or in the bars. Ashley Hall, a LDS spokesman, admitted that there are a few blackjack dealers in good standing within the church, "but they are the exception, not the rule." Las Vegas may be the only place in the world where Mormon doctrine has been altered to accommodate a city's economic forces.

"When I first came here, I assumed gambling was taboo. I assumed that anyone who worked in the industry or liked to gamble and wanted to become a Christian would quit," said Central's O'Bryant. "But a very significant proportion of our congregation works at the casinos, as blackjack dealers, waitresses, and cashiers." O'Bryant and other clergy are quick to point out that there is no reference to gambling in the Bible, and that it is not officially regarded as a sin.

"When someone comes to me and says they're a twenty-one dealer, there is no response from me," said Bob Perry, Pastor of Victory Christian Church. (Founded with six people in 1991, Victory now ministers to more than 500.) "We teach people that their identity is not derived from their vocation." Perry, in fact, was a car salesman before he attended Oral Roberts University, in Tulsa, where he was trained as a pastor. People assumed he was shifty, he says, because of his job. "I tell people their identity is who they are in Jesus Christ. Sometimes God will speak to a dealer and tell them to stay right where they are, because they are the only light in the whole darn casino."

■ ■ ■

Bearded and handsome, 42-year-old Kevin Odor looks like a folk singer. The pastor of Canyon Ridge has a kindly face and wears casual, woodsy clothing. Another Ohio native, Odor joined the staff at Canyon Ridge Christian Church in 1993, just as the congregation was getting off the ground. He knew right away that he wasn't in Ohio anymore.

"Back in the Midwest people have an image, a veneer they feel they have to maintain. It took a long time for them to trust me enough to air their dirty laundry," said Odor. "In this town I get it in five minutes. I had just arrived to help start the church and people walked into my office and said 'I've been divorced, I've been sexually molested, my boyfriend is beating me, my pregnant kid just ran away from home,' and I was like, 'Oh, is that all?' There is such a brokenness here. We don't have to convince people that they need help. They come in saying, 'Help.'" Kevin Odor likes the word "authenticity." It's what he believes separates megachurches like Canyon Ridge from other houses of the holy.

"We see a lot of self-doubt, spiritual hurt, festering wounds, the need for forgiveness. We tell people here to be real because authenticity frees people and honors God. We are real people in a real church and the pastors on stage are real people with real hurt, real marriages, real problems. And we are all people who really love God," Odor said.

Odor cites researchers who discovered that one of the main reasons Baby Boomers were driven away from traditional churches was because they didn't make them feel good. "People are used to being told by the church that they're wrong or sinful and guilty," Odor said. "They have been condemned but never helped. That's where we come in. It's all honest. It's functional instead of dysfunctional. You are allowed to speak, allowed to feel what you've always been told you can't see, talk or feel. And when that happens, it's like, 'Oh my gosh! Maybe I can be healed.'"

Canyon Ridge is Central Christian's sister congregation. As Central grew, a few hundred West Las Vegas congregants decided it was time to build their own house of worship closer to home. In 1993, with blessings and financial support from Central, Canyon Ridge was born. On the first Sunday of its existence, Canyon Ridge held services for six hundred people in a high-school auditorium. Since then, the number of attendees has more than tripled. In 1998, the congregation opened a new $20-million church on thirty acres of land in West Las Vegas.

■ ■ ■

Central Christian's motto, "Where Needs are Met," could serve as a slogan for the megachurch movement as a whole. More than two dozen "small groups" meet here during the week. Some discuss issues such as substance abuse and marital strife; others are purely recreational, like aerobics classes choreographed to Christian rock music.

"We have spent a lot of time trying to understand the unchurched Las Vegas Baby Boomers, and we have structured our whole ministry around that," said Kerry O'Bryant. "What we do is use objects and lessons and stories that the common man can understand. Jesus hung out with the common man, but many religious leaders of his day were out of touch. We want to be in touch with the needs of the common man and woman." Scanning a list of weekly activities at Central, one learns that what the common man, woman, and child in Las Vegas needs is help.

Sunday: Soul Insight: a spirituality group for teens
Monday: Tough Love Parenting Group
Tuesday: Divorce Recovery Group
Wednesday: Lydia Circle: a support group for senior women
Thursday: G.L.O.W: Girls Living Out the Word, a preteen ministry
Saturday: Ladies Co-Dependency group

Brochures advertising Central's many small groups are stuffed inside plastic envelopes that line the walls of the church's tennis-court-size lobby. There is something for almost everyone: Soul Invasion, a Senior High School Social Ministry; W.O.W. (Women Of the Word), a Bible-study group; Weigh Down Workshop; Too Busy Not to Pray, a support group for busy moms; Alcoholics Anonymous; Al-Anon; Survivors of Suicide; Pornography Recovery; and In His Image, a group "intended to assist women healing from damaged emotions and to help them form healthy relationships with God and others."

Because many Baby Boomers are familiar with twelve-step programs, they feel comfortable in small-group settings, say megachurch leaders. The groups also keep expanding megachurches homey enough so that people don't get lost in the crowd. "Becoming Christlike is a together thing, and that is what our big worship services are about," said Central's Whelchel. "On Sunday you could be sitting two rows behind someone who is going through a divorce or just declared bankruptcy and not even know it. That's what small groups are for. To be together and share. To stay accountable to the members of the group. Small groups are not just about Central, they *are* Central."

It is Wednesday evening, and Central's congregation has gathered for Exultation, a weekly ceremony billed as a "corporate worship experience" for believers. The chapel is a huge auditorium with beige walls and the kind of fold-down seats found at movie theaters. The room is dimly lit by several five-foot-tall candles alongside the altar. Pastor Gene Appel welcomes "the family" with an opening prayer, then asks the congregation to bear witness as baptisms are performed.

A door behind the dais opens and sentimental organ music wafts through the room.

"Kristin Reynolds," Appel says.

A gawky adolescent clumps down the stairs in a too-short white robe that barely reaches her calves. She bows her permed blonde hair before Pastor Gene.

"Kristin, do you accept Jesus Christ as your Lord and Savior?"

She nods yes.

Pastor Gene dunks her head in the stone baptismal font. Water dripping down her shoulders, Kristin exits the stage as the audience cheers, like fans at a basketball game. The baptisms continue for almost fifteen minutes. Most of the twenty or so people who commit to Christ on this evening are teens like Kristin, though a few older men and women come through the door.

The evening's sermon is about small groups. Senior Pastor Steve Thomason stands on stage in front of a giant easel, clutching a magic marker. "As our church grows larger, we must grow smaller," he begins.

The Wednesday-night crowd is smaller than the weekend service, attracting about 800 worshippers. It's mid-March and the desert air is getting warmer. A couple near the front wear shorts, the woman with a matching blouse and her husband with a Promise Keepers T-shirt. Thomason, like the crowd before him, is dressed down, in Dockers and a blue polo shirt.

"At our large services, anonymity is intentional," Thomason explains. "We want newcomers to be able to slip in, hear our message and leave without feeling like they need to commit."

Thomason draws dozens of dots on the paper, one to represent each small group at Central, until circles are splashed all over the page. "Every Christian is unique!" Thomason reminds the audience. "If there is not a group here to fit your needs, then we can help you start one." (Parishioners who decide to lead a small group must take a seven-week training course and attend a monthly meeting with other leaders.)

Slowly, Thomason begins to connect the dots until the scrambled marks make a single word: JESUS.

"You see," Thomason says with an I-told-you-so-smile. "All of the random dots together become HIM."

After communion, the crowd files out noisily, many picking up kids at one of Central's on-site child-care facilities. Some head to the back of the sanctuary to the "Decision Room," where they can meet with pastors and discuss their readiness to accept Jesus Christ as their Savior.

■ ■ ■

Megachurches in Las Vegas fill one of the Baby Boomers' most important needs: child care. The Infantree, a glass-enclosed room equipped with automated rocking swings, playpens, and three child-care workers, is open during every Central service. Parents check their infants in at the start of the evening and receive a number; if at any time a child begins crying or needs parental attention, the parent's number is flashed on one of several color monitors around the sanctuary. "Parents don't have to worry and they can really enjoy the service because their babies are in good hands," O'Bryant said. "If they see their number, they are free—and encouraged— to leave. They can always grab a tape of the sermon later on."

Older children are scattered about in rooms marked according to age. A small girl with a helmet of black curls waits in the five-year-olds' room for her mother. When she arrives, mom must show a photo I.D. before she can take her daughter by the hand. The girl has spent the last hour doing arts and crafts. A homemade medal, made from construction paper and shimmering with glitter, dangles from her neck; it reads, "God forgives me."

"Kids are people, too," Kevin Odor says. "If they can come to church and learn that church is fun and learn songs and stories about God, then you're planting seeds and investing in their morality."

Down the hall, a teen program called "Reality Unplugged" is winding down. Some boys shoot hoops, while clusters of girls stand gossiping and teasing one another. A spunky, twenty-something leader blows her whistle, calling the group to gather on the floor.

"Time to pray!" the leader says. Most heads go down immediately.

"Thank you, Jesus, for bringing us together tonight for fun with our friends. Next week may we see new faces here, Amen. We're outta here!"

■ ■ ■

Church leaders stay in tune with their congregants' needs by staying tuned themselves. They watch TV, go to movies, read popular magazines, listen to the radio, and use pop-culture tidbits to make sense of the Bible. A recent series of sermons at Central was called "What would God say to...Howard Stern? Dennis Rodman? Bill Gates?" (Answer B: Jesus would tell Dennis Rodman to reconsider his violent tendencies and the way he expresses his sexuality. "The freedom you are looking for is not going to come from cross-dressing or one-night stands, but through a relationship with God," Appel advised him.)

"Jesus was culturally relevant," Kevin Odor says. "He was always among the people able to relate to the culture. Instead of just saying, 'This is what is written in Corinthians 11:3,' we say, 'This is what was on *Nightline.'*" Central Christian attracts new members by appealing to their cultural and their religious tastes. Through market research, Central Christian determined that most of its members listen to classic-rock radio, so all religious music in the church is adapted to that format.

"We are pursuing the same message as old-school churches, but with a different medium—one that is relevant to our culture and time," says Whelchel. "If we were a Texas church, we'd use country music."

A recent weekend service was, in fact, designated a country-western celebration. Appel and the other pastors wore Stetsons and bolo ties. Five smiling performers burst onstage and broke into a country-style Christian song called "Too Many Voices." The male performers wore jeans and cowboy boots, the women layered, frilly skirts. With flair and emotion, the musicians invoked the name of Jesus. People in the audience clapped, swayed, and tapped their feet, singing along as the lyrics were projected onto a movie screen.

■ ■ ■

"God called me to start a church for my generation," says Joe Boyd, referring to "busters," twenty-somethings like himself who don't quite fit in with the Boomer-style megachurch. "I want to create a church inside a church."

Boyd listens to alternative rock, likes to watch movies, and is an avid sports fan. He say all of these pastimes make him a better Christian. "It is especially important for someone of my generation to know the difference between Sheryl Crow, Counting Crows, and the Black Crows," said Boyd. "That makes busters trust me and my opinion. After we talk about pop culture, then we can get to God."

Boyd, who is married, recently led a retreat called "The Real World: Las Vegas," borrowing the name of a popular MTV program. It was the first-ever outing of APEX, a group of singles and couples in their twenties which Boyd founded to bring "busters" together. The group spent the weekend camping in Arizona, discussing spiritual issues facing young people, such as premarital sex and homosexuality. Boyd played two popular alternative hits at the campground, both of which make references to God, and asked the group to discuss the lyrics. Like his Baby Boomer mentors, Boyd's goal is to make God relevant, so bits of pop culture find their way into almost every activity he leads and every sermon he preaches.

"There's an urgency to everything we do here in Las Vegas," Boyd said with a look of seriousness. "If we don't get them now, they'll slip." Boyd suddenly looks up, his face suddenly alive with optimism. "But at the retreat I baptized eight people! One person said, 'If it wasn't for this retreat I never would have found God.'"

■ ■ ■

It is Palm Sunday, the Sunday before Easter. Pastor Gene Appel is playing prophet, reminding his flock that the end of the world will come; it's just a matter of how and when. Instead of layering his sermon with biblical references, Appel begins with a cultural reference sure to resonate with the thousands of mediaphiles in his midst.

"You know, I was thinking about *Independence Day*," he begins, referring to the 1996 blockbuster movie about aliens who want to take over the world. "And you know, we are staring the end of the world in the face, whether it will be because of an alien invasion or something else. God is warning us."

Appel ticks off examples of some contemporary warnings: the eruption of Mount Saint Helens, the continuing depletion of the ozone layer, the nuclear leak at Three Mile Island, and a 1988 explosion at a plant in nearby Henderson. "Remember, destruction will come because of man's sin and evil. The Bible has its own *X Files*," Appel chuckles. Appel reminds his flock that since death and destruction may visit at any moment, it is imperative that they lead godly lives.

"There is an obituary column somewhere with your name on it and one with my name on it," says Appel, his voice now crackling. "Are power and popularity all that we want? Whether you have a little sin or a truckload, at death it is repentance that matters. God is patient, friends. He wants you to have the chance to call his name."

The auditorium falls silent. Appel paces along the stage and then hurls a question at his flock.

"RAISE YOUR HAND IF YOU ARE COMMITTING YOUR-SELF TO GOD!"

About forty hands shoot up.

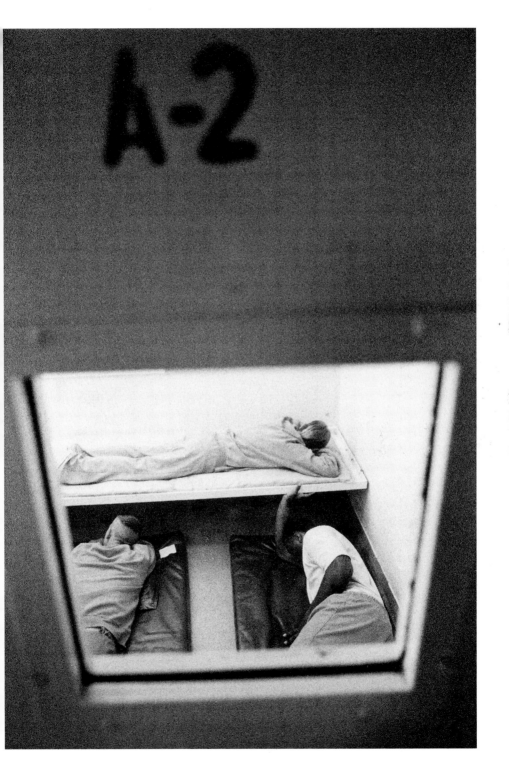

Organizing Las Vegas

Andrea Lampros

THE CLOUT OF 226

On the northern end of the Las Vegas Strip, outside the Frontier Hotel and Casino, five picketers sat on a brick landing with dog-eared "On Strike" signs propped between their knees, listening to salsa music on an old radio. Half a block down, four more workers listened to seventies soul on a beat-up boombox. Nearby, a taped message from the Culinary Union crackled from a kiosk, appealing to tourists to support the strikers by refusing to enter the Frontier.

Across the wide street, a woman impatiently waited for a walk signal. She held a Starbucks iced coffee in one hand as she gestured towards the strikers with the other.

"They're the laziest picketers I've ever seen," she said to her friend.

"Wouldn't you be after so long?"

"They should get it over with and get back to work. Find another job."

"Go tell them that."

"I can't. They don't even speak English."

Most of the Frontier strikers did speak English, in fact, though often with a Spanish accent. During the six and a half long years of their strike, they had heard all kinds of insults and seen the words "Union Scum" scratched into their ten-foot-tall sign on the corner of the Strip and Fashion Show Drive.

Quirino Campos, 47, who was on the line that day, flipped eggs and burgers at the Las Vegas Hilton Hotel Monday through Friday from 6 AM until 2 PM, then joined the picket line at the Frontier for five more hours. He's a Mexican immigrant who came to Las Vegas via Los Angeles nine years ago in search of a job to support his two teenage daughters. "I wanted a union for me, for everyone, for my family," he said, his face a leathery red. "I don't quit. I'm one hundred percent union."

■ ■ ■

Las Vegas may seem an unlikely place for the revival of a dormant national labor movement, especially since this city has an extraordinary number of service workers, a branch of the workforce that has traditionally been ignored by America's unions. The showy Strip may seem more a haven for ambitious entrepreneurs in sleek suits and ties (or for the world's middle class, on vacation in T-shirts and shorts) than for activist members of the working class. But this resort city in the southern Nevada desert is emerging as the national focus of union organization. It combines all the required ingredients: an abundance of jobs; a profitable and permanent basic industry (billion-dollar casino-hotels aren't likely to move to Mexico or Taiwan); millions of dollars from the AFL-CIO; and one of the mightiest union locals in the United States—Local 226, the largest local affiliate of the Hotel Employees and Restaurant Employees International Union, with 10 percent of its members. Las Vegas may be the only city in America where a cocktail waitress, making $11.25 an hour plus tips, can afford to send her children to college.

The Frontier Hotel strike, which ended with the owners selling out (in essence, a union victory) late in 1997, was the longest-running strike in the history of the United States, and certainly the most visible and pivotal union fight Las Vegas has ever seen. In the spring of that year, strike leader Joe Daugherty was watching tourists walk along the Frontier's groomed front lawn through thick eyeglasses. He leaned his foot on the low brick wall that edges the lawn, as comfortable as a kid in his own backyard. He had been here on the street with the strikers almost every day since the battle began. "We've got to finish it," said Daugherty, looking down at his worn Converse All-Stars. "We've got to see it to its end"—an end that was, in fact, just a few months away.

The very longevity of the Frontier strike was evidence of the union's strength and persistence. Five hundred fifty bellmen, maids, cocktail waitresses, and cooks walked out, and not one of them walked back in. (In fact, only about 350 of them were still around when the strike ended; at least thirty five of the original strikers had died.)

Towards the end, the remaining strikers had given up hope of ever winning a contract from the Elardis, the old-time, anti-union Las Vegas family that owned the Frontier. Some workers insisted they would never go back to work for the family in any case; their goal had changed to driving the owners away. In October 1997, it was announced that Margaret Elardi had sold the Frontier to Phil Ruffin, a hotel owner from Wichita, Kansas, for $165 million. The actual transfer took place on February 1, 1998, when Ruffin walked into the hotel hand-in-hand with Culinary Union officials; he had earlier signed an agreement to reopen the Frontier as a union hotel, and to rehire any of the strikers who wanted to return. The Elardis lost an estimated 40 percent of their normal revenue during the strike. A 1997 decision of the National Labor Relations Board, upheld in March 1998 after appeal, cost the new owner nearly $5 million in back wages and benefits for employees the Elardis fired in 1991.

Family pride and wealth inspired and enabled the Elardis to keep resisting the union while improving slot-machine odds and decreasing buffet prices in the hope of attracting wary visitors. But the 40,000-member Culinary Union had deep pockets, too. Members voted to increase their dues by seven dollars a month in order to support the strike fund and allow the demonstrations to operate 24 hours a day, seven days a week, just like the casino. Towards the end, the regular picketers, most of whom had other jobs, received $200 in strike relief for each week they were on the line for a total of 24 hours.

In image-conscious Las Vegas, the Frontier strike was unwelcome news. Former Frontier security guards claimed that the Elardis had used a bag of dirty tricks to intimidate union members, from stealing their signs and turning hoses on strikers to dumping heaps of manure near their eating place. They testified that the family kept watch on the strikers from a secret camera posted in a room in the hotel, and that Tom Elardi, son of owner Margaret, illegally taped conversations with picketers using a mini-cassette recorder concealed in a pack of cigarettes in his pocket. The strikers themselves appeared less malevolent, but a few years ago several of them were arrested and sued for beating up two tourists from California.

The Culinary Union won at the Frontier not because the union is either "right" or all-powerful, but because the heads of the corporations that now own most of the major Las Vegas hotels don't like the eyesore of picketers on their expensively remodeled, "family-oriented" Strip. They weren't necessarily praying for a union victory, but they did not want this awkward distraction defacing their profitable tourist haven. One neighboring casino-hotel even provided food and drink for the Frontier's picketers.

■ ■ ■

A few blocks north of the Frontier on Las Vegas Boulevard, the high-priced glamour of the Strip quickly runs dry. Just past the 1,149-foot tower of the financially troubled Stratosphere Hotel, one runs into small liquor stores, pawn shops, low-budget strip shows, and the headquarters of Local 226.

Thanks to well-publicized events like its victory at the MGM Grand in 1995, its dogged refusal to give up at the Frontier, and its more recent battles with Sheldon Adelson for a contract at the new Venetian, the Culinary Union has become the star of the Las Vegas labor movement. Local 226 has managed to unionize 80 percent of the casino-hotels on the Strip, which in turn employ a substantial fraction of the city's population. The union now takes on each new monster resort even before the foundations are laid.

March 1997, 9 AM: workers pack the upstairs union hall, filling more than two hundred brown plastic chairs. Another hundred or so are milling about in the room's unfurnished empty spaces. Young, old, and middle-aged, black, white, Asian, and mixed-race, they are dressed in Wrangler jeans topped with silver belt buckles, blouses and slacks, or the uniforms of bellmen and waitresses. Some have children trying to squirm off their laps. On the wall, a neon-orange banner reads, "Organize for Our Share of Gaming's Future."

Glen Arnodo's voice booms from the podium on the raised stage at the front. Another voice, that of his Spanish interpreter Lalo Cacias, comes from the center of the room, near five rows of Latino workers. Cacias listens to Arnodo's words and repeats them in Spanish a second later, punctuating his more spirited version by shaking his fist. Each speaker tries to make himself heard over the other.

"The Elardis are drunk drivers in the gaming industry—that's what they are, drunk drivers," shouts Arnodo, the union's political director. "And it's time to take their driver's license away."

The line gets laughter and big applause. Smoothly dressed in a black T-shirt and dark sports coat, Arnodo knows how to deliver the passionate pep talks that are stock-in-trade in the union business. Vilifying the Elardis always works well at Local 226.

■ ■ ■

In this same hall a month earlier, Bruce Springsteen's "Born in the U.S.A." rocked the room as 650 workers waited to hear AFL-CIO President John Sweeney sing their praises. "Who's got the power?" union leaders chanted. "We've got the power!" responded the faithful. Sweeney told the Las Vegas workers that their city was poised to replace New York—his hometown—as the "heartbeat of the American labor movement."

"Las Vegas is a union city. Now we want to make it a one hundred percent union city," said Sweeney, a soft-spoken man known more for his organizing than his oratory. "If America needs a raise, then the buck starts here."

In 1998, only 14 percent of U.S. non-farm workers belonged to unions, down from 35 percent in the 1950s. Just to keep that share of the workforce, the AFL-CIO has to recruit 400,000 new workers a year, every year. In 1995, the year Sweeney defeated Lane Kirkland for the presidency on a platform of aggressive labor organization, their membership declined by 338,000, to a total of about 13 million. Another 92,000 were lost in 1996. In 1998, their numbers were estimated at 16 million, but their overall percentage of the growing national workforce continued to decline.

Sweeney and the AFL-CIO picked Las Vegas as the nation's most promising union city mainly because Local 226, along with Local 711 of the United Food and Commercial Workers (UFCW), has been so successful at the kind of recruiting the AFL-CIO would like all its unions to undertake. The UFCW unionized every grocery store in Las Vegas by devoting most of its budget to recruitment. Local 226 has put more than a third of its total budget into gaining new members over the past ten years. (Few locals, in Las Vegas or elsewhere, spend more than 5 percent.)

Sweeney's idea of a "100 percent" union town would be an impossible goal almost anywhere in the country, in the light of labor's steady decline since the organizing triumphs of the CIO in the 1930s and 1940s. But in Las Vegas, a "can-do" city accustomed to achieving the impossible, it seems almost possible. According to the 1994 census, 18.4 percent of the Las Vegas workforce was unionized; John Wilhelm, President of the national Hotel Employees and Restaurant Employees Union (HERE) and a former Las Vegas organizer, claims membership in the area is closer to 30 percent. Sixty-five thousand workers in Las Vegas belonged to unions as of April 1997, and thousands more are covered by union contracts. Since Nevada is a right-to-work state, unions cannot require membership even of an employee working under a contract won by the union. In some sense, this restriction makes the unions even stronger, because their workers have *chosen* to join and pay dues—twenty-six dollars a month, in the case of the Culinary Union.

But even more important than numbers may be the sense of union identity, which seems stronger here than in other American cities. Ask a cab driver to take you to Culinary headquarters, and he knows exactly where to go. Mention the Frontier strike, and every local citizen has a vigorous opinion. Big drugstores in strip malls list the union health plans whose cards they accept. That is not to say there is no skepticism about, even disdain for, unions in Las Vegas, as there would be in any city. The difference is that in Las Vegas, unions become a target for active admiration or disgust because they still hold genuine power.

■ ■ ■

Elmer Alton Bramlet drove a Lincoln Continental, wore leisure suits, smoked long cigars, and ran the Culinary Union for twenty-four years. In 1977, on his way back from a business trip to Reno, he phoned his daughter from McCarran Airport and told her he would be home in half an hour. His body was later found in the desert, punctured by several bullet holes. The sixty-year-old Bramlet had reportedly resisted some Chicago gangsters who were trying to take control of the union's health plan. He had other other enemies as well: hotel owners were upset over a sixteen-day strike in 1976 that had cost them an estimated $26 million in lost business. The federal government was investigating several million-dollar loans he had made to friends from the union's pension fund.

Nobody knows who killed Bramlet. But the murder threw the Culinary Union into a tailspin. Bramlet had always been the sole decisionmaker, and had not allowed other union leaders to develop.

For ten years after his death, Bramlet's successors kept their office doors locked. Appointments were hard to get, and callers were thoroughly screened. Ben Sweeney and Jeff McCall, who followed Bramlet as secretary-treasurers of Local 226 (secretary-treasurers tend to be more powerful than presidents in many U.S. union locals) weren't taking any chances.

Jim Arnold was around in the Bramlet days, too. But as a matter of principle and good public relations, he has always kept his office doors open. Arnold, the secretary-treasurer in 1997, is fifty-four years old and has spent most of his adult life in the Culinary Union. He is a native Las Vegan whose father worked in the local building trades, back when that industry was solidly union. His first job after high school was at the Sands Hotel, where he picked up and delivered laundry; later, he served as a shop steward, and helped to negotiate contracts at a time when shop stewards played a token role at best. In 1974, Arnold became one of Bramlet's union representatives.

Like other Culinary leaders, Arnold gets nostalgic for a time before the corporate takeover of Las Vegas's casino-hotels, when families like the Boyds and the Binions ran their establishments like private estates. Maybe the Mafia was involved, they concede; but that was better than being ruled by out-of-town corporations whose policies are driven by distant stockholders, New York financial analysts, and the everlasting need to maximize short-term profits.

"These family-run casinos really believed in making a profit. But they believed that the workers should get a percentage of that," says Arnold, his diamond pinky ring flashing as he lights a cigarette.

Political Director Glen Arnodo was shocked when he arrived in Las Vegas in 1989 and heard workers glorifying the good old days of the mob. "Old workers will tell you that it was so much better to work for the mob," says Arnodo. "They say that because, to the extent that there may have been union troubles, at least the mob wasn't out to bust the union."

Culinary leaders insist that there are no union-mob ties nowadays. But in 1995, after two years of negotiations, the U.S. Department of Justice took control of HERE because of persisting evidence of mob connections and other abuses. By the end of 1997, sixteen Hotel and Restaurant Employees locals had been audited, and ten of their officials were banned from union membership by Federal Court Judge Kurt Muellenberg, the appointed monitor, because of ties to organized crime, embezzlement, and other abuses. Arnold says that the federal investigators had full access to Local 226 records and found no evidence of anything shady. In fact, as part of the deal the Department of Justice made to release HERE from its control, the union's Chicago-based president was obliged to resign, and John Wilhelm of Local 226 was appointed to take his place. (Wilhelm also served on President Clinton's National Gambling Impact Study Commission, one of three "Industry-friendly" members, along with J. Terrence Lanni of MGM Grand and William Bible, former head of the Nevada Gaming Control Board.)

Major changes in the Culinary Union began in 1984, when the national HERE leadership sent several of its best organizers to help salvage a badly run strike that pulled 19,000 workers out of the major Strip hotels. Several of the hotels settled after sixty-seven days; others held out for as long as fifteen months. Six hotels hired new strikebreaking workers, who then voted to decertify the union. "Basically, everyone in this town, from workers to casino owners and politicians, felt that the union was pretty well finished," says Arnodo, who came to Las Vegas in 1989 for what was supposed to be a six-month campaign.

If the 1984 strike was a low point of Culinary's recent history, the MGM Grand victory in 1995 was definitely the high. Before the MGM Grand Hotel—currently the world's largest, with more than five thousand rooms—even broke ground in Las Vegas, the company educated job applicants (an estimated hundred thousand people applied for eight thousand positions) by showing an anti-union video and warning them of the perils of organizing. It then offered its workers more than the going union rates, and an equivalent benefits package. Local 226 had to work hard to convince workers that without a union, these wages and benefits could be withdrawn at the whim of the corporation, under pressure from stockholders if profits ever started to dip.

Local 226 won that fight, in the end, by developing hard-core union committees inside the MGM Grand and using provocative street tactics outside the gold lion that guards the hotel's main entrance on the Strip. At the MGM Grand's gala opening in January 1994, set to a *Wizard of Oz* theme, union leaders dressed up as the Tin Man, the Scarecrow, the Cowardly Lion, the Wicked Witch, and Dorothy handed out flyers denouncing CEO Robert Maxey's union-busting tactics. More than four thousand union supporters rallied outside the gigantic green-glass-walled hotel. The union directed its efforts nationwide at stockholders' meetings and other investor groups. Bold tactics like this drove Maxey nearly apoplectic, and the negative publicity they caused helped persuade owner Kirk Kerkorian to replace him as CEO in 1995. In his place, Kerkorian hired the more levelheaded Terry Lanni away from Caesars Palace. Lanni declared the hotel neutral in the battle, and let workers decide whether they wanted a union or not. The workers voted yes.

High off the MGM Grand victory, the Culinary Union moved into the world of electoral politics in 1996 by putting together a doorbell-ringing, neighborhood-by-neighborhood campaign to defeat incumbent state legislator Sue Lowden, owner of the off-Strip Santa Fe Hotel and Casino, which had also resisted efforts to unionize its employees. Lowden had been expected to win big before the Culinary Union decided to make use of its political weight and available manpower to bring her down. They visited thousands of houses and apartments, and bused union members to the polls. The union's contribution to the campaign of Valerie Weiner, Lowden's Democratic opponent, was estimated at $140,000 (almost all in donated staff time), which more than equalized the two candidates' war chests. Their victory (Lowden lost by 9 percent of the vote) gave Local 226 the confidence to start its own political fund, raised through voluntary dollar-a-month contributions from members. They plan to use it to run hotel and casino employees for public office. In 1998, the union's door-to-door campaigning helped to defeat candidates supported by Sheldon Adelson, owner of the new, non-union Venetian Hotel.

One current target of the union's efforts—which they hope to make the MGM victory of the decade's end—is the ARK Corporation, a New York-and Washington-based company which employs nine hundred non-union workers at several restaurants inside the hippest new hotel in Las Vegas, the New York New York. Although the impressive, $460 million hotel, owned jointly by MGM Grand and the Primadonna Corporation (the two companies merged in 1999), opened in January 1997 with a union contract, the owners had subcontracted most of its restaurants to ARK, leading the union to cry foul.

Unionizing ARK Corporation employees would seem to be a cinch compared to organizing MGM Grand, because of the vast discrepancy in wages and benefits. In 1997, a typical ARK kitchen worker made $5.50 an hour; if she wanted health insurance benefits, she paid, out of these minimal wages, $50 a month for herself, $100 a month for herself and a spouse, $200 for a family of three, and $500 for a family of four. Under the contract signed by Local 226 and the New York New York, a union kitchen worker would have earned $9.62 an hour, and pay nothing for health insurance that covers her whole family.

William Sherlock, CEO of the New York New York, told the *Las Vegas Business Journal* that subcontracting was not a bid to undercut the union, but simply a cost-cutting effort to free the hotel's budget from the burden of restaurants. (In-house restaurants often serve as loss leaders for adjoining casinos; they have traditionally lost money in Las Vegas Strip hotels. But this is generally not the case with upscale, "name" restaurants, whether hotel-owned or subcontracted.)

Kevin Kline, a veteran of several Culinary Union fights and the lead organizer against ARK, fears that if the New York New York gets away with subcontracting its food operations to non-union companies, other resorts will follow suit. Industry insiders disagree. MGM Grand subcontracted its Studio Cafe in 1996, but reversed its decision a year later, when it realized that it was giving up quality control and suffering as as result. Kline says that ARK made less than a million dollars in 1996—a sum smaller than the budget of the union itself. He doesn't think ARK has the resources to pay union wages, and hopes the company will be driven away by labor pressure, leaving New York New York to assume control of its own restaurants at union wages. "I am absolutely confident we will kick ARK out of town," says Kline.

■ ■ ■

Cheryl Bunch is a general in the ARK battle, although she wouldn't describe herself that way. "My job is to teach workers how to stand up together to get what they need," she says; "not to fight for them, but to show them how they can do it." She was once a hotel worker herself, waiting tables at Circus Circus and the Excalibur.

Bunch grew up in Wildwood, New Jersey, and became a waitress at thirteen. She worked at a restaurant on the Jersey shore in the early 1980s, earning two dollars an hour plus about forty dollars a night in tips. At that (non-union) job, she says, she had to wait "for the last drunk to leave" before ending her shift. Her ex-husband paid no child support for their three children, and the fact that she worked in an East Coast resort town meant that she was unemployed four months a year.

She finally packed the kids into her car and left for Las Vegas to join her mother, then a waitress at the Silver Slipper. (The old casino, torn down in 1988, was located in what is now the parking lot of the Frontier.) Bunch arrived in Las Vegas just before the ugly, drawn-out Culinary strike of 1984, and went straight to Local 226 to find a job.

"I always thought union workers were like steel workers," she says. "I thought a waitresses' union was kind of bizarre." But she could now afford medical care for her whole family—an unattainable luxury in New Jersey.

Bunch soon became a rank-and-file activist; she would protest, walk picket lines, and lead meetings for the union. While working at the Excalibur, she was active in other union fights, and got arrested alongside her mother for acts of civil disobedience.

Two years ago, the Culinary Union asked Bunch to become a full-time union organizer. "I'm forty years old now," she says, "and I've finally found what I'm supposed to do."

Bunch is in charge of the English-speaking cooks, waitresses, hostesses, and bus people at the New York New York's America restaurant—a huge, buffet-style place where a giant cartoon map of the United States hangs suspended over the tables. She and her partner, Ramón, who is in charge of the Spanish-speaking staff, have formed a workers' committee that meets once a week. They spend off-duty hours talking up the union to their coworkers.

At the New York New York, as in most union campaigns, the committee stays underground at first, in order to avoid management repercussions. The America restaurant committee suddenly went public in March 1997, pinning on union buttons and sending a list of their names to the managers and executives at the hotel and at ARK. Such a public display can help protect workers, because under the terms of the 1935 Wagner Act, it's illegal to fire a worker for union activity.

Even so, some of the committee members claim to have been harassed by management: their shifts were suddenly changed, their days off taken away. If a worker believes he has been intimidated by management because of his union affiliation, he can file a grievance with the NLRB. If successful, he could ultimately win compensation. If he has been fired because of union membership or activity, the NLRB can order his employer to give him back his job—as it recently did at the Frontier.

Bunch drives out of the Culinary Union parking lot in her blue "travelling office" van to meet Donna Wilson, one of her committee members. Wilson's home, in one of Las Vegas's many new planned communities, is decorated with baskets, shells, and three-foot-high classical statues. Outside is a tiny swimming pool. In any other city, this might pass for the home of a member of the suburban middle class. Wilson, 51, is one of Las Vegas's more than 300,000 service workers.

The appeal of the Culinary Union for her has more to do with protection from age discrimination than a need for higher wages or benefits. Since Las Vegas casino-hotels prefer their female serving personnel to be young and attractive, Wilson feels increasingly at risk of losing her job.

Wilson hands Bunch five new cards signed by America Restaurant staffers indicating that they want to become union members. She has already talked dozens of her coworkers into supporting the union, and she tells Bunch that the restaurant managers called an impromptu meeting the night before to persuade workers that unionizing was a bad idea. Company spokesmen told workers that ARK had a twenty-year lease with the New York New York, and that it would be futile to join. "I had three buttons on," says Wilson, defiantly. "I was in their face."

■ ■ ■

While the ARK drive was the union's major campaign of 1997, Local 226 is big enough to mount more than one organizing effort at a time. In May of that year, the union was negotiating new contracts, and pressuring Sheldon Adelson, the owner of the former Sands Hotel to go union even before his proposed new three-thousand-room replacement (now called The Venetian) was completed. They were also working with the Service Workers International Union (SEIU) in their battle to organize hospital workers at Columbia Sunrise Hospital and Medical Center, the largest hospital in Las Vegas.

Although the Columbia Sunrise workers were in their second year of fighting for a union, the hands-on support of Local 226 boosted their drive enormously in 1997. The Culinary Union mobilized its own rank and file to go to SEIU's demonstrations, and wrote letters in support of their cause. Thousands of patients at Columbia Sunrise are union members (or relatives of union members), which adds considerable clout to their campaign.

At the Local 226 hall on a Friday afternoon in March, about forty Culinary organizers and volunteers showed up for a "secret action." At exactly 11:02 AM, dozens of Culinary organizers, in groups of four and five, started to enter Columbia Sunrise Hospital carrying flowers and balloons and delivering the message "Hi, we're members of the Culinary Union. We're your patients, and we support your union drive." The demonstrators had strict instructions to visit the nurses on designated floors, but not to disrupt patients or get into arguments. They were to talk to as many people as possible and to be out of the building within eight minutes.

Back at union headquarters after the "secret action," SEIU campaign director Adair Dammann got a call from a pro-union nurse at the hospital who said that the staff there had been ordered to throw away the flowers and balloons. At this news, the Local 226 crowd roared with laughter and applause: their message had gotten through, and management was mad.

B-TOP: CHANGING THE FACE OF THE BUILDING TRADES

The powerful Culinary Union has had more difficulty trying to work with local building trade unions than it has had with its own employers or the Service Workers Union. The men (and a few women) who belong to the fifteen building-trade locals have trouble getting along with one another, much less the maids and cocktail waitresses of Local 226. One problem is that, while the Culinary Union prides itself on its racial diversity (its president, Hattie Canty, is black, and many of the rank and file are people of color), the building-trade unions continue to be dominated by white men with exclusionist attitudes. This problem is compounded by the fact that most of the new workers in Las Vegas are people of color. Latino men currently fill most of the non-union jobs in residential construction.

A coordinated drive to organize construction workers, from general laborers to high-skilled specialists like electricians and pipefitters—a drive that includes Latinos and blacks as well as whites, women as well as men—has rarely been tried elsewhere, because of the traditional divisions (in race, pay scales, and levels of skill) among construction workers. For this reason, the Las Vegas Building Trades Organizing Project (B-TOP) is being watched closely by unions and building contractors all over the country.

■ ■ ■

They call it the war room. It's the Las Vegas office of the Laborers International Union, where determined, angry men smoke Marlboro Reds and talk about beating the bosses. The room is not much bigger than a one-car garage. When a cellular phone rings, five guys reach at the same time for their back pockets. The names of building contractors and workers are scribbled on pieces of butcher paper and taped to the walls. The war room has no other decorations, and no windows to distract its occupants from the mission at hand: a short-term, high-energy recruitment drive to draw more workers into the union.

In northeast Las Vegas, where Bonanza Street tails off into the undeveloped desert, a gang of young organizers is spending most of its waking hours in and out of this room, trying to do for the off-Strip construction industry what the Culinary Union has done for Strip hotel and casino workers. Several national unions (like the laborers) have dispatched their brightest organizers from other U.S. cities to Las Vegas to help what they believe to be one of the most important unionizing drives in the country.

Jim Grogan, the lead organizer for the Laborers' International, was working in Alabama with the Amalgamated Clothing and Textile Workers Union when he heard about the excitement in Las Vegas. He left ACTWU, joined the laborers, and headed west. "I really wanted to be a part of it," says Grogan, 26, a New Jersey native. "Labor has realized that it has got to get off of its ass." He definitely sees this facedown between Clark County building contractors and the unions that are trying to organize their workers as a war as mortal combat.

B-TOP kicked off in January 1997 with a $6-million war chest: $2 million contributed each by the Carpenters and Joiners, the Laborers' International, and the AFL-CIO. The goal of the project was to unionize at least ten thousand of the city's thirty thousand non-union construction workers within the next two years, and to persuade the historically divided building trade unions to work together.

Construction workers employed in major casino-hotel building and enlargement along the Strip have been unionized for many years, so B-TOP focused on the other kinds of construction that have contributed to

Las Vegas's overwhelming expansion over the past decade: the ever-spreading housing tracts, apartments, and condominiums, the strip malls and other retail centers, the schools and civic buildings, the warehouses and light industry, all of which are built almost entirely by non-union workers.

■ ■ ■

Stefoni Aragon is one of the few women to show up in the War Room. With her heavy boots, khaki shorts, silver nose ring, and hair pulled back in a neat ponytail, she looks more like a casual western college student than a feisty union organizer.

The twenty-two-year-old daughter of Mexican immigrants, Aragon grew up in Las Vegas. After high school, she attended a two-year nurse's-aide training program in Phoenix, where her mother lives. But she found that she couldn't stand the bedpan routine, so she returned to Las Vegas in 1996 to become a building-site laborer like her father.

She immediately found work hauling debris at the Monte Carlo Hotel (then a non-union site). A few months later, she signed up with the Laborers Local 872 and took a union job at the Luxor, where she earned eleven dollars an hour plus sixteen dollars for every hour of overtime. As one of the rare women in this sweaty man's world, she put up with daily taunts and catcalls from her fellow workers. ("Shouldn't you be home making tortillas?") But when her boss began making sexual advances, she turned for help to her union rep.

She didn't expect Tony Valdez to take her complaint seriously. But "the next thing I know, he's on the job site a week later, watching everything, asking questions, talking to my boss, trying to get it straightened out." She quickly became a union devotee.

"When I reached out for help, someone was there for me. I was pretty wowed by it. I felt like angels were around me. I sat there and I just felt so protected. After he left, I stayed smiling—like I was important. Like whatever happened to me mattered."

Valdez was quick to see that Aragon—a young, bilingual Latina laborer—could be a major asset to the union's membership drive. He encouraged her to go through a six-week B-TOP training program, where she was chosen as the group's first and only female apprentice organizer. Now she's working fifteen-hour days and making $700 a week recruiting concrete-pourers.

No other city has attempted an organizing drive of this magnitude among the building trades—dirt-haulers and fine craftsmen united by a common product but rigidly divided by their separate lines of work. Iron workers, for example, refuse to regard themselves in the same class as laborers. The competition for control of B-TOP mirrors the competition on the job site. Some trades, like the iron workers, claim superiority because of their skills; others, like the laborers, because of their numbers. (Nationally, laborers outnumber iron workers five to one. But iron workers demand long apprenticeships, and earn considerably more.)

Why did the big national unions and the AFL-CIO devote so much energy and money to so risky an effort—and in Las Vegas, of all places? The main reason is the sheer number of workers involved. Construction is now the number-two industry in Clark County. Builders are putting up not only the giant new hotels and hotel extensions, but also houses, stores, and schools in record numbers, to accommodate the more than 5,000 new residents who move here each month.

The abundance of new work has called for an abundance of new workers, about 25 percent of whom may be Hispanic immigrants, "legal" or "illegal." If the building-trade unions permit this burgeoning workforce to remain almost entirely non-union (as the Southern Nevada Home-builders Association would prefer), they may find themselves swallowed up by the boom, with their relative share of the workforce decreasing, despite their lock on the higher-paying jobs along the Strip.

■ ■ ■

The building-trades organizers have borrowed the Culinary Union's training center at the Holiday Inn on Fremont Street to hold an open house for non-union construction workers. One or two representatives from each of the fifteen trades, from bricklayers to roofers, sits behind a table waiting for the masses to arrive. Stefoni Aragon, the only woman in the room, is posted at the reception table, ready to welcome the workers as they come in for the free buffet and a chance to talk about unions.

By four o'clock, almost no one has shown up. It looks like a reading room at the Church of Scientology: plenty of eager believers, few new converts. An hour later, the room is half-full of men in overalls and dirty work pants, most of them speaking Spanish.

As I walk down the center of the room, between the U-shaped tables, many eyes follow me. An iron workers' rep darts a glance at me, then looks away. I hold out my hand and introduce myself; he can hardly bring himself to return the gesture. When I ask how the open house is going, he gives me a suspicious grin.

"How do I know that you're really a writer?"

I point out to him that I have already interviewed dozens of labor organizers in Las Vegas, including his boss. If I were a management spy—which is what he appears to suspect—I'd have to be a pretty good one.

It's clear that these workers aren't accustomed to questions from reporters. Until now, the national press has focused on the Culinary Union, with its colorful history, its cutting-edge strategies, and its attention-getting marches on the Strip. The reluctance to talk may also be related to the very real possibility that contractors are in fact spying on the unions, just as the unions are spying on the contractors—by, among other things, rummaging through their trash.

Jim Rudisil, the first B-TOP director, a veteran of the International Brotherhood of Electrical Workers, was unconcerned about spies and reporters; his immediate problem was getting his own house in order. With millions of dollars at his disposal, he hired eighteen full-time organizers, thirteen apprentices, and ten interns to work all day, every day recruiting workers from four of the county's largest building contractors. Each of the fifteen national building-trades unions donated one organizer to Las Vegas to work with B-TOP—almost all of them English-speaking white men in their forties.

B-TOP organizers visited job sites every day to talk up the unions and invite workers to small-group meetings, where they could air gripes about their bosses and talk about safety violations on the job. These were held in the evening, at either the Laborers' war room, the B-TOP office, or one of the other union locals' headquarters. They offered free food and a chance to talk strategy. Labor leaders call this "bottom-up" organizing.

"The first part is internal education," says Rudasil. "We're trying to get our members to open up, which isn't always easy."

Leslie Curtis, Nevada director of the AFL-CIO, says it's hard to persuade local union leaders and members in the historically exclusive building trades to welcome new recruits, especially among the large numbers of Latino immigrant workers who arrive in Las Vegas daily. These local leaders have restricted their numbers for decades, partly because of inbred suspicion, partly to guard their numbers against competition for jobs. The history of racist exclusionism in the southern Nevada building trades dates back to the construction of the Hoover Dam in the 1930s, when only white men could obtain jobs. Family or other connections have often been crucial in obtaining building-trades apprenticeships.

"If the labor movement wants to survive, then it has to bring in the people who are doing the work," says Curtis. "And the people who are doing the work are the minorities." Curtis is one of fifty new directors hired by John Sweeney to supervise organizing drives in every state. "They are realizing that they cannot continue to be as cavalier about who they try to exclude."

After years of squabbling among its constituent unions over how—or indeed whether—to recruit new workers, the first few months of the B-TOP campaign were fairly rocky. Ruticell began taking heat for paying B-TOP leaders high wages and for hiring seven secretaries. Jim Grogan of the Laborers Union was kicked out of a B-TOP meeting for criticizing the group's timid start-up. At a demonstration at Precision Concrete during President Sweeney's visit, Grogan claims that B-TOP tried to steal media attention from the laborers and detracted from the purpose of the event, which was intended to focus attention on a fired concrete-pourer who had been beaten up by non-union workers. "They didn't even know this man," says Grogan, blue eyes blazing. "It was just a photo op for them!"

As the trades try to get their troops in order, they must also worry about opposition from the industry. At the first hint of the B-TOP drive in October 1996, the Southern Nevada Homebuilders Association sponsored a multi-page insert in Las Vegas's largest-circulation (and pro-business) newspaper, the *Review-Journal,* comparing union leaders to Communists and warning the public of the un-American menace of the AFL-CIO's organizing drive.

Joanne Jensen, a spokeswoman for the Southern Nevada Homebuilders Association—an umbrella group for contractors, seen by labor as their number-one adversary in Clark County—has a lot to say about the presence of unions at casinos and hospitals, but little about their role in the building trades; for the moment, at least, she would appear to be downplaying their threat. Mark Smith, former director of the Las Vegas Chamber of Commerce, was openly skeptical about B-TOP. "I would be interested to know what they are spending their money on, member for member," says Smith. "I don't think their success will be anywhere near what they think it will be."

■ ■ ■

Tony Valdez, the local Laborers' representative, is both awed and disturbed by the hordes of out-of-town organizers who have moved into Las Vegas over the last few months. The thirty-one-year-old San Jose, California native says that after B-TOP is gone, Las Vegas laborers will be left with no more than his own union, Local 872.

It's 5:05 AM. Valdez is drowsy as he pours coffee into the automatic urn at union headquarters. Stefoni Aragon is slouched in a chair in the small kitchenette, still angry at Valdez for making her get up so early. A crescent moon is still visible in the dark sky. Aragon and Valdez are on an early-morning mission to join other B-TOP organizers at a non-union employment service, where workers show up at dawn in the hope of finding jobs for the day.

Al Balloqui, who manages the service (called "Labor Ready"), has agreed to permit union organizers to talk to his low-skilled, mostly homeless workers, as long as they provide coffee and donuts. Like a handful of similar agencies in Las Vegas, Labor Ready can quickly supply non-union workers for short-term building jobs off the Strip. The workers are paid five dollars an hour to do basic cleanup jobs that would earn a union worker $12.77. Balloqui doesn't think the unions are a threat, so he opens his doors.

At Labor Ready, a crowd of workers is talking to a handful of union organizers. "Most of us need money now to get a place to sleep tonight," says the tallest man in the room.

"We understand. We're not asking you not to go to work today," says Valdez, surrounded by a crowd of rough-edged men. Most of these workers can barely afford a meal, let alone the $500 it costs to join the Laborers local. But several workers appear eager to hear what the organizers have to say, and few seem opposed to unions on principle: who wouldn't want to earn eight dollars more an hour?

A man in the corner wearing a beige down jacket identifies himself (after some game-playing with me) as Anthony Jones.

"They're playing a defective slot machine," Jones says of the union organizers. He holds a Styrofoam cup of black coffee. "I worked for three union companies back east, but they all shut down and went to Mexico. The problem is not, 'Will I join a union?' I would love to be in a union. But every time I get in a union, the company goes bye-bye."

Jones says he's just waiting for the summer sun; then he'll drive his motor home back to Juneau, Alaska, where he spends most of the year. In Las Vegas, he is a "working tourist"—he picks up construction jobs in the daytime and plays the casinos by night.

As itinerant farm workers follow the crops around California's Central Valley, many construction workers, like Jones, come to Las Vegas for seasonal work, or just to pick up a few bucks before moving on. But unlike the Central Valley, here a worker can cash his paycheck at a casino and lose a day's pay or more on the blackjack tables or slots in a matter of hours. Some 200 people a day drift through Labor Ready; between 100 and 150 find work. Balloqui claims that 20 percent of his workers already belong to building-trades unions. They come to him because the unions don't have enough work for every member.

He's right. At the Laborers Union local, for example, five hundred workers are laid off at any time. Most of these workers could take short-term, less desirable union jobs, but they choose to keep their names on the union's list, waiting for a long-term gig on some colossal Strip project. In the meantime, some take non-union jobs and hope that their union brothers don't find out.

After the event, B-TOP organizers insist that they didn't go to Labor Ready in the hope of signing up throngs of workers, but rather to offer a sort of union Welcome Wagon. If there is a building-trades walkout or strike, the union organizers hope these workers will think twice about crossing their picket line.

The Building Trades Organizing Project in Las Vegas was one of the most important experiments in the U.S. labor movement's current attempt to recover from its moribund state. Within eight months, Rudasil claimed 2,800 new union members (and 255 new union contractors) in Las Vegas as a result of the project's efforts, as well as thirty-seven NLRB charges filed against employers—despite the entrenched resistance of groups like the Associated Builders and Contractors of Southern Nevada, who gave legal advice and moral support to members trying to resist the unions' tactics. At the end of 1998, B-TOP unions and non-union construction companies—notably Lewis Homes (the largest homebuilder in Las Vegas), two concrete companies, and the general contractor of a $92 million freeway interchange project—were still filing charges and countercharges against each other with the NLRB.

If B-TOP is ultimately successful, its success will resonate well beyond Clark County. It may mean that building-trades unions across the country are finally ready to shed some of their exclusivity, infighting, and white bias to embrace a new and broader kind of trade unionism.

■ ■ ■

Many things that happen in Las Vegas are hard to imagine happening anywhere else. The growth and style of this one-of-a-kind city are as curious as its location in the middle of an inhospitable desert. But the organizers, pickets, meetings, strategies, and war rooms that help to compose the Las Vegas labor movement *can* be replicated in cities elsewhere. The "New Labor" movement here may have been more successful than it has been elsewhere because of the unique nature of the gambling industry (which is both unusually rich and unusually eager to conciliate potential adversaries) and the astonishing economic and building boom it has fostered. But it was not growth alone that spurred the labor movement in Clark County. In fact, growth on this record scale could have allowed industry to drive the local labor movement into the ground.

Las Vegas was an activist union town long before the national labor movement took any notice of it. Back in the 1950s, Al Bramlet was able to assure the town's casino-hotel proprietors that he would supply them with good workers, and guarantee labor peace, if they would recognize Local 226. The owners, whether local families or their mobster friends from other cities, needed the stability of an eager and tranquil workforce, and (with a few exceptions) paid the price of unionization. This ability to galvanize a labor movement in the early stages of an economy, and to turn it quickly into part of the local establishment, remains part of the history and legacy of Las Vegas.

John Sweeney pumped $35 million into the 1996 U.S. Congressional elections as part of an AFL-CIO "education" campaign. His investment may have helped ensure a number of key Democratic victories; but the Republicans took over Congress even so. Considerable attention today is being paid to younger, more activist union leaders who have been winning local elections around the country. "Union Summer 1996" gave 1,200 college students and other young people a three-week experience of union organization in drives across the country. Major changes in the status of American trade unionism—in numbers, power, and nature—do seem to be taking place.

But there is no question that the AFL-CIO needs a major victory soon—a victory bigger than isolated campaigns among janitors in Los Angeles, health-care workers in San Diego, or policemen in Baltimore. It needs to come up with an American city—a whole city—that is once again proud of its own working-class and trade-union identity.

Las Vegas may be John Sweeney's best bet.

Pawnshops

LENDERS OF LAST RESORT
Joe Heim

Anthony Bock takes an enormous bite of his corned-beef-on-rye, pulls himself out of his chair, and begins speaking, unconcerned with the crumbs falling from his mouth and the piece of lettuce hanging from his chin.

"You're a journalist. Ask the questions. You ever interview a lawyer before?"

"You're a lawyer?"

Bock stares back at me for several seconds before answering. He is of average height and build, and his doughy white face is almost expressionless.

"Well, never took the bar, but, yeah, I'm a lawyer. Finished with law school. UNLV. But I started doing this full-time a couple of years ago and I happen to like the business. You got more questions?"

Bock's hair is dark brown, almost black, parted in the middle. His eyes are dark and narrow, and he has a habit of looking away when he is talking. He is standing behind the counter of John's Loans, a pawnshop on North Third Street in downtown Las Vegas. His grandfather, Irving Starr, opened the store in the early 1960s. Bock, 29, has now taken over as manager and part owner.

It is mid-December, and "Seasons Greetings" is spray-painted on the store's window in seasonal snowy white. A green Christmas tree has been freshly painted. Inside, the store itself is plain and dreary. Its off-white stucco walls are cracked and peeling, and the only decorations are a portrait of a sea captain smoking a pipe and a yellowing *Las Vegas Sun* article with the headline "You Can Bet on It: Pawnshops Abound." The grey carpeting is thin and worn, and there are water stains on the ceiling. A fluorescent bulb overhead can't decide whether it is on or off.

Gold chains, electronic equipment, necklaces, rings, and watches fill the glass cases lining either side of the store—items that customers have pawned and never returned to claim.

The store is empty, yet Bock is reluctant to talk about his clientele. He wants to preserve their anonymity, he says. When he finally does talk about them, he alternates between expressions of sympathy and barely disguised contempt.

"There is a tendency to laugh at people who are not in the best position in the world, but if you work here and you understand anything at all about lack of fortune, you realize this can happen to you."

A few minutes later he sounds less compassionate.

"I've seen people trying to pull stuff off all the time here. We have people coming in trying to tell us all sorts of stories, telling us how bad all of our stuff is or trying to get us to take all sorts of shit. You realize they don't know what the fuck they're talking about."

While Bock is discussing the pawn business, a slender, young black man enters the store. Bock undergoes a seemingly effortless transformation from tough-talking businessman to street-talking salesman.

"What's up, bro?" Bock calls out warmly.

"Nothing Tony, how you doing," the man responds. "I just came to pick up."

"You got the bracelet, right?" asks Bock as he scrolls down a computer screen. "...What's your name again?"

"Antoine."

"Right, right, Antoine. My man Antoine. I tell you what I'm going to do Antoine, I'm gonna give you a Christmas present. You see those colognes over there on the wall? Take your pick."

Antoine looks over to a small section of one of the display cases which contains seven or eight boxes of cologne.

"Yeah? Are you serious? Hey, that's all right, Tony. That's pretty cool. Merry Christmas."

"Well, we like to treat our customers right, Antoine. You're gonna come back, right?"

"I'm not going anywhere, Tony. You take pretty good care of me here."

Antoine redeems his pawn ticket and pays back his loan plus the 8 percent monthly interest. After he walks out of the shop, Bock sits down to finish his lunch.

"Like that guy who was just in here, I know I can trust. After a while you get to know if someone's bullshitting you. If they're B.S.-ing you, you don't play. You can't trust everybody."

Behind the counter, ancient-looking ledger books collect dust on a shelf. Empty coffee cups and paper wrappers are tossed on the floor. A few feet from the cash register, and out of view of the customers, a large handgun in a holster hangs from a peg.

"As a pawnbroker in this city you see people at their worst," continues Bock. "You see man at his darkest, because they don't have anything going. They are at their very end."

As Las Vegas Boulevard crosses Sahara Avenue heading north, the winks and hisses of the bright lights of the Strip give way to a dismal commercial stretch. Cheap motels, run-down strip joints, and dilapidated bars separate the check-cashing stores, quick-loan outfits, and pawnshops. Bleary-eyed drunks stumble on the sidewalk. An occasional panhandler approaches strangers asking for change. With signs promising instant credit and E-Z cash, the storefront windows offer the last flickering hopes to casino casualties. The pawnshops stand out like unwelcome reminders of the flip side of this gamblers' paradise.

In a block-and-a-half you pass Bobby's Jewelry and Loan ("The oldest pawn shop on the Strip"), the Hock Shop ("Want more money in your pocket? Hock it!"), and the Gold and Silver Pawn Shop ("We never close. 24 hours. 7 days a week"). Closer to downtown and just off Las Vegas Boulevard is Pawn Shop Plaza, home to Stoney's ("The prestige store") and John's Loans ("We Loan the Most"). A block away, across from Binion's Horseshoe Casino, is Pioneer Loan and Jewelry, a Vegas institution where owner Bill Drobkin boasts "Las Vegas is becoming famous for its pawnshops." Around the corner is Ace Loans; two blocks away, the prosaically named Pawn Place.

Heading into the city of North Las Vegas, the string of pawnshops along the boulevard continues with Bargain Pawn ("The Smart Way to Shop"), EZ Pawn, and Poor Richard's. A massive billboard for First Class Pawn and Jewelry tries to be clever: "Need Cash? Give Us A Ring." A picture of a diamond-solitaire engagement ring aids those too dense to get the joke.

The slogans might appear tacky or tasteless, but Las Vegas pawnbrokers, like pawnbrokers everywhere, will tell you that they are providing a service. Pawnshops, they maintain, have traditionally been the legal lender of last resort for customers whose checking and savings accounts have finally run dry, whose credit-card companies have spurned their requests for another advance, and whose relatives have rejected "I promise I'll get it right back to you" pleas for the last time.

Civic leaders in Las Vegas aren't crazy about the number of pawnshops located in popular areas frequented by high-rolling tourists. Ask about growth in Las Vegas and you will hear stories of the exploding gambling industry and the phenomenal rate of home and hotel construction it has created. You will hear how it has brought about new schools and hospitals, restaurants, freeways, laundromats, golf courses, gas stations. You will hear stories of a 24-hour city of a million people that is expanding in every direction.

But even though the number of pawnshops in Clark County has gone from less than a dozen ten years ago to forty-five today, you are unlikely to find a city or county official boasting of the role of pawn in Las Vegas's booming economy. No matter how much pawnbrokers object, their business is still seen as seedy and objectionable. Jan Jones, the mayor of Las Vegas, doesn't want tourists leaving town with the image of streets full of pawnshops floating in their heads. In a January 1997 article in the *Las Vegas Review Journal,* Jones was quoted as saying, "It is very possible that Las Vegas Boulevard's highest and best use is not pawn shops. The City may have to look for ways to both assist and relocate those into a district that meets the needs of their customers." In other words, get them out of here. One of the first casualties of the $70-million "Fremont Street Experience," a 1996 exercise in civic glitz designed to draw more tourists away from the Strip into Downtown hotels and casinos, were the many pawnshops that once lined Fremont and adjacent scruffy streets. The casino owners and civic officials who put up the money for the FSE decided that pawnshops didn't fit the new image they were after, although the nude Girls of Glitter Gulch were allowed to stay.

Long time Vegas pawnbrokers seethe when they encounter such attitudes from elected officials. "The city fathers are crazy," says Henry Kronberg, the seventy-seven-year-old pawnbroker who purchased the legendary Stoney's pawnshop in 1964. "They are not business people. It seems like the city thinks the pawnbrokers are undesirables. Our business is conducted in a professional manner. We are running a very clean operation. This is a legitimate business."

Perhaps no one in Las Vegas believes that more than Steve Mack. A fifth-generation pawnbroker whose family moved from Oakland to Reno when he was a year old, Mack has singlehandedly introduced a new face of pawn to Las Vegas and Clark County. Mack is president and CEO of the Las Vegas-based SuperPawn, the largest privately owned pawn chain in the west. The fifteen new stores he has opened in Clark County in the past five years are the local symbol of the industry's amazing growth nationally, and have established Mack as the reigning king of pawn in this desert resort.

Casually yet stylishly dressed, this affable thirty-eight-year-old with boyish looks is attempting to redefine the image of the pawnbroker with single-minded enthusiasm and the earnest style of a Rotarian entrepreneur. At SuperPawn headquarters, located a few blocks from the Strip's shimmering new casino hotels, Mack sits behind an enormous desk in a spacious and playfully decorated office: a twelve-foot motorized surfboard used in a James Bond film leans against one wall; an oversize golf bag with SUPERPAWN printed on its side in large block lettering rests in a corner. Mack talks sincerely and passionately about his vision for the pawn industry and about Las Vegas, his own ideal of American opportunity.

"There's an entrepreneur coming to Las Vegas every single minute of the day, and they are figuring out they can make a living here," says Mack. "This is a can-do place. And the business environment is a can-do thing in the sense that the imagination, the creativity, and the execution happen here. The business environment here is so progressive and so stimulating that it keeps people like myself interested in keeping the ball rolling. I've been doing this for almost twenty years. This place is a Disneyland for visionaries."

And what is Steve Mack's vision? He is eager to share.

"We've been able to redesign and create a business for the nineties that recognizes that our customers have been underserviced and misunderstood. Our company philosophy is that we're going to take advantage of that knowledge and give these people what they need and deserve. We're becoming what I call a specialty finance company. As the bigger banks consolidate they become less customer-oriented and the costs of their services become prohibitive to some people. Others just don't want to deal with a depersonalized banking setup. So our company has been strategizing expansion through check cashing, Western Union, money wire transfers, foreign exchange, and, of course, pawn services, which we're very good at. Now we're also getting into selling life insurance, auto insurance, and annuities."

In other words, SuperPawn is becoming a one-stop financial center for low- and moderate-income customers. But that's not the only aspect of

Mack's vision. While most pawnshops don't like having to deal with the retail end of their business, Mack has made it the key component of SuperPawn's success. Mack says that retail sales account for 70 percent of SuperPawn's profits, and he sees his stores eventually competing with major "new merchandise" retailers. Sometimes that means having to buy new merchandise just to have items available to sell. "We want people to come into our stores to buy," says Mack. "If they come in and we don't have merchandise, we have an inventory problem. So we'll buy overruns and other items just to have the merchandise that makes it possible for us to compete with places like WalMart and Circuit City."

Mack says he is not really interested in having his stores serve the needs of tourists and gamblers in Las Vegas. In fact, he estimates that only 5 percent of his customers are out-of-towners. Increasingly, other pawnshops in Las Vegas are following Mack's lead and moving away from the Strip and Downtown, turning up in new lower- and middle-class residential communities that have sprung up to house the area's burgeoning population. Pawnbrokers are focusing on the resort community's permanent population rather than on gambling tourists hocking a wedding ring for a last gasp bet on the craps table.

In addition to the SuperPawns that have opened on West Cheyenne and South Decatur, North Nellis and East Charleston, The Pawn Place has added stores on West Charleston, on Tam Drive, and in Green Valley, to the south. Sahara Pawn has opened on South Jones Boulevard, and First Class Pawn (owned by Michael Mack, Steve's younger brother) on Rancho Drive.

Although the famous old pawnshops still operate Downtown and on the Strip, and well-known places like Desert Inn Pawn and Cash-4-U carry on elsewhere, Steve Mack's stores now dominate the pawn landscape in Vegas. His bright teal and gold buildings with teal and gold signs are distinctive even in a city famed for its visual excess. In front of the stores, yellow, white, and teal balloons flutter in the breeze above signs announcing a 20-percent sale on diamonds. Inside, the sales floors are different from the haphazard, often junky arrangements typical of many old-fashioned shops. Department store-type signs designate each section of the immaculate, brightly lighted stores. Salespeople, polite and smartly dressed (all the men wear white shirts and ties), greet customers at the door. "Anything I can do for you today, sir? Just looking? Okay, well, let me know if you need anything. We're having some great sales." Dividers at the sales counter offer customers privacy as they negotiate loans with sales clerks, trying to get at least twenty dollars more for their "almost brand-new TV set."

With a total of twenty-seven stores in Nevada and Arizona, 300 employees, and plans for major expansion in the next three years, Mack's SuperPawn vision has grown into one of the ten largest pawn chains in the country. Cash America, with 300 stores, and EZ Pawn, with 250, both publicly traded companies, are the nation's biggest chains. If the growth of SuperPawn continues on schedule, Mack concedes that the possibility of taking his company public will be actively considered.

Ask locals and experts what has spurred the rapid increase in pawn shops and you get several answers. Some tell you that when Clark County introduced legislation in 1991 that relaxed restrictions on new outlets, pawnbrokers jumped at the opportunity to open new branches. Others cite the county's huge population growth. Almost everyone mentions Steve Mack. But the major causes for the upsurge in Las Vegas are the same ones that lie behind the remarkable growth in the pawn industry nationwide over the past decade.

■ ■ ■

The existence of pawn chains may come as a surprise to people familiar only with small, family-owned pawnshops in run-down parts of town, but chain stores have played a major role in the recent growth of the industry. The number of new pawnshops in the United States increased by an average of 10 percent a year between 1988 and 1995, with much of the growth occurring in the southern, southwestern, and mountain states. The total number of shops grew from eight thousand in 1988 to nearly sixteen thousand in 1996.

Mack relates an anecdote to show just how fast pawn shops have grown in certain areas. "I have a store in Atlanta, Georgia. I opened it four years ago. When I went there, the state of Georgia had a hundred and eight pawn shops, which is quite a few. I felt Atlanta was a fantastic city, more liberal, and had great opportunity for people of all races and colors. It was a high-interest-rate environment [referring to the rates that shops are allowed to charge customers], and I had to prove that my stores could work outside of the gaming market. I felt I had to do that because there are people who, when I'm trying to tell the story of Super-Pawn and get financing, just say 'Yeah, it's a great idea here in Nevada, but where else is a pawnshop going to work any better?' I just knew my concept would work somewhere else, not just in a gaming state, so I took it to Atlanta.

"Now, four years later, there are sixteen hundred pawnshops in Georgia. The state legislature there is committed to reducing the number of shops and trying to reregulate, but it gives you an indication of how quickly everything took off. Even though having so many stores eroded our opportunity, we still did very well there. And we were able to tell our story successfully."

In his 1994 book *Fringe Banking: Check Cashing Outlets, Pawnshops, and the Poor*, Swarthmore College economist John Caskey argues that the boom in the number of pawnshops and resultant usage is due in large part to the increase in the number of American households without bank accounts.

Among all low- and moderate-income families, writes Caskey, "the percentage without bank accounts of any type rose from 9.5 percent in 1977 to 13.5 percent in 1989. However, for families with less than $11,970 in income, about 20 percent of the population, the percentage of families without bank accounts rose from 30 percent in 1977 to 41 percent in 1989." Caskey asserts that as banks have increased fees on small accounts, they have become less accessible for low- and moderate-income families, so pawnshops and check-cashing outlets have become the principal lenders for 10 percent of American households.

"What I've become more and more convinced of is that the biggest barrier for most people is not physical access to a bank, but financial access," says Caskey today. "These are people living paycheck to paycheck, and they have no savings. They don't have bank accounts, because at the end of the month their account would be zero, and banks won't let you keep an account like that. People living from paycheck to paycheck have no financial margin of safety. They're juggling bills, and any little interruption or unexpected expense can interfere with their ability to pay bills or rent on time. As a result, they end up with bad credit records."

Another important factor for the increase in pawnshop use, Caskey believes, is that the incomes of working-class households have stagnated or declined.

"There are lots of reasons why people have no savings. If you're a single woman with two kids and you're making sixteen thousand dollars a year, it's just extremely difficult to build up savings," says Caskey. "It's also true that if you're single and living in Vegas and make twenty two thousand dollars a year, it's not difficult to spend all of that and not live that high. You might have a car and an apartment and just have no savings. As a consequence of that, you may have a credit card that may quickly be at the max, and at some point you start missing payments. You get a bad credit record, you need to borrow money. You go to a pawn shop."

■ ■ ■

Pawn is one of the oldest and most basic of financial transactions. A customer presents an item to a pawnbroker as collateral on a loan. The customer then has a fixed period of time in which to repay the loan, plus interest, or forfeit the item. The amount of the loan is usually between 10 and 50 percent of what the broker believes he can sell the merchandise for, should the customer not return to claim it. In Nevada, the maximum interest rate a pawn broker can charge is 10 percent a month (or 120 percent a year). The customer has 120 days in which to repay the loan before the pawned item becomes the property of the broker.

Most pawnbrokers will allow customers who can't afford to pay off the entire loan to pay simply the accrued interest after 120 days, and renew the loan at the same rate. If a customer pawns a diamond ring with a value of $500, the pawnbroker might offer her $100. After 120 days, she would have to pay $140, plus a $5 handling fee, to get her ring back. If she chooses only to pay the $40 interest, the customer would then be given another four months before she would lose possession permanently. Over the course of a year, the interest she would have paid on the $100 loan would be $120, plus the five-dollar handling fee.

Pawnbrokers insist that they need to charge high interest rates if they are to survive, but customers and critics often decry these rates as usurious. In some states, such as Florida, Georgia, Texas, and Hawaii, pawnbrokers are allowed to charge customers from 240 to 300 percent interest a year.

While no states ban pawnshops outright, many states have effectively kept their numbers down by strictly regulating them and the interest rates they can charge. In New Jersey, for example, pawnshops are allowed to charge only 3 percent interest a month, or 36 percent a year; the state has only thirteen pawnshops.

"We don't really know what hardships that creates," says Caskey. "Are people better off when pawnshops are abundant but expensive, or when pawnshops are scarce but relatively cheap? I can't answer that question."

As the pawn industry grows and gains power, state legislatures are lobbied to reconsider their rate ceilings. In 1992, when the maximum interest rate pawnbrokers could charge in Indiana was, as in New Jersey, 36 percent a year, the state had thirty-eight pawnshops. That same year Indiana passed a new law allowing pawnshops to charge customers as much as 276 percent a year. Within six months the number of pawnshops had doubled; in 1997 the state had more than 100.

With its 10-percent-a-month interest ceiling, Nevada actually ranks near the middle of states in rates that pawnbrokers are allowed to charge.

Until 1993, the maximum rate in Nevada was 6 percent; in that year, the Nevada Collateral Loan Association, the pawnbroker's lobby, founded by Mack in 1981, successfully pushed a law through the state legislature which raised it to 8 percent. Pressure for a second increase led to the legislature's approval of a 10-percent rate in 1997.

Whatever rationale the pawnbrokers provide for their interest rates, negative perceptions of their profession persist. The image of pawnbrokers as Shylocks, as greedy money-grubbers preying on the poor, permeates nearly every cultural or historical depiction. In *The Pawnbroker*, a 1965 film directed by Sidney Lumet, the title character, portrayed by actor Rod Steiger, is a pitiless businessman who reviles his customers, treating them with contempt while (as another character puts it) "sucking away their life's treasures in exchange for a dollar or two." Shot in black and white, the pawnshop in the film is a gloomy labyrinth of shelves and cages, and Steiger a prisoner of its darkness. "There's a pretty good portion of people with negative images of pawnshops, and the Rod Steiger movie was very effective in creating that," says Steve Mack, who believes that changing this image is one of the greatest challenges he faces.

"I've been quoted many times saying that we're the second-oldest profession in the world, with the reputation of the first," says Bob Stogner, chairman of the National Association of Pawnbrokers. "Of course, we got that reputation unjustly. But still we do have the reputation of raping the public."

Stogner's group has made improving the way Americans view their industry its number-one goal. Las Vegas pawnbrokers agree that their image is in need of an overhaul. "I say I own a pawnshop and everybody gets quiet. It's like I'm on crack or something," said Bill Drobkin, who, with his wife, Erminia, owns Pioneer Loan and Jewelry. Another Las Vegas pawnshop owner is even more direct: "A lot of people have got that New York Jew-mentality image of pawnbrokers, and that's the image we're trying to get rid of," he said. George Bramlett, owner of Bargain Pawn, voices another common pawnbrokers' refrain. "People charge a thousand dollars on their credit card and they think nothing of it," he said. "Here they come in to borrow a hundred dollars and somehow they feel bad just because they're in a pawnshop." No matter how hard the industry tries to improve its image, many people continue to view pawnshops as either dismal last refuges for the down and out or, worse, semi-criminal fencing dumps for burglars and muggers.

■ ■ ■

Pawnbrokers argue that the days when their shops took stolen goods are long gone, and are quick with statistics "proving" that only a small percentage of stolen goods ever finds its way into pawnshops. Most brokers parrot an industry line that only "one-tenth of one percent" of the goods found in a pawn shop are stolen. According to Stogner, however, "statistics show that we get less than one-tenth of one percent *of the stolen merchandise* in the country." The wording is only slightly different, but the potential difference in the quantity of stolen goods handled is enormous.

Pawnbrokers contend that they are one of the most strictly regulated industries in the country, and thus have little chance to traffic in stolen goods. The police department in almost every major American city has a pawn unit. Marjorie Love, supervisor of the ten-person pawn detail of the Las Vegas Metropolitan Police Department, says that "pawnshops are a necessary evil," but she has nothing but praise for the pawnbrokers she works with. "We get one hundred percent cooperation from our pawn shops," she insists, in tracing stolen property.

■ ■ ■

"I don't dial 911. I dial .357," reads a sign behind the counter of the Hock Shop on North Las Vegas Boulevard. While pawnbrokers deny that they knowingly sell stolen merchandise, crime remains a topic of conversation. With so much cash and jewelry on hand, pawnshops are a natural target for holdups. While they have insurance coverage, many proprietors have adopted their own get-tough approach to crime in their stores. It is a rare pawnshop where workers are not armed with at least a handgun, usually holstered and strapped to their waist.

No Las Vegas pawnbroker is as prepared to deal with crime as George Bramlett, whose Bargain Pawn shop was broken into twice before he moved into his present location, a building he designed with security in mind. The outside of the building is guarded by waist-high, concrete-filled metal poles to protect Bartlett from the latest fashion in burglary: thieves wait until the stores are closed and drive stolen vehicles through windows or doorways. They then grab as many valuables as quickly as possible and make off with the loot before police respond.

Having foiled would-be smash-and-grab artists, Bramlett concentrated next on holdups that take place while the store was open. On a recent visit, Bramlett led me into his second-floor office, from which he can keep an eye on the his entire sales floor below, from behind a two-way mirror window. A rack of more than a dozen rifles, shotguns, and semi-automatic weapons stands next to Bramlett's desk. Bramlett pulled a shotgun off of the rack and pointed to a 4 by 6-inch opening in the wall at floor level. "If we ever have a hostage situation inside the store, I can just pick up this shotgun, which I've got loaded with a soft lead bullet so it won't spray all over, lie down on the floor, take aim and fire. That bullet will pretty much blow someone's head off."

When it comes to security issues, Steve Mack takes a different approach from that of many traditional pawnshop owners. He shakes his head solemnly when the subject comes up. "It really sickens me to have to worry about my employees going through such a traumatic experience. We're sensitive to the opportunity of that happening and we take precautions. When you walk into our store we have twenty-four hour camera surveillance, but we don't allow our people to wear firearms and we don't have armed guards in any of our stores. I fear for my employees' safety, but I still want to create a friendly environment for my customers. I don't want them thinking that they are walking into a place that is any different than any retailer."

Mack also recently decided that SuperPawn would no longer sell guns in its stores, even though guns are staples at most pawnshops. "I just didn't feel selling firearms was part of our social nature," said Mack. But the moral voice was not the only one that Mack was listening to when he decided to change his policy. "That decision is going to help us develop and open our stores in what we call nontraditional pawnshop locations."

By nontraditional pawnshop locations, Mack means parts of town that are not run-down or economically depressed. People living in poverty may occasionally use pawnshops, but, according to Mack, "the real story is that those aren't our customers. You need to take out the word 'destitute' to describe a customer coming into a pawnshop. They're not destitute; they just don't have any money today. Maybe they're getting their paycheck on Friday and they don't have any money on Wednesday. They need to go buy brand-new tires for their car and they don't have a credit card. So they use their TV or stereo or a pocket watch to borrow a hundred bucks so they can do that and come back in forty days and pay us sixteen bucks. [The rate when we talked was 8 percent a month.] And ninety-two percent of them do come back, so pawning simply gets them through this tough time. If everyone was destitute they wouldn't be borrowing; they'd be selling to get more money."

Mack can make his vision for SuperPawn sound like part of a social-reform movement. "I really believe in what I'm doing and I think there's a real philosophical commitment to do something good for our customers," he says. "Fortunately it's not all motivated by creating a lot of wealth for myself. If you could see some of the testimonials, the customers are so overwhelmed by how they're treated and the environment they go into. It makes everyone around here feel really good about what we're doing."

■ ■ ■

Besides the old charges of usury and fencing, Las Vegas pawn shops have another image they would like to disown: they are often seen as overpriced banks for gamblers. Some pawnbrokers insist that gamblers make up only a small percentage of their customers. Location is obviously relevant here; Kronberg guesses that up to 50 percent of his customers pawn possessions in order to continue gambling. Players can make last-chance bets by giving up valuables, from a watch or a wedding ring to gold teeth and even cars. "Need Money Fast? Call Auto Pawn." Parachutes and rodeo saddles are among the items Las Vegas pawnbrokers recall crossing their counters. At Bargain Pawn, two human skulls (presumably from a medical school, though one never knows) are proudly displayed by owner George Bramlett as "trophies" in a glass case in his office.

The value of items pawned by gamblers varies widely. At John's Loans, Bock routinely makes small loans of ten or fifteen dollars. At the other extreme, Bill and Erminia Drobkin remember offering a $150,000 loan on jewelry worth over $600,000 to a man who was losing badly on the poker tables at Binion's Horseshoe, across the street. Several hours after receiving the loan, the man returned to let the Drobkins know that he had lost that money as well.

Every Las Vegas pawnbroker can tell riches-to-rags or rags-to-riches stories about casino habitués. "As a pawnbroker, you hear so many horror stories, especially in this town—because of the gaming," said Bill Drobkin. "This is a different town. This is not Miami, friend. This is not Chicago. This is Vegas." Carole O'Hare, executive director of the Nevada Council on Problem Gambling and a recovering problem gambler herself, says she is grateful she never reached the point where she had to resort to pawning. "The idea of pawnshops is frightening," she says. "It's almost like selling yourself for the sake of your gambling."

For John Caskey, the tremendous growth in the number of pawnshops nationwide raises serious issues about the American economy, particularly as it relates to working-class and low-income families. He talks about possible solutions—consumer-education groups, low-income credit unions, more effective ways to help people salvage their credit records, increases in the minimum wage. But none of these, he acknowledges, will "help the person who is truly poor and just can't maintain savings." In the meantime, he concedes, "There's no political pressure to change the way pawnshops operate. The people who use them aren't organized, and they don't have a political voice."

Caskey's attitude toward pawnshops reflects an ambivalence shared by many who are familiar with the industry. "On the one hand, I think there's a real problem," he says. "You have here a lot of moderate- and low-income people paying extremely high fees for basic financial services. That lowers the quality of life for families in real need. On the other hand, I don't think you can just ban pawnshops. They are filling a need."

■ ■ ■

John Jones isn't destitute, but he is poor. In many ways, he is a typical customer of a Las Vegas pawnshop. Jones, 35, moved to Las Vegas from San Diego two years ago in search of a job. He lives with his wife and son in a $450-a-month apartment in the shadow of the Stratosphere, the landmark (and, incidentally, bankrupt) tower with an unobstructed view of the seemingly endless ocean of sand and rock that surrounds Las Vegas. With his dark, tired eyes, longish mustache, and pale, thin face, Jones looks like a man who has seen hard times. He is neatly but simply dressed in a black baseball cap, a knit shirt tucked into blue jeans, and hightops. A furniture deliverer, Jones doesn't have a bank account. "Well, I just don't make that kind of money yet. Don't really have the finances to open an account. I'm still trying to move my way up at work." He says that he has only pawned his personal property once before: several months earlier, he pawned a hundred-dollar camera for a ten-dollar loan. Three weeks later he paid nearly twenty dollars to get it back. (In addition to interest, shops may charge a "transaction" fee.)

Standing in line at a SuperPawn on St. Louis Avenue holding an old, beat-up VCR in his hands, Jones tells me that he is hoping to get a fifteen dollar loan for it because his family "had just run short of groceries and my paycheck's not coming until the first of the month." It is Good Friday, and Jones wants to be sure that he'll be able to put food on the table for Easter dinner. He has brought the VCR to pawn because it is the only real item of value in his apartment and "Anyway, I guess we don't rent too many movies these days."

Jones approaches the counter where signs cheerfully remind customers of pawn and loan options. "Ask about auto-title loans. You get the cash. And still keep your car!" Other signs encourage customers not to pay off their entire loan but simply the interest due. "Don't Pick it Up! Keep Your Cash! Renew It!"

The clerk is polite but firm. She can't provide a loan because the VCR is more than five years old. "I'm sorry, we just can't offer you anything for it." Outside, Jones is discouraged but not bitter. Walking away with his VCR in his arms, Jones stops momentarily, turns to me, and says quietly, "You know, nobody really wants to pawn something, but sometimes you're just short on cash."

Skin City

Maia Hansen

As you drive into Las Vegas from the airport or the edges of town, it's hard to miss the army of billboards that confronts you along every major road. Giant, garish images and verbal invitations promise free slots and cheap buffets, while larger-than-life lines of dancers grin from static poses above the freeways. Casino showrooms offer beautiful, near-naked showgirls in "Splash II" at the Riviera, "Enter the Night" at the Stardust, and "Folies Bergère" at the Tropicana. Showing a surplus of cleavage fore and aft, these dancers perform to sold-out houses where customers have paid up to fifty dollars a ticket. On a slightly smaller scale, the advertisement for another popular show called "Crazy Girls" is displayed on the sides and backs of taxis and shuttle buses (in addition to numerous billboards); it sports a row of bare female bottoms with the caption "No ifs, ands, or BUTTS."

But the more serious skin shows lie off the Strip, out of view of most family tourists. Once you arrive in the city itself, a new array of smaller signs touts the town's nude and topless clubs. Along with its fame as the country's gambling capital, Las Vegas's reputation as a sex bazaar has long been a key part of the city's identity, however much local residents and city officials deny or ignore it. You can even purchase a guide to commercial sex in Las Vegas—where to find it, what to expect, and how much to pay. The University of Nevada at Las Vegas offers a course on "The Sociology of the Sex Industry." Deke Castleman, managing editor of the *Las Vegas Advisor*, has written a futuristic novel in which sex takes over as the city's main attraction and economic foundation. Some people have reckoned that, in time, the loosely defined "sex industry" in southern Nevada may actually overtake the gambling industry in revenue.

Although sex and gambling may be linked in the public image of Las Vegas as the two most common forms of commercial "sin" available here, some industry insiders consider the two to be in competition. After all, time and money spent in sex clubs and on other forms of "adult entertainment" is time and money that could otherwise be spent on gambling.

Most of the city's sexually oriented businesses—nude and topless clubs, adult video, book and novelty stores—are located off the Strip, but near enough that interested tourists can easily find them. Several of these establishments line Las Vegas Boulevard North, on the extension of the Strip that lies between the resort-hotel zone and Downtown. More are strung out along Industrial Road and Western Avenue, northwest of and parallel to Las Vegas Boulevard South.

Recent efforts by Clark County and the Nevada Resort Association (the casino-hotel owners' lobbying group) to "clean up" the Strip have led to the periodic removal of visible smut, and prompted hookers to advertise their wares through outcall agencies rather than in person. Until the city passed an ordinance in 1997 forbidding their distribution, leaflets and flyers advertising more than two hundred licensed "outcall entertainment services"—i.e., room-service "dancers"—were thrust at pedestrians walking down the Strip, by immigrant workers earning five dollars an hour. Filled with full-color photos of naked women (their nipples and crotches covered with colored stars and hearts), the brochures are now available in free distribution boxes on the sidewalks.

The agencies that publish the brochures advertise "private dancers" who will perform nude in your hotel room, or for bachelor parties or banquets. Thumbing through the Yellow Pages of the Las Vegas phone book, you will find more than 100 pages of full-color ads for these "Adult Entertainers," most of whom are under contract to agencies run by a handful of owners. One outcall agency was reported to have spent $50,000 a month on its phone-book ads alone. Protesting the 1997 ban on flyer distribution as a violation of its rights to free speech, another agency owner was quoted in a Las Vegas newspaper as saying that his agency had served over 33,000 customers in the last year.

The twenty-four-person Las Vegas Metro Police vice squad calls the majority of outcall agencies fronts for prostitution. Through a series of sting operations, the police have arrested over six hundred "adult entertainers" connected to outcall agencies for soliciting prostitution in the past six years. Lieutenant Carlos Cordiero says that the vice squad is unable to make arrests when girls (as sex workers universally call one another) catch on to the fact that they are dealing with cops, and leave the room before any actual offer takes place.

The agencies themselves cannot be held liable, since they oblige the girls to work as independent contractors. An agency gets $100 to $125 for each girl it sends out, and insists that whatever services she might offer "other than dancing" are her business, not theirs. Police have also arrested high-end call girls—not listed in free flyers or the Yellow Pages—who charge their clients as much as $3,000-$4,000 for their services. But sting operations are costly and time-consuming, and in recent years the vice squad has concentrated on the more troubling issues of underground child pornography and prostitution. (Sixty-eight juvenile prostitutes were arrested in Clark County in 1996, compared to twenty-seven the year before.)

So even though casino executives and other city-proud Las Vegans will remind you that prostitution is illegal in Clark County (unlike most other counties in Nevada), and will point out that the once-ubiquitous street-walkers have been swept off the Strip, prostitution remains a major industry in the city.

The city is currently trying to tone down its image as a sex haven in order to improve its status as a "family destination." Arcades full of children's games, mini-theme parks, and water rides for kids are supposed to be taking the place of Folies Bergère showgirls and cocktail waitresses wearing thonged leotards. A security guard at Wild J's, a topless club, shakes his head in dismay. "This city was built on greed, sex, and gambling. Now they want to take away all the good stuff! They should leave us alone."

■ ■ ■

One thing you won't see on Las Vegas billboards or in street brochures is an ad for any of Nevada's thirty-four legal brothels, three of which lie fifty miles west of the city in the town of Pahrump. It's illegal even to advertise prostitution within Clark County, for although the brothels are only an hour's drive or cab ride away, Las Vegas would rather its visitors spent their time and money in town. Yet the number-one industry in Pahrump depends for its survival on the number-one industry in Las Vegas, and the millions of tourists it attracts to southern Nevada each year.

■ ■ ■

Bill's limo is a black stretch with tinted rear windows and personalized license plates: "4 YR PLSR" in the front, "ITS 4 PLSR" in the back. The sunroof is broken however, the result of a recent bachelorette party. Seven women had been standing up through the sunroof flashing their breasts to passersby on The Strip, he tells me, when one of them slammed into the edge and jammed the window open. It is now permanently closed, but that hasn't seemed to affect business.

The business cards Bill passes out to people who just want rides around town simply say "Limousine Service." But the ones he leaves in plastic card-holders at the topless and nude dance clubs around town are bordered by drawings of women draped in loose togas, each with one breast exposed. The cards advertise service between the clubs, and outings to Pahrump brothels for a round-trip fare of $100. Bill also maintains a Web site (called "Cathouse Limo") on the Internet.

"I'm old and fat," Bill says. "I don't want to deal with other aggravations in life. This is an easy way for me to make a living. My main objective is to take men from Vegas to the ranches to get laid." But as often as he shuttles customers to and from the ranches, Bill chauffeurs the young prostitutes who work there to and from the city, the airport, the shopping mall, and the STD clinic for their monthly AIDS checkups. He also chauffeurs many of the porn stars who fly into Las Vegas to do special feature promotions at the local dance clubs.

A heavyset man in his mid-sixties, Bill has a soft, warm smile and a jovial manner. With whitening hair receding from a ruddy, round face and one eye that doesn't fully open, he could be anyone's father, even grandfather. And for many of Las Vegas's working girls, Bill is the only father they know.

"They need somebody to take care of them," says Bill. "A lot of these girls never got that sort of attention, either growing up or from their boyfriends." Leery of the "boyfriends" who hang out in parking lots waiting to pick up the dancers when they get off their shifts, Bill says that most of the ones he's met don't have jobs themselves. He thinks they're no better than pimps.

A resident of the Las Vegas area for thirty-seven years, Bill has done his share of work in both of the city's major industries. He's dealt blackjack and poker and tended bar in the casinos; he also used to tend bar at Sheri's Ranch, one of the brothels in Pahrump. "If you're gonna live here," he says, "you've got to work in the Industry. I tell ya, it's hard to hear about the recession when there's so much money being thrown around this town...."

He points to the multifaceted, $460 million New York New York casino-hotel as a vivid example of the city's surplus wealth.

Bill raised three children here, and lost two of them here as well. Two years ago, his twenty-six-year-old daughter was strangled to death by her second husband, who is now in prison. Bill's three grandchildren are being raised by his daughter's first husband (their father) and his parents. Last December his son, who was "in a bit of trouble with the law," died of a gunshot wound. The police told Bill that his son killed himself when a SWAT team cornered him in a hotel room, but he doesn't believe that. "I'm an old man. They're the ones who should be burying me," he says sadly. "I shouldn't be burying them."

Bill is heading out on one of his regular runs to pick up some girls just ending their three-week work shift and going home for a week off. "Home" for each one is somewhere outside Nevada. He says the girls prefer to ride with him than in a cab because they know him, and he treats them with respect. "Most of these girls have a very low self-esteem. I always tell them they're worth something. I say, 'You'll be okay, there is a niche for you somewhere. I know you're just doing this temporarily.'"

A short way down Interstate 15, he leaves the highway at Exit 33, an inconspicuous off-ramp that leads toward the high desert via State Route 160. After about half an hour, a mileage sign to Pahrump and Death Valley appears, followed by another sign offering firewood for sale.

We encounter little oncoming traffic as the road winds steadily through the hills, then straightens into a long, arrow-like track paralleled by power lines and telephone poles. "This road has killed a lot of people," says Bill. "They fall asleep at night. The road is so narrow, when they wake up and try to overcorrect their turn, they end up flipping the car right over." The Nevada Highway Patrol recorded 264 accidents on the road in 1996 alone.

Bill is used to the journey since he does it several times a week, sometimes several times in one day. He drives with a continuously replenished six-pack of Diet Coke within reach on the floor of the passenger seat. Bill says his limousine service gives clients the opportunity to sleep on the long, curved seat in the back on their way to a brothel, or to drink and party with their friends—and, in either case, leave the worry of driving to him.

On the outskirts of Pahrump, we drive down some dusty backroads past littered lots full of tumbleweeds and broken-down, rusted-out cars. Tattered-looking mobile homes and small shacks give way to huge, lush green fields of the Valley Sod and Turf Farm. Soon after, the road dead ends at Sheri's Ranch. Chicken Ranch—the second of Pahrump's three legal brothels—is next door.

According to George Flint, head of the Nevada Brothel Association, Chicken Ranch is the most profitable brothel in the state, followed by Mustang Ranch and Mustang II, near Reno. Although the number of working girls varies from season to season—and owners are uncomfortable discussing income and profits—the Pahrump brothels employ between ten and twenty girls each, and pay quarterly license fees of $7,500. Their combined fees subsidize the Nye County Health and Welfare budgets.

■ ■ ■

"She'll probably yell at me 'cause I'm early," mutters Bill, referring to Sheri's manager. The one-story, ranch-style house is inconspicuous except for some short, white Greek columns planted haphazardly around the driveway in front. At the driveway entrance, a solitary post supports a spinning red light, a reminder of the red-light districts of the past. A sign reads "Valley Inn Cocktails," and a banner over the door promises "Girls, Girls, Girls!" Both announcements look out of place in the stark light of morning and these quiet, pastoral surroundings.

Bill and I walk through the back door and down a windowless, carpeted hallway with seventies-style wood-paneled walls to the lobby. A large room with a full bar faces the front door, its floor tinted by a red-neon Budweiser sign in one of the front windows and a Bud Light sign in the other. Shadowed by a broad fan, a pool table occupies one corner of the room. On the other side of the door, a glass display case holds souvenir merchandise—colored caps (including one in army-camouflage greens), T-shirts, and coffee mugs, all imprinted with the Sheri's Ranch logo—and palm-size "menus" listing some of the services the girls offer, though not their prices; clients can select such items as a "fantasy" package, an "extended stay," or a "half and half" (combination intercourse and blowjob).

Next to the display case stand a cigarette machine and a jukebox offering songs by Olivia Newton-John, Neil Diamond, Lionel Ritchie, Cher, and Julio Iglesias. Behind them, a sign in big, bold letters invites customers to "Use Your ATM Card!" The Visa and MasterCard logos are imprinted below; alternate business names, I learned, show up discreetly on customers' credit-card bills.

It's now a little past 9:30 AM, early for Sheri's girls to be up and about, but the three on leave are ready to go. Their pink and flowered luggage completely fills the large trunk, and they sit in the roomy back. Just down the street, Bill stops at a convenience store so they can pick up a six-pack of beer and some munchies. One of the girls returns with a handful of small, porcelain-faced dolls clothed in colorful, baggy clown suits and gives one to everyone in the car, including me. Having had a good month, she was apparently feeling generous. Bill leans over and whispers, "I'll betcha each of those girls is carrying close to eight thousand dollars—cash."

On the road again, back-seat talk turns to a coworker who had tested positive for something and hadn't returned to work that month. Before starting a new shift, and once a week thereafter, all legal prostitutes in Nevada are checked for chlamydia and gonorrhea, and they're checked once a month for AIDS and syphilis. At the beginning of a shift, they must spend two days in the brothel without working, waiting for their AIDS test results. All legal prostitutes are required by Nevada law to use latex condoms, and they do: their health, as well as their jobs, depends on it. Since 1984, when regular AIDS testing began, no cases of HIV have turned up within Nevada's legal brothel industry, a fact George Flint cites in defense of the institution.

The girls' conversation shifts to a discussion of last month's customers, and Nicky complains that so many guys had asked for her as "the one who looks like Michele Pfeiffer" that she's considered changing her name. She is thirty-two years old, married, and has two children aged fifteen and eighteen waiting for her at home in Oklahoma. (Her husband is their stepfather.) She started working in the sex industry when she was fourteen.

"I made some mistakes, but I took care of my responsibilities," she says, referring to her kids. She spent ten years working as a dancer for entertainment agencies in Las Vegas, doing conventions, banquets, and private parties before she and her husband "got sick of Vegas" and moved back to Oklahoma. She returned to Nevada to take a job at Sheri's, and now commutes the eight hours home by bus every month because she hates to fly. "In Las Vegas, you don't know what you're getting into. It's lots safer and better working in Pahrump," she says.

Sarah, sitting next to her, nods in agreement. She is in her early twenties, and has straight, shoulder-length brown hair. A slight gap between her two front teeth gives her a mischievous smile, and large breasts push the bottom of her short white T-shirt away from her slightly exposed tummy. Bill confides that she has just gotten "a new set."

As we enter the city, we stop at a light next to an attractive young couple. The other girls tease Sarah that the man is eyeing her through their open window. "Flash 'em, Sarah, flash em!" challenges Sammy, a short, bleached blonde with kinky hair, a slightly upturned nose, and a loud voice.

"Should I?" Sarah asks, her eyebrows raised and her hands wavering at the bottom edge of her shirt. Giggling, they try to make eye contact with the man to see if he is still watching. "Go on, do it!" they urge. But the light turns green and the car pulls away.

"Shit, if I had boobs like that, I'd have flashed 'em," says Nicky.

After coaxing Bill to pull over at a 7-11 so they can buy another six-pack of beer, the girls prance up to the door and allow a young black man to hold it open for them. They get a visible kick out of the stares drawn by the limousine, and when they get back in the car they are laughing uncontrollably.

"Did you hear what that guy said?" asks Nicky, peering out the back window. "He said, 'I'm sorry I don't have no red carpet for you ladies, but you sure deserve one!'"

Sammy seems the most excited to be getting out of Pahrump. A friend of hers is meeting her in the city tonight, and she's not coming back for two weeks.

"Two weeks?!" says Bill. "But you're a blonde. They need you!"

"Naw, they've still got a couple of blondes," she replies, unaffected. But before Bill drops them off at their hotel, she leans over the front seat with a serious look on her face. "Bill, watch out for me tonight. Just keep an eye on me, okay?" she asks him in a low voice, handing him a card with some writing on the back. "This is where I'm staying, and this is my room number. That's the room number of my friend."

Bill nods, takes the card and slips it into a breast pocket inside his jacket. "Okay honey, I'll watch out for you," he says softly without turning around, keeping his eyes focused on the road in front of him.

■ ■ ■

On her first day off in six weeks, a hot and sunny Monday, Amy sits in a motel room with the curtains drawn and the television on. After anxiously peeking out the window a few times and pacing around the room in bare feet, she alights on the arm of the couch and picks up the phone.

"Where *is* he?" she asks, dialing Bill's number and replacing the receiver when his voice mail picks up. She is expecting his limo in the parking lot, ready to take her shopping for some new clothes at one of Las Vegas's many malls. After driving her around to several hotels in search of a vacant room, Bill had dropped Amy off at this motel so she could get a few hours of rest first. "It's not so bad for eighty dollars," she says, looking around at the beige-toned unit, with its queen-size bed and kitchenette. Amy pays $35 a night for room and board at the brothel where she works, but she says this place is much larger and quieter. And no one has knocked on the door since she arrived.

Most brothels charge working prostitutes a daily rent of $25-35, which includes a cooked breakfast and dinner, and food to make their own lunch. But at one house where Amy used to work, the owner charged extra for all the food ("like four dollars for a baked potato!") and made the girls buy all of their work outfits from his pre-selected wardrobe. He also charged exorbitant prices for their daily necessities, from soap and condoms to panty hose.

"He thrives on the game of manipulation," she says, and stole money from some of the girls. "He doesn't care if they use drugs—he likes to keep them fucked up so he can take advantage of them." She says his business attracts the type of girls who are generally irresponsible, and who need the kind of discipline and power play that he offers. Amy has worked at three brothels in Nevada over the past two years, but says she's happiest where she is now because the owner seems fairest to the girls.

At twenty-five, Amy has a round, deeply tanned face with a few freckles, large, blue eyes, and lashes heavy with mascara. She has a broad smile, which rarely lasts more than a second; more often, her full cheeks dip below the sides of her mouth, giving her a childlike, pouty look. She is used to being called "cute."

The reason Amy is staying here tonight is that she can't go back to the place she's been sharing with her "old man" for the last five years. He split town a couple of weeks ago, when they broke up, and put all her belongings in storage. "Yeah, I have this guy. He's black, and I love him," she says. "But I know he's no good for me. I've lost a lot of myself trying to make him happy." And, she adds, a lot of money.

Tomorrow she'll fly to Seattle to visit her sister and mother, but she has nothing to wear other than the clothes she's got on: a bright-white cotton sports bra beneath an unbuttoned denim shirt with the sleeves rolled up, and a pair of loose, jersey-style shorts tied below her exposed brown belly. She's dying to go shopping.

She looks around the room uncomfortably, and fidgets with the phone. "When you come out from working for three weeks, you feel like an oddball," she says, gesturing at the closed curtains. "I guess I get kind of paranoid." She plays with the ponytail that spouts colored blonde hair from the top of her head, and alternately tightens and loosens the white cotton elastic band holding it in place. "You feel like everyone stares at you. I say to myself, 'No, they're just looking at you because you're pretty.' But I think they know."

During their shifts, prostitutes in Pahrump are confined to the brothel where they work. They don't get out much, except to go to the clinic for their weekly checkups. "We have a swimming pool," says Amy. "We get drunk sometimes. We have fun. But when it comes down to it, we're all in it for the money. I don't have any girlfriends. You never really have friends in this business. You might have your drug friends, or friends on the surface. Maybe you click with one person. But three's a crowd—everyone's competition." Living in Nevada, Amy has seen how easy it is to get caught up in either gambling or drugs, and feels lucky that she isn't hooked on either. "Some girls have to get high or drunk in order to work. I don't."

■ ■ ■

Amy began working in the sex industry when she was a senior in high school. "I was never molested. I had a fucked-up life, but I wasn't molested," she says in defense of her family. Her father kicked her out of the house when she was fourteen, and after living with an aunt for three years, she took a job dancing in a topless club. "That's why I didn't finish school. I couldn't go home. I had to do what I had to do." Amy describes her mother as a poor, hard-core drug user, "physically and mentally fucked up." Her mother was fifteen when she had her first child, Amy's brother; Amy was born slightly after.

After traveling and working in topless and strip clubs in several other cities, Amy started prostituting in massage parlors and private clubs. "Let's face it," she says. "Lots of girls are prostitutes in one way or another. This way, it's right to the point." It was easy for her to make the transition from dancing to prostitution, she says; she uses the same tactics with her tricks that she used with customers at the clubs. "I'm really good at dancing. It's about seducing, changing and adapting to each guy. I may not be the best-looking girl around, but I can adapt," Amy says, looking down at her hands that continuously fold and unfold a napkin on her lap. "You have to approach each guy differently." Many topless and nude dancers in Las Vegas, on the other hand, hate to be associated with prostitutes, and take offense when people refer to them as "sex workers."

Amy first came to Las Vegas after a friend flew out here to work the dance clubs during Comdex, the annual November display of new computer technology that has become the largest convention in the world. Among Las Vegas cab drivers, sex club workers, and prostitutes, the convention's 200,000 annual attendees—mostly men—have become notorious for their fascination with the city's adult diversions.

When her friend came home with a bundle of money, Amy was easily persuaded to leave her job in a Seattle massage parlor and head for Nevada; the money in Las Vegas sounded too good to be true. Having heard that the legal houses of prostitution were safe environments for working girls, she decided to give them a try.

■ ■ ■

At the house where she works, customers view a lineup of fifteen to twenty girls who enter a dimly lit lobby, declare their working names in turn, and wait to be selected. Most houses offer a similar lineup; some allow men to mingle with the girls at the bar before making their choices. Amy's house has a bar, but she says the girls aren't allowed to linger there. Some houses require girls to wear floor-length evening gowns between six and midnight; before or after that they can wear lingerie. In others, there is no dress code, and they can wear what they like.

"I guess I get picked because of my smile, my 'innocent face,'" she says, lighting up the one-second smile with exaggerated charm. "They say I look friendly. It's really how you look when you come around the corner." Some guys, she adds, are repeat customers and will ask for the same girl every time; other men like to try a variety of different girls. Many are intimidated and apprehensive, and will choose the face that looks most inviting. A lot of them only come through Vegas once, she says, which makes their visit to Pahrump something special. Whether or not she is picked, or attracts repeat customers, Amy has learned not to take it personally.

After she is chosen, a girl leads the customer to her room and negotiates a fee for the services he wants. Semi-permanent workers have rooms of their own, which they can decorate with whatever they like, from flowery throw pillows and puppy-dog posters to leopard-skin bedspreads, black lights, and *Playboy* calendars.

Before any "activities" begin, all cash, travelers' checks, or credit cards involved are given to the manager, who listens to fee negotiations through intercoms in the bedrooms. Most houses follow this procedure, and managers will often check a girl's person and her belongings for unreported cash before she leaves for her time off.

Like other girls in the business, Amy says there is no such thing as a typical customer, although one former prostitute suggested "a common denominator of curiosity and loneliness." Locals keep business going during the hot summer months, when the out-of-town traffic slows down; but it's rare, says Amy, to meet a true "desert cowboy," a man actually born and raised in Nevada. Some men want to get in and out of the house as fast as they can; others want to linger. Some customers try to please her, but Amy tells them not to bother; she doesn't enjoy sex, she says, although she hopes that someday she will learn to. In addition to using latex condoms, Amy says there's another sacred rule of the trade: absolutely no kissing on the mouth. Too many germs are passed that way.

The majority of international customers at Nevada's brothels seem to come from Japan and Germany. According to one of the brothel managers, these clients drop large sums of money in the houses, a fact Amy confirms. Weekends are almost always busy, and everyone in the business knows they'll be swamped when a big convention is in town. Amy says she has serviced up to ten customers on her busiest nights.

"You get lots of guys on vacation who are just up for having some fun, but we get sickos too—guys who are into dominance and all that. They want to drink your pee, or they want you to shit on them. One guy begged and pleaded with me. Or they say they won't come unless you're pulling on their balls as hard as you can," she reflects with disgust, shaking her head. "I can't do it—I start laughing! One guy wanted me to wear my hair in pigtails and say, 'Hi, Daddy, can I suck your dick?' I mean, come on! They're sick." One girl she knew had a guy pay her $5,000 to walk him naked through the desert with a collar and leash, like a camel.

"The most normal-looking guys—they want the weirdest things."

■ ■ ■

The unspoken house minimum where Amy works now is around $150, but the average date pays her between $400 and $800. All fees are negotiated. Amy says she realizes that to some people $150 is a lot of money, and she will occasionally negotiate a lower fee. At least once or twice a week, on the other hand, she gets a client who drops $1,000. "Then a thousand dollars starts to seem like it's not enough, and you think you can get more…" she says, as a knowingly greedy smirk crosses her face.

While conventions in Las Vegas bring in more customers, Amy makes the most money over the Christmas holidays, when many other girls are gone and there is less competition. "There are usually only seven or eight of us around. Mostly we get guys that are lonely, or just divorced."

Last year, Amy cleared $95,000. Considering that the house gets half of all the money a prostitute negotiates with her customer, and that she has to tip the management, cleaners, and kitchen staff, she probably brought in over $200,000 for the year. Not bad for a twenty-five-year-old without a high-school diploma—and this is considered an average salary for a prostitute in Pahrump.

"I enjoy my money. But money is the root of all evil, right?" she asks rhetorically, shrugging her shoulders with another fleeting smile. "One hundred dollars to me is nothing. I can spend one hundred dollars in two seconds. But I figure I'd better save a little." She just opened her very first bank account this year.

In Pahrump, she says, girls can stay with a customer for as long as they want, once a fee is negotiated. "Up north [i.e., in the brothels near Reno], they sell time with the activity. There's more hustling from the bar and more stress involved in getting a date. Guys from up north have no class," she adds, sneering. "They think we're all the same."

Ideally, Amy would like to work in the brothel six months a year and in dance clubs the other six months. "I've probably got about ten good years left in me. When it gets to the point where I can't make customers happy, then it's time to take a long break." Industry insiders say that most girls in the business last between four and ten years.

Eventually, Amy says, she wants to get married and have children. At that point, she'd look for a job outside the sex industry. But so far, the only man she's ever been in love with is the one who just left town.

"What's love, anyway?" she asks me. "I think you can be content. There's no white picket fence. If you can be relaxed and happy, that's enough."

■ ■ ■

After an hour of conversation, Amy is fidgety, and tries again to call Bill. There is still no answer, so we go out to get something to eat.

As she locks the door to her second-floor room, a young man below looks up and pulls his sunglasses down low on his nose. He lets out a slow whistle and utters an admiring "Je-sus Christ." As we reach the bottom of the stairway and turn to walk through the parking lot he shouts, "Wait! Take me with you!" his arms outstretched and a big grin on his face.

She looks over her shoulder and smiles coyly as we walk away. "I like to flirt," she says. "But that's all."

A few minutes later, as we're approaching a combination 7-11 and Del Taco, she glances down at her shirt, her shorts, and her spanking-white Keds, and asks, "Do I look like a prostitute?" Actually, I think, she looks more like a beach girl from southern California. I tell her no. "I can always tell other girls who are prostitutes. Something about the way they look...it's either their clothes, their makeup, the way they carry themselves. I dunno, I can just tell."

As we enter the store, several heads turn to watch Amy walk by. Marching directly to the takeout counter, she orders a burrito, a quesadilla, large fries, and a Coke. The tall, thin, dark-haired man who takes her order continues to watch her across the store as she plays a few fifty-cent slot machines. When her number is called, she grabs a fistful of hot-sauce packets and another of ketchup, throws them into the paper bag, and snags a few fries before closing it.

"Thank you," says the dark-haired man, staring directly at her. "Thank you, very much." He watches her intently as she walks away from the counter. "That guy's a trick," she whispers. "I can tell."

Outside, she looks with disgust at a couple of young guys with short haircuts, baseball caps, and athletic builds who climb into a truck. Amy says she can't stand "those college frat-boy types. They think they know everything." But cab drivers, she says, are the worst. "They always say, 'Oh, you don't have to pay, just give me a blowjob.'" It drives her crazy. "Especially Middle Eastern ones. Middle Easterners in general—they're all tricks, every one of them."

On our walk back to the motel, Amy is quiet and contemplative. After a while, she opens the fast-food bag and begins popping fries into her mouth, one at a time. "Men are scum," she says flatly. "I didn't used to think so, but I do now."

■ ■ ■

The dressing room at Crazy Horse, a topless club just off Paradise and about a mile from the Strip, is dingy and small. It has one mirror splintered into a starburst, rendering about half of it unusable; there is a dirty makeup counter, and a wall of rusty lockers where dancers store their clothes. A threadbare piece of cloth hanging in the doorway offers little privacy from the interior of the club.

Loud dance music beats against the club's high walls and ceiling, filling the spaces between the dozen or so customers scattered among small tables and seated at the bar. They are all watching a topless woman in very short shorts slide sensuously up and down a firehouse-style pole mounted on the stage.

"Watch this one," says Gail, nodding towards a hefty dancer at the end of a row of tables. The girl is facing away from her customer and rubbing her very large, nearly nude bottom in a fast, circular motion over his groin. "She'll make him come, just wait."

Technically, lap dancers are only allowed to touch their customers in "nonsexual ways," and customers are not supposed to touch the dancers at all. Watching these two, you'd never know such rules existed, and in any case, a harmless hand on the neck, arm, foot, or even the behind is usually permitted. If they think the tips will be worth it, some dancers let customers get away with more; others make them sit on their hands during a dance.

In most clubs, dancers are scheduled to perform on stage several times throughout the night, from which they'll collect tips at the end. During the rest of their shift, they roam the floor in bikinis, lingerie, or skimpy dresses, soliciting lap dances or table dances, where the customer pays for a girl to dance and strip for him (or, occasionally, her) personally. The going rate is about $20-25 for the length of a song, but satisfied customers—or those who have been well hustled—usually tip more.

Gail, my companion for the evening, runs a small costume-jewelry store, which is closed more often than it's open. But business has never been better. In this city that never sleeps, her best customers are just starting work. On Thursday, Friday and Saturday nights, she sets up shop in the dressing rooms of the city's topless clubs and sells her jewelry to the dancers. "They weren't coming to me, so I decided to go to them."

Two bored-looking black women are sitting at a table near the entrance to the dressing room, complaining about how slow things are. No one is pulling in much money tonight. A few other girls stop by the jewelry case to see what's new since last time, but no one buys. Gail decides to move on to the next club, hoping to catch girls coming off their shift who have more money to spend.

Most topless and nude dancers in Las Vegas work eight-hour shifts as independent contractors. In the better-known establishments, they can expect to bring home about $300 on an average weeknight; on Fridays and Saturdays that jumps to $500. Some pay a percentage of their earnings— about 15 percent—to the club, while others pay a nightly fee (between $30-70) but get to keep all their tips. In 1997, a Las Vegas attorney filed a class-action lawsuit on behalf of the dancers, with the aim of forcing club owners to treat them as regular employees, entitled to keep all their tips.

At Cheetah's, the dressing room is smaller, and choked with cigarette smoke. As soon as Gail sets down her trays, the girls are on them like bees to honey. "Oooh, you got new rings!" says one of them, her eyes widening as an excited smile spreads across her face. Five girls crowd around the tray to try on fake pearl, silver, and rhinestone earrings, necklaces, tummy chains, and toe rings. Whenever one leaves, another takes her place.

"I tell them they gotta glitter," says Gail. "You've gotta wear jewelry to make the money out there." Guys pay more for a girl who looks expensive, she explains to them, and they listen. After a long process of trying on several necklaces and looking at herself from different angles in the mirror, hair up and hair down, a girl named Storm decides on a fifty-dollar rhinestone choker. Gail instructs her to tell her customers that she has to make enough money to pay for it. Obediently, the girl runs out of the room with the choker sparkling around her neck. Within half an hour, she returns with the cash in hand and a big smile on her face. "I told him it cost eighty," she says slyly, and tucks the extra money into her stilleto-heeled shoe. (At Cheetah's, dancers are required to wear three-inch heels.)

Another girl, just off her shift, is too tired to pay much attention to the jewelry. She sits down at the makeup counter, rubs her feet for a few minutes, then disappears into the locker area. She reappears with her thong bikini in hand, and proceeds to dry it with a hair dryer just as a girl from the next shift walks in, pulls her own thong out of a bag, and doses it heavily with perfume.

■ ■ ■

The dressing room at Crazy Horse Too, on Industrial Road, is in a whole different league. Two long walls of mirrors, lined with rows of globular makeup lights over bright-pink counters with matching cushioned stools, run down the middle of a huge, multichambered room. On one side, multiple tiers of lockers separate low padded tables where chiropractors work on dancers' backs for a few hours every night. There are tanning beds, hot showers, and a hairstylist, all of which are put to good use.

A kitchen on the other side of the mirrors is furnished with a long couch for catnaps, a television suspended from the ceiling, and a dining table and chairs. This is where Maria, a woman in her mid-forties, serves the dancers a hot, home-cooked meal for five dollars a plate. She also brings them Band-Aids, snacks, nail glue, and perfume, and listens to their daily complaints. On occasion, when a girl has had too much to drink, Maria will help clean up the mess. She works the late shift until 5 AM, and then returns to her six children at home. It's not a glamorous job, but to the dancers, Maria is indispensable. They all call her Mom.

A continuous parade of girls marches in and out of the dressing room; at least twenty of them are napping, eating, dressing and undressing here at any given time. They nonchalantly run around in nothing but a pair of high heels and a thong bikini bottom, tugging it out of their crack or playing with their hair. One or two walk around fully nude, their severely shaved pubic hair barely visible. Small tattoos on hips and shoulders are popular, as are anklets, toe rings, and tummy chains worn around the waist.

Under the bright dressing-room lights, one can see their over-bronzed chests and behinds shedding small flakes of dry skin. Bottles of lotion litter the countertops; the girls douse themselves with it every time they pass by. Before going back out to the club, each one bends over and checks her thonged behind in the mirror. Someone later explains that the black lights on stage pick up anything white, "including the smallest bits of toilet paper."

"I've had it with this place," snarls a girl who calls herself Champagne, as she marches in and flops down in a chair. She complains to Maria about a customer who stiffed her. "Guys here have no class. They don't know how to treat a lady. And I am a lady, I'm not a tramp!" Maria nods sympathetically and rubs her back. (Two weeks later, Champagne quit her job, and went to work as a cocktail waitress in one of the casinos.)

■ ■ ■

"The girls here in Las Vegas, the way they hustle is they tell the guys what they're going to get for their money...." says Wendy (a.k.a. Chantel), an attractive bleached blonde with a slim figure and a quiet voice. "But a lot of them lie about what he's going to get." Wendy worked as a dancer at Crazy Horse Too for two years before quitting the business and getting a job as a customer-service representative in a supermarket.

Before moving to Las Vegas four years ago "for the money," Wendy worked both in topless clubs and as a go-go dancer in southern California. Within three weeks of arriving, she had signed a contract and was working full-time. "In California, it was all stage work. We made our tips from the bar. There was no hustling, or mingling with the customers on the floor. Here, it's *all* hustling." On a really busy night, such as during a big convention, Crazy Horse Too can have up to two hundred girls working one shift, and things get competitive.

"Lots of guys are just after the fantasy of having a pretty girl make him feel special for the night," says Wendy. They come to Las Vegas for business or pleasure, and curiosity draws them to the clubs. Sometimes they go just so they can tell their friends they've been.

"Onstage, I was great. I'm a very intense dancer, very emotional, and I could perform whatever I was feeling at the time," she says, smoking a cigarette in the gay and lesbian bar where she and her girlfriend play pool on Wednesday nights. (Wendy estimates that, like her, about half of the girls who work at Crazy Horse Too are bisexual, although no one she knew considered herself solely a lesbian.)

"I enjoyed doing what I did on stage, I was real. I could be raunchy, down and dirty, and guys would throw money at me. But stage work is the easy part. Getting down to the nitty-gritty, when it's one-on-one, that's hard. It's so much easier to know a guy just wants to talk to you and to be with you. Most guys here, they buy a dance and then it's, 'See ya!'" She holds up her hand and waves it with a short flick of the wrist.

When she first started working in Vegas, Wendy had none of the practiced skills of the other dancers; she says she got her job on looks alone. She learned by watching others work. "It was scary—really scary. Crazy Horse Too is more for tourists, and that's why the girls hustle so hard."

She worked the 9 PM-5 AM shift, and after her first night she went home with $100. "I guess I didn't have an aggressive enough personality." If she got no takers for lap dances after circling the three stages of the club, she would change her outfit. On a bad night, she might change up to ten times. Only once, she says, did a guy ever approach her to ask for a dance. Eventually, she brought her nightly average up to $200, but she saw other girls taking home $300-$400 every day.

Like many dancers in Las Vegas, Wendy decided to get breast implants in the hope that they would improve her appeal. The city's phone book contains ten pages of ads for plastic surgeons, whose base price for silicon implants runs about $4,000, but Wendy found that in Ogden, Utah, a five-hour drive north, the operation cost only $2,400. Unlike many of her coworkers, she regrets the decision. "It just wasn't the same afterward. A lot of my regular customers said, 'Don't do it!' They were all ass men—I was blessed with a good ass. I should have listened."

Things only got worse from there. Wendy finally quit dancing when one of her friends at the club died. "I went to pick her up for work, and her roommate said, 'I've got something awful to tell you.'" The roommate had found her friend hanging from the curtain rod over the bathtub, half-dressed for work in one of her costumes, a stars-and-stripes skirt and stars-and-stripes Reeboks. Her makeup was partially applied. Wendy believes that someone close to the dancer had her killed.

"I couldn't go back to work after that. I just couldn't," she says, slowly shaking her head. After three months of unemployment, she landed the supermarket job, where she says she's happy enough. But the money doesn't compare. She still thinks about going back to dancing, but is afraid she would be haunted by the death of her friend.

"The worst thing is, I can't even visit her grave. Her father had her cremated, and he keeps the urn on his mantel."

■ ■ ■

"I hate topless clubs," says Suzanne, a short, spunky, green-eyed dancer with long, thick, auburn hair and a huge smile painted in dark-red lipstick. "I've had fewer problems working at nude clubs than I've ever had at topless clubs. Guys at topless clubs get drunk, they get irritated, and they want to see more. But they can't because it's against the law. In a nude club, there it is, all spread out like a TV dinner for them to see, and they don't get upset. Topless clubs are a waste of time."

In Clark County, topless clubs can serve alcohol but cannot offer full nudity, whereas the fully nude clubs cannot serve alcohol. The one exception is the popular Palamino club, in North Las Vegas, which fell under a grandfather clause when the law was established. As one insider remarked, "You can either have booze or pussy, but you can't have both."

Many other dancers say they have no problem dancing topless, but that a combination of modesty and the "bad image" associated with fully nude clubs keeps them from stripping all the way. At the same time, some prostitutes insist they could not do either. They say it would be much more difficult to perform nude or even topless in front of an audience than to have sex in private with an unknown individual.

"The general conception of Las Vegas is that it's Sin City," says another nude dancer, a tall, leggy blonde with enormous breasts, a raspy smoker's voice, and sleepy doe eyes set in a longish face. "But we work in a safe, enclosed environment, and we have a support group of coworkers within our building. It's like a terrarium."

The dancer's name is Mona, and she is introduced as a "feature" at Little Darlings, the Western Avenue club where she and Suzanne work. It's one of a chain of about a dozen Deja Vu nude dancing clubs in larger cities across the country. "Most of the guys here treat us like we're queens of the world," says Mona. "They know why we're here—to make money."

And they had better be prepared to spend it. After paying a thirty-dollar cover charge, the men (women are not allowed) can sip non-alcoholic drinks from plastic tornado glasses at ten bucks a pop; three dollars of the drink money goes to the house, and seven to the girl who gets him to buy it. Couch dances cost twenty dollars—more if you have one in the VIP or "fantasy" rooms—and tips are always appreciated. Little Darlings is equipped with a Victorian-style living room for watching porn movies, individual viewing booths with more than one hundred porn channels, and a series of fantasy rooms (actually just partitioned spaces) made up like movie sets, including a bedroom, a Bondage Room, and an Oriental Room.

On a typical Wednesday night, a smattering of men in suits, boys in T-shirts and baseball caps, and a group of nicely dressed young Japanese men are seated at small tables surrounding a central stage. Near a corner of the room sits a pair of big boys in black cowboy hats and boots, Western-style shirts, and bolo ties. They are slumped down low in their chairs with their legs stretched out and their arms crossed. The two have been silently watching dancers perform costumed strip routines onstage for over half an hour, refusing couch-dance solicitations and dancers' requests for drinks.

A woman in a ragged leopard-skin outfit and a huge teased-hair wig strip-dances to the theme song from *The Flintstones*; she is followed by a woman in an Egyptian costume who swallows a fiery sword with a flame so big it sets off the fire alarm. The two boys remain unfazed.

But when a lanky young girl comes out doing the two-step in a red-and-white checked shirt tied above skin-tight jeans, with a five-gallon hat resting on her mass of frizzy brown hair, the cowboys come to life. Sitting up straight in their chairs, they start tapping their feet to the country-western beat. As the dancer begins to take off her shirt, they each let out a loud "Yee-haw!" and lean forward for a closer look. After a bit more dancing and a few more hollers, the dancer gives her jeans a fast tug. They split down the side seams with a Velcro "r-r-r-rip," and go sailing offstage behind her. By this time, the club has turned into a room full of hand-clapping, yee-hawing men. When the dancer finally loses the bikini underneath her clothes, the cowboys have their hats in their hands and are swinging them around in the air above their heads. She knows who her big tippers are tonight.

Oblivious to the ruckus out front, Mona smokes another cigarette in her chair in the dressing room, one foot up on the counter and one knee pulled up to her chest. "Heck. We've got nothing to hide—we're naked most of the time!" she laughs. Surrounded by a small group of women who are all talking, smoking, or playing with their hair in the mirror, she looks at ease in a baby-blue velour bikini top that's several sizes too small to hold what appears to be a pair of double-E breasts.

Having starred in "adult films" (she hates the term "porn flicks") for three years, through which she acquired a sizeable fan club, Mona became a feature dancer through a booking agency that trained her to dance at topless and nude clubs around the country. When she got tired of traveling, she and her husband decided to move to Las Vegas, where she retired from films and took up dancing permanently. She now maintains her own Web site (which her husband helped her create), where she sells her videos, as well as T-shirts and various other paraphernalia imprinted with her image. She says it gets more than ten thousand hits a day, and that her fan club is bigger than ever. But at twenty-eight, she regards herself one of the "dinosaurs" of the business. Most dancers are between eighteen and twenty-three, and Mona finds it funny that people still want to see her dance at her age. She is also one month pregnant.

"In Las Vegas, most of the people we deal with are in and out of here. They're traveling a lot," she says, shrugging them off like flies. "They're kind of like cheap dates—you see them one night, and then you never have to see them again!" In a month or so, when her pregnancy becomes more obvious, she won't be coming back.

"The difference between working in Las Vegas and working in other places is this," chimes in her green-eyed friend Suzanne: "Money, money, money, money, money!" She flashes a fiendish grin. "Other places are bogus in comparison." Standing just four feet, ten inches tall in a black, sleeveless, body-hugging dress that accentuates her own remarkable breasts, Suzanne has a surprisingly commanding presence in the snug, crowded room. In the business for over ten years, she was Mona's dance trainer when the two worked for a booking agency, and is now her roommate and best friend. The two share a townhouse in Summerlin, a new residential suburb about twenty minutes northwest of the city, with Mona's husband, a pet ferret, and two prairie dogs.

"I enjoy what I do. I chose it as my profession," says Suzanne. "Ever since I was a little girl, I've always, my whole life, wanted to be an actress or an entertainer. It was my dream."

Standing next to her, a thin, fair-skinned twenty-two-year-old with long, curly blonde hair says she spends ten days at a time working in Las Vegas followed by ten days in Ohio, where she lives with her boyfriend. "I will not work in Ohio. The dance clubs there are basically whorehouses. And they're extremely racist." She earns enough money at Little Darlings to make her commute worth the trouble.

"Contrary to popular myth, the average customer who comes into a club here is not a dirty old man," says Mona. "He's someone who's not getting attention from his wife at home. You know, he's got three kids, the sex drive is gone, and he just wants somebody to pay a little attention to him."

"The majority of them are just out to have a good time, a little R-and-R. They want to let loose," says Suzanne. "They don't have any perversions, there's nothing wrong with them. They don't want to take you home—they may try, but they're just doing it for laughs. They want to yuk it up for the night. So what? If I can make them laugh for twenty minutes, hey, I'm in there. My job is done."

Well, almost. As in every Las Vegas strip club, if a dancer wants to go home with more than her tips, she's got to go out and earn it hustling the floor. To keep the money flowing, Little Darlings has a "blue-light" break every half-hour or so: the stage show stops, spinning blue lights flash throughout the club, and all the girls have to be out on the floor working the customers one-on-one. They either put themselves on display by standing on the tables and dancing, or they approach customers individually.

■ ■ ■

A number of Deja Vu's "little darlings" have husbands, fiancés, or steady boyfriends, though most of those with children seem to be raising them on their own. Their partners are more often than not managers, disc jockeys, bartenders, or owners at other nude and topless dance clubs. One girl who had dated a guy not in the business said it didn't work out because he was constantly put down by his friends for having a stripper for a girlfriend.

"This is like our own little club," says Mona. "We don't mingle much with people on the outside." Her own husband is a deejay at the other Deja Vu club in town. "And it's very hard to have female friends who aren't in the business." Most people on the outside, she explains, don't understand or can't relate to their lifestyles, not to mention their working hours. And the dancers themselves feel somewhat isolated from the rest of the world; they have unlisted phone numbers and addresses, and their driver's licenses show only a post-office box. "Outside of the club," says Mona, "most of us are so modest. We don't go out, we don't party, we don't wear makeup. And I never dress to show that I have large breasts."

"Our stage names represent a totally different personality from who we are in real life. We are TOTALLY not the same person," adds another woman. "We walk differently, we talk differently, and obviously we dress differently." A single mother with three young kids, her specialty at the club is the Shower Room, where for twenty dollars a song customers get to rinse off a soaped-up girl with a hose. This activity is advertised on an electronic sign inside: "Are you man enough to wash off our Little Darlings?" The message flashes repeatedly across the screen.

"During Comdex," she says, "I had up to sixty guys in the shower room. The line to get into the club went clear around the corner."

"Conventions are the bomb," agrees Mona. "But we get pissed off and jealous of the girls who come in just to work conventions." Most clubs in Las Vegas have a steady stock of "weekend warriors," women who commute from all across the country just to work weekends and conventions because the money is so good. Many of them work a continuous circuit, following conventions from city to city. According to Las Vegas police, call girls and prostitutes do the same.

While most dancers admit they work in topless and nude clubs for the money, they often claim to be doing it either to raise children or to pay for an education. And while they say that most customers treat them with respect, dancers get tired of being propositioned. There are clubs in Las Vegas where, according to police, girls turn tricks every night; but this is obviously not the case everywhere. Every dancer has at least one story to explain why she deserves to make as much money as she does: dancers have been bitten, slapped, punched, and called names they wouldn't repeat.

"One guy actually asked me, 'What happens if my dick accidentally ends up in your pussy?'" said one girl. "I told him, 'Then my shoe lands in your dick!'" Mona rolls her eyes. "We have to deal with stupid questions a lot. This one guy asked me, 'If I give you five dollars more, can I lick you?'" She sneers. "Right! Like 'Oh, that five dollars is really going to make my day!'" She then grabs the fair-skinned blonde and insists that she tell her tale.

Reluctant at first, the girl gives in to her coworkers' pleas and describes an incident that occurred when she was doing a couch dance. These dances (which don't actually involve a couch) are performed inside a phone booth-size cubicle with a padded bench for the customer on one side (partly hidden by an outer partition), and a metal bar running across the top of the other. In this confined space, the girl—either standing, mounting the bench, or hanging from the bar—dances, shimmies, slithers, wriggles and shakes her breasts and behind, sometimes wrapping her legs around the customer's neck or brushing her bare flesh over his face. The dancer can get as close to her customer as she wants; but once again, he is not supposed to touch her in any sexual way.

Just before the end of her dance, when the dancer was looking in the other direction, her customer pulled out a lollipop and tried to shove it up her rear. She yelled for one of the security workers, and the man was escorted out the door. "The worst part was, he was licking it on his way out."

■ ■ ■

An only child, Suzanne was raised mostly by her father and stepmother in a trailer park in Ohio. "It was nice enough, but it was a trailer park. I wore garage-sale clothes to school, and the other kids made fun of me because, basically, I was wearing their hand-me-downs."

She took ice-skating and gymnastics as a kid, and then dance lessons when she got older. In high school, when she thought she wanted to become an attorney, she began taking college courses for credit and got a job as a topless dancer to pay her tuition. But after club managers repeatedly yelled at her for studying on the job, she quit school and went into dancing full-time. Both sets of parents supported her ambitions.

"My parents love to watch me perform. My mom even went with me to my first audition. She asked me, 'Do you think you can do that?' and I said, 'I don't know if I can get naked, Mom.' My knees shook so hard, I don't remember dancing."

After working in topless clubs for a few years, she auditioned for *Cats*, Kings Island, and Disney World. "At Disney World, all they could offer me was a *Smurf* costume. For two hundred dollars a week, I could walk around as a *Smurf*!" She spits out the word. "But going to audition after audition was killing me. It was always, 'We're looking for someone taller,' or thinner, or with this or that. I'd tell them, 'I'll wear three-inch heels!' I'd do anything to get a job.'" Eventually, she was hired as a feature trainer with the booking agency, where she spent five years teaching dance, music theory, and a little bit of everything else.

"I taught these kids everything they needed to know, from doing their taxes, to child care, to 'You got a guy, he's not doing nothing? Get rid of him.' I'd tell them, 'Make him work at McDonald's! But don't take him on the road if he's excess baggage.'" But even she had to learn the hard way. Her first husband quit his own job a few months after they were married. When she discovered he'd been stealing money from her, she ended the marriage then and there.

Suzanne admits that she fell prey to the party atmosphere of the club world, and—like many dancers, she says—she battled alcoholism for several years. After going through a detoxification program, she followed her new friend Mona out to Las Vegas, at first hoping to get a part in one of the big casino shows on the Strip. "Then I realized these people had been studying dance since birth. Here they could do pirouettes and stuff on either foot. I could only do them on one foot. I could only kick with one leg, only spin in one direction." Although she got a part as a chorus dancer, she says she felt out of her league.

"But you learn how to accommodate your dreams. When I learned that I could perform every night, and be the writer, director, producer and star of my own little one-person show, I said, 'Hey, I'm there!' And I had total autonomy." That's when she joined Mona as a dancer at Little Darlings. While she does use traditional dance moves, Suzanne's strip routines rely more on humor than anything else. At four feet, ten inches, she says it's hard to carry off "sexy." "I do better with 'funny' or 'powerful.'"

At the club, when the disc jockey plays the Three Dog Night song "Joy to the World (Jeremiah Was a Bullfrog)," Suzanne comes bounding onstage fully outfitted in a bright-green sequined costume, complete with a frog's head and bugged-out eyes. Bouncing around on stage, alternately stepping out with pointed toes and snapping her fingers, she looks like a cross between Kermit the Frog and an aerobics instructor. To Van Halen's "Jump," she strips down to a green sequined bikini. During "Jump for My Love," by the Pointer Sisters, she teases her audience by turning her back and slowly inching down her bikini bottom. She plays peek-a-boo with her breasts, peeling back her top, then putting it back on. For her finale, Suzanne lies down fully nude on the stage, throws her legs up over her head, and thrusts her arms—with frog puppets on each hand—up between them. Over her rear end, the puppets face each other and lip-synch to the *Sesame Street* favorite "Ma-nuh-ma-nuh" (sung by the Muppets).

By this time, everyone in the audience is laughing out loud. Men in the bar shake their heads, unsure what to make of the whole froggy scene. But Suzanne receives hearty applause and smiles all around. The performance and costume, she explains, are copyrighted. One customer told her he'd enjoyed her show so much he wished he'd brought his wife. "This is part of my dream. I get to be on stage and entertain every night. Yeah, the money's great, but the thing that keeps me going on that stage every night is that applause, that sound. There's that immediate gratification, making people smile and laugh. That's what I do."

Suzanne was engaged to be married at the end of June, and wanted to go back to school to get her high-school diploma, and then a teaching credential. "I have never been in this business for the money," she declared.

"I've made four point six million dollars in the past twelve years. Ask me where it is. I have no clue. But you know what? I've had a blast."

Law and Disorder

Heather World

Gordon Dickie, director of security and surveillance at Harrah's Hotel and Casino, slides a video cassette into a VCR in his windowless basement office. When he presses "Play," the grainy black-and-white surveillance film of the casino's first and only armed robbery pops up on screen, with the date (4/24/94) and time (2:45 AM) noted in the corner.

The silent story of the robbery unfolds in a leap from camera to camera, each panning, tilting, and zooming to catch the action. The clip opens with a shot of the glass doors of a ground-level rear entrance, empty but brightly lit. Suddenly a dark minivan pulls up to the curb. Four young black men (later identified by police as members of the Las Vegas Crips) leap from the van. Seconds after the four men disappear from the camera's eye, the screen is filled with a shot of patrons running out the same doors.

The picture switches to inside the casino, where the four men run down aisles of slot machines and jump over the counter of the cage, where each day's working cash is kept. In the lower corner of one camera's view, one of the men waves a Colt .45 pistol, warning people away. Inside the cage, the robbery (more than $100,000 was taken) is performed over and over again, from every conceivable angle.

The camera pans to the man with the gun, who grabs a hostage. The image is fuzzy and dark, but clear enough to show the hostage being dragged along the floor until he is finally let go.

"He probably owns a piece of Harrah's now," says Dickie with a slight smile on his sunburned face.

Zoom, pan, switch to another camera. The four men run out of the casino and jump into the waiting van, which speeds out of the parking lot. As the van slips off the screen, another camera shows a Datsun sports car leisurely leaving the premises. Las Vegas police caught the van after a high speed chase, but they believe the money—which was never recovered—went in the Datsun to Los Angeles, along with the masterminds behind the robbery, Melvin "Poppa" Foster and Chet "Shortdog" Govan.

The 1994 Harrah's robbery fits into the traditional history of Las Vegas, in which urban criminals come in to stir up the dust of this Western desert town. The man who first gave the Strip its name was a former Los Angeles police captain and vice-squad commander who had operated illegal gambling parlors back home. When the mayor of Los Angeles decided to crack down on illegal casinos in 1938, Guy McAfee moved to Las Vegas and began operating legal casinos there. The domination of Las Vegas casinos and hotels by the mob, a generic term for the organized-crime syndicates based in cities throughout the U.S., began with the arrival in 1941 of Benjamin "Bugsy" Siegel, a front man for the Chicago gang who used millions of dollars of organized-crime capital to complete and run the glamorous new Flamingo Hotel. Siegel was shot to death (presumably by his mob associates) at his home in Beverly Hills in 1947.

Most of the crimes for which mobsters and their agents in Las Vegas were eventually convicted—mainly hidden ownership arrangements, and the skimming of casino profits (both to avoid paying taxes on them, and to repay illegal mob investors)—were of interest more to federal than local agencies, and did not make Las Vegas any more dangerous to most residents and tourists. But the out-of-town gangsters who owned most of the Strip hotels in the 1950s and 1960s—often with the backing of mob-arranged loans from the Teamsters' Pension Fund of Chicago, and with moderately respectable front men—were responsible for the city's own "Green Felt Jungle" legend, in which cheaters were beaten or mutilated by casino security forces, minor criminals were shaken down by major ones, police were paid off, and dead bodies of rival gangsters were discovered buried in the desert sand. A mob code, supposedly, required that major offenders be offed outside Las Vegas. So ex-Flamingo boss Gus Greenbaum, who antagonized *his* Chicago employers in 1958 while managing the Riviera Hotel, was, like Siegel, murdered at his out-of-state home.

Howard Hughes' purchase of the Desert Inn and several other casinos between 1967 and 1970 began the businessmen's takeover of Las Vegas's gambling industry, in which more or less respectable hotel and resort corporations gradually displaced the mob. One may or may not admire the business practices of the Hilton Corporation, Mirage Resorts Inc., or MGM Grand, but they are not likely to involve smashing fingers, planting car bombs, murdering opponents, or defiantly cheating the government. Even so, a major skim of doctored slots continued at the Stardust and Fremont Hotels, largely for the benefit of Chicago mobsters, until 1976; at least four murders (and one attempted murder) have been related to this operation. The last took place in 1985, when the body of Tony "the Ant" Spilotro, a ruthless career criminal and Las Vegas crime boss who may have been involved with the other murders, was found stripped, tortured, and buried in a cornfield in Indiana shortly before he was to testify regarding the Stardust Hotel skim and other mob operations.

Many Las Vegans today happily recount such tales from their city's past, although with the implicit understanding that such things never, of course, happen anymore. These days, if the police find a body in the desert, it is more likely to be that of a prostitute than the victim of a Mafia hit. Robbers are more likely to target banks than casinos. People who live here are quick to defend their city against outsiders' persisting suspicion that the gambling, drinking, and prostitution of the Strip and Glitter Gulch spill over into the rest of Las Vegas, or in any way represent the morality of the city itself.

"It's really no different here than in any other big city," said Officer John Loretto, of the Las Vegas Metropolitan Police Department, one chill December night, on his way to helping with a crack bust in a Latino housing project. I often hear this remark, along with "It's really very safe here," when I asked people about crime in Las Vegas. Police officials and residents alike blame gangs and growth for the influx of drugs and the high rate of violent crime.

It may be true that many residents of Clark County have a conservative, suburban attitude that contrasts with the careless, hedonistic behavior encouraged by the casinos. But it is also true that the Strip and Downtown continue to have a major impact on the city's crime statistics. The gambling industry's free-floating cash economy attracts con artists and pickpockets; the lure of easy money attracts people who sometimes lose everything but their desperation; and the gambling boom and resulting population explosion have created serious growing pains in the police department. The city's casinos also affect the way crime is handled. To remain the nation's number-one tourist destination, Las Vegas—like the roller coasters, medieval tournaments, wild-animal acts, and mock volcanoes on the Strip—must seem to be safe, but with an exciting, dangerous air.

■ ■ ■

The days of mob rule may be over, but Las Vegas still has more than its share of violent crime—the kind of violent crime that affects residents, not tourists. National statistics show that Clark County has higher rates of murder, rape, and robbery than do comparably sized resort cities without legal gambling. In 1995 Clark County had 14.8 murders per 100,000 residents, whereas Honolulu and Orlando had 4.3 and 5.7 respectively. Furthermore, Clark County had fewer people in the eighteen to twenty-four year old range—those who typically commit most violent crimes—than those cities did.

The links between crime rates and the county's major industry cannot be demonstrated conclusively. But the presence of large numbers of gamblers and immense amounts of visible, tangible cash redefine the very nature and value of money, to a point where players become unusually susceptible to cheaters, thieves, scam artists, and high-priced prostitutes, as well as the irrational appeals of gambling itself. The frustration of the unemployed and underpaid in a city so obviously awash with dollars drives some to seek out extralegal ways of sharing the wealth. During major boxing matches in Las Vegas, when many commodities on the Strip leap upward in price, people well known to the police and FBI pour into the city from other places. Drug dealers find it easy to make sales for large sums of cash in a city where hundred-dollar bills are standard supermarket change. As almost every U.S. city has learned, any substantial increase in drug dealing brings with it an increase in violent crime, as dealers and subdealers try to defend or extend their turf or pay off rivals or welshers. Las Vegas's gambling boom is at least in part responsible for the city's own manic, unstructured growth, which has created a large population of transients working graveyard shifts, many in service jobs in the big hotels—not the best recipe for a stable community. The county's population of young people—white, black, Asian, and Hispanic—is unusually unsettled, volatile, and violence-prone.

■ ■ ■

To keep pace with its growing and changing population, the county has expanded its public services, including the Metropolitan Police Department. Metro, as it is usually called, was formed when the city of Las Vegas and Clark County merged their police forces in 1973. The department has jurisdiction over the county's unincorporated areas (including the Strip) as well as Las Vegas proper. In 1996, residents passed a bond measure to pay the cost of adding eight hundred police officers to a force of 1,326 over a two-year period; but such rapid, wholesale increases can make it difficult to screen out unsuitable officers, and to train new ones properly. Stories about rogue police officers dominated the newspapers around the same time the bond measure passed. One was charged with threatening to arrest prostitutes unless they had sex with him. Another was charged with forcing a couple to engage in sex while he watched. And then there was Ron Mortensen.

Ron Mortensen turned thirty-one on December 28, 1996, and he celebrated his birthday by drinking himself sick. Mortensen and his partner and friend Christopher Brady started the night with a bang, downing tequila and beer. Feeling playful between bars, Brady sped down side streets, skidding and spinning his 1974 Dodge pickup.

"Ron was laughing," Brady would later tell a grand jury. "He thought everything was funny, especially the way I was driving."

The pair pulled up to people they assumed to be drug dealers and stared at them. "There was so many people out there selling dope, so many people that are like your bangers and your dopers that are out there, and it was just easy to pull up and talk to them or sit there and look at them and harass them," Brady testified.

Daniel Mendoza, 21, was hanging with his friends on a small dead-end street just north of Flamingo when Brady and Mortensen drove up. The group of Latino boys signaled that they had no drugs, but the pickup didn't leave. Instead, according to Brady, Mortensen pulled out his pistol and fired six shots into the group. The pickup screeched off, leaving Mendoza's friends with his dead body.

Brady sped away from the scene and drove to the next bar. He and Mortensen walked into a room full of their fellow police officers at PT's Pub on Spring Mountain Road, where the two men joined their coworkers for more tequila and beer. They partied until Mortensen threw up several times and was, in the words of one friend, "falling down drunk."

Mortensen, described by his captain as "nothing spectacular, nothing stellar, nothing negative, nothing positive," had started his job only sixteen months before the shooting. During his six-month partnership with Brady, two accusations of excessive force had been filed against the pair. In one incident, they arrested eighteen-year-old Raul Luis Mosqueda for possession of a pair of scissors and being under the influence of a controlled substance; Mosqueda ended up in the hospital because of the injuries he sustained during the arrest. Hospital staff tied him down and pumped his stomach on the orders of the two officers, who said they suspected an overdose. Nothing was found in Mosqueda's system, and the District Attorney later dropped all charges against him for lack of evidence.

At first glance, Mortensen and Brady seem not unlike most of their fellow officers: white, male, and relatively young. The average age of a Metro cop in 1997 was thirty-four, according to department estimates, but that number doesn't reflect the large number of young recruits hired since 1996.

After the Mortensen incident, *Las Vegas Sun* police reporter Cathy Scott wrote a series of articles exposing the department's inability to perform adequate background checks on new officers. She discovered that the officer who reviewed Mortensen's previous work history as a department-store security guard had advised Metro not to hire him based on his performance reviews, which described him as "aggressive and combative." Metro's personnel director overruled the objection and hired Mortensen anyway.

Furthermore, Scott says, there's a new generation of cops on the force. "The older cops here joined the force to make the community a better place," she says. "For the new cops, it's not a career, it's a job."

Inexperience and inadequate background checks have repercussions beyond bad publicity. In 1994 Las Vegas had a high rate of violent crime, but the lowest rate of violent crimes ending in arrest, according to FBI statistics comparing major U.S. cities. Lieutenant Dennis Cobb, a sixteen-year veteran of the force, faults the department for not making training a priority. The police academy has only six staff officers and runs only two classes a year, even though Las Vegas has one of the largest police forces in the country. When money does come in, he says, it goes to hire more officers, not to train the ones they have. "The police force has a corrupt gene pool of ideas," says Cobb, who would like to start a public-justice magnet school to create an influx of new ideas.

Cobb also faults the department for its lack of communication. "When there is this much growth, you spend a lot of your time figuring out your job." As an example, he cities the relationship between Metro police and the police of North Las Vegas. Although Metro patrols the city of Las Vegas and the unincorporated areas of Clark County, it has no jurisdiction over North Las Vegas, Henderson, or Boulder City, each of which has its own force. The superiors of the North Las Vegas and Metro police force jealously guard their separate autonomy, he says, to the point where the two forces even use different radio frequencies. Anytime they work together they have to trade an officer out of each car, so that each has one North Las Vegas and one Metro officer. Only then can they communicate by radio.

■ ■ ■

Las Vegas suffers under the pressures of rapid, barely controlled growth and gambling-related social problems; but it also suffers from pressures imposed by the gambling industry to make the city look safe. Rare among police jurisdictions, Clark County doesn't issue a "police blotter" (a daily listing of crimes used by police reporters in search of news stories); too many stories about crime in local or national newspapers might make the city look dangerous, and thus keep tourists away. Reporter Cathy Scott says she has to get her crime-story leads from the police scanner, police-issued press releases, or phone tips.

Charlene Barrett, a young mother who moved here from southern California in 1995, worries that police priorities may be misplaced. "Everything here is catered to the tourist trade," she says. She mentions two serial rapists who molested a number of local children in the summer of 1996, then disappeared before the police could catch them.

"The police didn't inform the community," says Cathy Scott. "They didn't want the bad publicity." When Scott asked Lieutenant Brad Simpson about the molestations, he said he hadn't even heard of a serial rapist in his precinct. Scott didn't know what to make of his comment. "I don't know if one hand didn't know what the other was doing, or if they honestly didn't know they had a serial rapist."

"There's pressure to keep crime statistics low to make Las Vegas seem safe," she adds. Scott covered the murder of rap star Tupac Shakur, who was shot on the Strip on September 7, 1996, after the Mike Tyson-Bruce Sheldon fight. Hours before he was killed, Shakur and his friends had beaten up Orlando Anderson, a reputed member of the Los Angeles Crips, at the MGM Grand. The police came, says Scott, but Anderson didn't want to press charges, so the police never filed a report.

The Las Vegas police frequently blame out-of-town (primarily Los Angeles) gangs for much of the city's violent crime, just as earlier city officials blamed mob-related crime in Las Vegas on criminal syndicates from other cities. Las Vegas has a way of making its problems look imported—an easy out, considering that 30 million people visit this metropolitan area of one million every year. Police who deal with "imported" crime blame outsiders not just for committing crimes, but also for attracting them. When the number of homicides in Clark County jumped 36 percent (to 163) in 1996, homicide chief Wayne Peterson laid responsibility on "a very small percentage of the [tourist] population that is inclined to criminal activity."

Lieutenant Dennis Cobb agrees: "There is an unnatural proportion of criminals from out of town." He says local gang affiliates scout out the stores for their Los Angeles counterparts to rob; or Las Vegas gangs rob the stores themselves, and sell the loot to their Los Angeles brothers; or— the most invasive scenario—gangs of tourist criminals (like the 1994 Harrah's burglars) come up from L.A. to take advantage of Las Vegas's floating-cash economy. "A robbery here is likely to net you more money," says Cobb. "Think of the rich guy who comes here with his mistress. The guy wants to buy her a diamond necklace, but he doesn't want the wife to know, so he brings cash for his purchases. That cash stays at the store until evening."

Bob Larsen, the assistant public defender, disputes these claims. The sixty-five attorneys in his office handle 60 to 70 percent of all major crimes in Las Vegas—more than fourteen thousand felonies in 1996. "Most of the crime occurs through the people who live here," he says. Moreover, he says, the city and state are very tough on crime: possession of marijuana here is a felony, not a misdemeanor; using a weapon to commit a crime doubles your sentence, as does committing a crime against someone over sixty-five.

■ ■ ■

There is one kind of criminal unique to legal-gambling centers like Las Vegas, who troubles casino owners and managers more than he does either residents or tourists: the casino cheater, whether dealer or player, cash-room skimmer, cardsharp, or slot-machine manipulator. Visitors, in fact, often find themselves sympathizing with such craftsmen (who are doing what they only dream of doing—beating the house odds), to the chagrin of casino executives. Cheating a casino is a felony that can get you up to twenty-five years in jail in Nevada, but such criminals cannot always be pursued into non-gambling states. So it is often up to the casinos themselves to prevent, detect, catch, and even punish such people.

The state of Nevada goes a long way toward making gambling-related crimes seem minimal, and to keep "undesirables" out of its casinos. The Nevada Gaming Control Board publishes a list called the Black Book, which includes the names and pictures of the twenty-eight men and one woman who are forever barred from Nevada's casinos. Since it began publishing the book in 1960, the Board has sought primarily to ban gamblers with links to the mob: here you still see names like "Tony Ripe" Civella and "Nappy" Pulawa.

Forbidding in name only, the innocuous pamphlet (which is covered in silver, not black) tells less about declining mob influence in Nevada than it does about the rise of corporate ownership of the state's casinos, and the desire of the new managers to appear squeaky-clean. Nevada created the Black Book to fend off federal attacks on legal gambling, former governor and attorney Grant Sawyer told the *Las Vegas Review Journal* in 1992. "We felt threatened by Congress," Sawyer said. "Nevada was being blasted in headlines all over the country."

UNLV professors Carole Case and Ronald Farrell examined each entry for their own book, *The Black Book and the Mob*. "It's used as a symbolic gesture," says Case. "The Black Book allows the state to say it has the gambling industry under control." For example, she says, as slot machines began to account for an increasing share of casino revenue, the Board entered a few token slot cheats. (Douglas Barr, Sr., entered the book in 1990; four years later, his son, Douglas Barr, Jr., joined his father.) "Obviously these few are not the total population of slot cheats," says Case. "The Black Book only bars people from going into casinos. These people can still go into rooms that don't have table games, like 7-11s, the airport, and bars."

The casinos' pit bosses, floor managers, and surveillance personnel, whose job it is to keep undesirables out, rely on a guide that is more helpful (though less regulated and legal), put out by Griffin Investigations. The four volumes of the Griffin Book contain about two thousand entries: the names and pictures of petty thieves who snatch purses or steal coin cups from slot-machine players, con artists who impersonate casino employees, sophisticated blackjack cheaters who use computers and hand signals, even card counters. (Card counting—a system of tracking high-point cards in blackjack as they are dealt and played—is not illegal in Nevada, but a casino has the right to banish players skilled enough to use the technique successfully.) Each entry also lists the person's "associates," which may be simply a list of the people sitting at the same table, for example. Bob Griffin, a private detective and former police officer, and his employees visit casinos, scout out entries for the book, and send monthly updates to their clients.

One professional gambler I spoke to (who did not want his name used) says that Griffin employs six to eight agents. Some of these, he claimed, are former Drug Enforcement Agency officers convicted of felonies. "Griffin buys mug shots from cops on the take," says the gambler, who adds that it is illegal to publish police mug shots.

Andy Anderson, a tall, silver-haired investigator who has been with the agency for sixteen years and acts as its unofficial spokesman, won't say what he did before coming to Griffin. Nor will he say how the agency gets its pictures, or how many investigators Griffin employs, or even which casinos use Griffin Investigations. He will say that Griffin has two hundred clients worldwide, and that Anderson is an assumed name: "The less people know about me, the better."

Some people listed in the book have filed class-action lawsuits against Griffin, claiming that an entry in the book is the equivalent to being labeled guilty of a crime without due process. Griffin is frequently sued, acknowledges Andersen, but he insists that the agency has won every case that went to court.

Like the police, the casinos do their part to keep crime statistics low. Dave Kuhl, a security officer at the Mirage, says that most tourists who have been victimized never report the crime to police, often because they are embarrassed. "Let's say they run into a big trick roll [a prostitute who robs her john]. We ask if they want to press charges, but we tell them Metro takes a while to come." When the visitor declines, the Mirage simply keeps a report in its own files.

"The casinos don't report a whole lot of crimes because it would make them look bad," says Lieutenant Cobb. "A lot of times they just compensate someone."

■ ■ ■

On the surface, it is surprising that the rate of larceny is much lower here (3,695 per 100,000 Clark County residents in 1995) than it is in Honolulu and Orlando (more than 4,000 per 100,000 in each). After all, 30 million tourists visit Las Vegas each year, many of whom carry cash in one hand and a drink in the other. Millions of elderly visitors (and thousands of local senior citizens) are vulnerable to a quick purse or coin-cup snatch when they sit down for an afternoon at the slots or video-poker machines. Many visitors from smaller towns may be unwise to urban dangers, such as pickpocketing.

But look about you on even a brief visit to the Strip and you will see one explanation for the relatively low rate of larceny: the ubiquitous private security forces. Casinos on the Strip employ a private security force of at least four times the size of the Metro Police.

At the Mirage Hotel and Casino, about $3 million changes hands daily, and a staff of 250 security and surveillance personnel keeps an eye on that money.

"We don't necessarily look for ex-cops or ex-military," says Steve Koenig, the tall former Villanova football player who, as director of security and surveillance at the Mirage, hires security staff. "We want ambassadors in customer service." About sixty such "ambassadors" patrol the floor of the Mirage during any one shift, most of them in uniform. In this atypical American town, anyone who is *not* gambling is regarded as suspicious, and carefully watched.

"Criminals prey on people's weaknesses, their greed or naiveté," says Koenig. Some slot players, for example, become so engrossed in finding a winning machine that they move dazedly from slot to slot, leaving behind a jacket or purse. Other guests, intent on their game, accept the offer of anyone who is dressed like a hotel employee to take their bills and change them. More often than not, says Dan Williams, assistant manager of the hotel's slots, the casino will reimburse a ripped-off client. "It's peanuts," he says. "Cheap advertising."

Fewer security guards carry weapons than they did ten years ago (in part due to prohibitive insurance premiums), yet their presence is still daunting. A casino security officer has the right to detain and question anyone on his employer's premises, just as a grocery-store employee can detain a suspected shoplifter. As a guardian of private property, a security officer can also expel anyone from a casino—or an apartment complex.

The presence of so many uniformed security guards is intended to intimidate potential crooks, say directors of security and surveillance. But it can also create an atmosphere strange to most visitors; people entering Las Vegas casinos may feel that they are always being watched. And they are.

The elite of the security industry are surveillance officers, culled from the ranks of pit bosses, floor managers, and dealers. Some are even former cheaters who decided to put their skills to legal use. They watch the casino floor through hundreds of cameras hidden in the ceiling, Las Vegas's famous "eye in the sky." Harrah's alone has three hundred cameras and seventy VCRs in its new, upgraded million-dollar surveillance system.

More than anything else, these cameras are used to resolve customer disputes, says Pat Cipolla, who heads casino surveillance at the Mirage. Assistant slot manager Dan Williams says that about three times a day a casino patron will argue that a machine has malfunctioned. Williams knows the machines are correct almost all of the time, but the casino often pays off even patently fake claims "to keep the client happy." (Williams admits he uses a criterion for deciding who gets paid off: "You look at the caliber of the shoes, old or new. You can tell a lot by shoes.")

The cameras are also used to watch employees. John Palumbo transferred twenty-six years of experience on a New Jersey police force to a job as a security officer at Bally's, where he worked for two years. "It seemed liked they watched us more then they watched the floor," he says. "One time I was talking to one of the girls in the coin cage. I talked to her for about ten minutes, but I was watching what was going on around me. I got a call on the radio to call the office. They chewed me out and said I wasn't doing my job."

Palumbo grew tired of the casino's rules and regulations and quit. Now he delivers pizzas, sometimes earning more money than his peak wage of $8.40 an hour at Bally's.

Palumbo's profile is typical of security guards: a retired police officer or armed-forces veteran supplementing his income. He received little formal training for the job. "Security work is nothing more than common sense, just like policing," he says.

The combination of low pay and minimal training can create costly problems, according to E. Les Combs, a personal-injury lawyer who sues casinos when security guards overstep the bounds of their responsibilities. "We're talking about relatively low-paid employees, minimal background checks to their criminal history and experience," he says.

Combs also prosecutes cases involving bar bouncers and security guards at apartment complexes. The national trend toward private security forces, in fact, may have reached a peak in Las Vegas, where residents often seem as obsessed about guards and gates as do casino security managers. These jobs do not pay well, says Ray Eicher, of Holman Security. Holman employs about eighty guards, who make between $4.75 and $5.50 an hour. "That's why we don't get ex-military," he says. Holman hires recent high-school graduates, older undereducated people who need jobs, and retired people. "We're looking for people looking for an extra something to do."

Holman guards do not carry weapons. "If you need a guard with a gun, then you don't need a guard—you need a police officer," says Eicher, adding that weapons raise insurance premiums for the company.

An armed guard is a deterrent, he says, but it can also escalate the level of violence. "Training doesn't cover upstairs," he says, tapping his head. "Regardless of how much training you have, there's always the possibility that someone's going to shoot someone else." The purpose of most security guards is simply to deter, to observe, and to report.

"The old Las Vegas used to have the cowboy-with-the-gun-on-the-hip kind of security," says Eicher. "Most casino security now wear suits or sports jackets." As Las Vegas changes from a family-owned town to a corporate-owned city, many casinos have to answer to corporate shareholders who do not like to hear about lawsuits over the use of excessive force. Even Binion's Horseshoe Club, a notoriously rough casino opened by Benny Binion in 1951, mellowed in the nineties.

The modern Horseshoe is a far cry from what it was in 1979, when the casino's security kicked out a thirty-eight-year-old Nevada Test Site worker named Rance Blevin who became unruly after losing two hundred dollars. Blevin responded by breaking the Horseshoe's windows. Moments later he was shot, execution-style, outside the casino. By the time police arrived, Benny Binion's son Ted had locked himself and the pit boss suspected of the murder in the casino cage in an effort to escape arrest. The police had to kick in the cage. According to the *Las Vegas Sun*, the pit boss served three years' probation.

Six years later, Benny's grandson Steven Fechser helped two security officers beat up two men suspected of counting cards. Both Barry Finn, a professional gambler and retired airline pilot, and Allen Brown, an engineer, went from Binion's interrogation room to the hospital; Brown suffered five broken ribs and a ruptured spleen. Binion's later made a private settlement reportedly worth $675,000 with the two men. In the criminal case that followed the settlement, Metro detectives testified that they could not find the surveillance tape for the night of the beatings.

Les Combs, who represented Finn and Brown in their civil case, says he sues casinos for excessive force a good deal less often these days. "From the lack of business in that area, I assume they must be learning," says Combs, who has prosecuted about a hundred such cases in his nineteen-year career. He thinks the flurry of lawsuits in the eighties led to more training for security officers, which led to fewer charges of excessive force.

■　■　■

Murders and petty thefts—even the occasional armed robbery of a casino—are crimes that could be transposed to other gambling cities. But geography sets Las Vegas apart from places like Atlantic City and Biloxi, Mississippi. It sits in a valley surrounded by unaccommodating desert, which means that visitors must stay in the city's lodgings. This captive audience is prey not only to the casinos, but also to criminals who have adapted themselves well to the peculiarities of this strange terrain.

Fraud Detective Larry Duis has seen many crimes that have an "only in Las Vegas" ring in his eighteen years with Metro. His office in the Municipal Building, one block from Fremont Street, is decorated with posters of Chevrolet Corvettes (which he races) and an FBI "Wanted" poster of a woman he admires: she robbed a Brink's truck and got away.

Duis describes one case from the summer of 1995. He pulls a mug shot from a thick file: the man in the picture looks pleasant but sleepy with calm, droopy eyes. His origins are not obvious: European? Hispanic? Middle Eastern?

That's what made him so good, says Duis (who would not reveal the man's name). This middle-aged man would hang around the bell desk of the busier, larger casinos, waiting until he heard a pair of tourists speaking one of the three foreign languages he understood: French, German, or Spanish. When he found his prey he would chat them up, feign familiarity with their hometown, and ask them to dinner. Later he would get to know them better and find out where their parents lived. "I'll say hello when I return to Europe tomorrow," he'd promise.

And say hello he did, according to Duis. He would call from his hotel room, assume the role of policeman, district attorney, or lawyer, and tell the parent that their child had run into trouble in the States, advising them to send money immediately. He used the names of real Las Vegas attorneys, but added his own post-office box address.

Duis doesn't know exactly how much the man made, but knows that he asked for a larger amount with each new victim. "He lived like a king," says Duis, thumbing through snapshots found in the man's belongings after his arrest. In one picture he leans against the rail of the balcony of his suite, the lights of Las Vegas spreading behind him. In another, two undressed women lounge on couches inside the suite. Apparently he moved from one hotel to the next, living in style, gambling when he wasn't working.

The detectives got a break in the case when they recognized one of the man's aliases in a case that the forgery division had prosecuted. Duis and his men copied the mug shot and sent it to bell desks and casino security and surveillance directors throughout the city. One director called back: "Your man is staying here," he told the detectives.

The man turned out to be a well-traveled Algerian who sent money to his wife and child in Germany, where he was also wanted on unspecified charges. The case was expensive: the Clark County District Attorney had to hire an interpreter ("All of a sudden all he could speak was French," says Duis), and pay to fly victims from Germany to Las Vegas. Despite the difficulties, they got a conviction.

McCarran Airport is another easy place to make quick illegal money. The tourist who puts her expensive-looking bag on the X-ray conveyor belt unwittingly hands it over to a thief when she gets in line for the metal detector: a con artist, wearing enough metal to cause a delay, can jump in line in front of her. While the line is held up, his partner on the other side can make off with the bag. It could happen anywhere, of course, but McCarran is the perfect airport for this scam, because tourists there tend to carry a lot of cash. "This is Las Vegas!" detectives Kevin Johnson and Keith Blaskoe of Metro's tourist-safety unit exclaim in unison. "People come here to gamble," says Johnson, "to double their money. They've always got a couple thousand U.S. on them."

■ ■ ■

Most people carry a lot of money in Las Vegas, but some people flaunt their wealth, wearing flashy gold jewelry and sleek designer clothes, and carrying expensive bags.

"Las Vegas is the Mecca of the nouveau riche," says Lieutenant Cobb. People with money flock to big events, like the 1991 prize fight between Razor Ruddock and Mike Tyson at the Mirage. "There were forty thousand people trying to get into that fight," he says. Outside, people tried to buy scalped tickets. Inside, fans modeled their wealth, those with $5,000 ringside seats proudly displaying their tickets in breast pockets. Metro officers wove in and out of the crowd, looking for signs of a scam.

When one ticketholder, an older gentleman with a twenty-nine-year-old date, paraded down the corridor, the officers saw their catch. A group of Latinos had surrounded the old man, talking to him, talking to each other, annoying everyone. "The officer who saw this said they looked like bees around a flower," says Cobb. The old man, distracted by the buzz of conversation around him, didn't even notice when one of the crew lifted his ticket from his jacket's breast pocket.

When the officers made the arrest, they realized they had nabbed three generations of a Central American family: a grandmother, a mother, and a few kids. "The fourteen-year-old had ten thousand dollars in his shoe," says Cobb. "I think they had a total of fourteen thousand."

Counterfeiters also make a bundle in Las Vegas, since it is a money town, and the money moves fast. In 1996 a group of counterfeiters printed Clark County payroll checks in Los Angeles using a high-resolution scanner. They brought the blank checks to Las Vegas, embossed the amount, and waited until payday.

"Fraud usually takes place in these high-pressure environments," says Cobb. Casinos encourage people to cash their paychecks inside, offering free drinks and drawings for cash as incentives. Payday in the casino means long lines and impatient check holders, making it an ideal time and place for counterfeiters to cash their fake checks.

■ ■ ■

Inside the casino of the New York New York Hotel everything is squeaky-clean. There is no smell of urine in the alleys of Little Italy, no gum stuck to the sidewalks of Greenwich Village. The only traffic jams are those caused by crowds gathering around the occasional jackpot, or waiting in line at the restaurants and bars.

The casino industry has constructed the same kind of sanitized image for the story of crime in Las Vegas. "Bugsy's Lounge" is now just a second-string showroom at the Flamingo, which has installed a bronze plaque honoring its infamous founder in its rose garden. Residents of Las Vegas, playing their own part in maintaining the city's image, have been insisting to outsiders for years that "It's just like anywhere else."

It isn't. The number of crimes and criminals in Las Vegas today may be no higher than that of other major cities. But because of the unique sets of pressures under which this remarkable city lives, the kinds of crime and criminals—and the forces deployed to arrest them—are both different and more colorful, as they were in the days when mobsters and their agents, instead of publically traded corporations, called most of the shots.

Why They're Mad

SOUTHERN NEVADA VERSUS THE UNITED STATES
Randolph Court

EDITOR'S INTRODUCTION

Few regions of the United States are at the same time so dependent on, so suspicious of, and so hostile to the federal government as the extensive, largely barren counties of southern Nevada.

The more one talks to southern Nevadans—whether natives, residents of long standing, or relative newcomers—the more one hears of a proud, defiant self-image: to be a Nevadan is, even today, to be a kind of freelance homesteader, a don't-tread-on-me entrepreneur. The long legacy of liberal codes unlike those of other states—relaxed requirements for marriage and divorce, legalized prostitution and gambling, freedom from taxes and speed limits—has become a part of the state's self-definition and claim to uniqueness. By now corporate, environmentalist, and other pressures have just about killed the actuality of the truly independent pioneer. But the gambling mentality, the hostility to regulation and taxation, and the remaining wide-open spaces of southern Nevada foster its perpetuation as an ideal.

In the case of Clark County, it was the federal government that first widened and paved the highway to Los Angeles, making Las Vegas accessible to its primary source of investors, tourists, and new residents. During the 1930s, the federal government spent more than $70 million (ten times that in current dollars) in the area, building Hoover Dam and Boulder

City, originally a government-owned company town for dam workers. During World War II, Washington paid for the three-million-acre gunnery training center that would become Nellis Air Force Base, and the magnesium-processing plant that grew into the town of Henderson. The Nevada Test Site, north of the city, attracted tourists, contractors, controversy, and employees in the years after 1951.

During the Depression, while it was still under construction, the Hoover Dam became a national magnet for tourists, as well as unemployed men seeking work. It attracted up to 300,000 people a year, most of whom stopped in Las Vegas, which came to serve as the administrative and supply center for the mammoth project. Dam workers, meanwhile—like airmen and metal workers later on—flocked to Las Vegas's casinos and brothels. The giant project helped to guarantee Clark County cheap water and electricity for many years to come. New Deal funding, channeled to Nevada by powerful Democratic senators, helped expand Las Vegas's sewer system, pave its streets, and build a public school, the first city park and golf course, and the first convention center.

As the benefits of the Hoover Dam project and other New Deal spending began to dry up in the late 1930s, World War II came along to give southern Nevada a second major boost. Washington's decision to concentrate new defense plants and military installations on inland Sunbelt cities proved an immense boon to Las Vegas and its neighbors. Nellis Air Force Base—originally a wartime school for pilots and gunners, later the nation's primary training center for tactical air combat—expanded the population of North Las Vegas and enriched the local economy through three major wars and the periods of anti-Soviet arsenal building in between. Basic Magnesium, Inc., a federally controlled processing plant south of Las Vegas, gave birth during World War II to another company town, now the burgeoning suburb of Henderson. The vast BMI industrial complex was later sold to the state, which in turn handed it over to its corporate tenants. In 1951 the Nevada Test Site, its boundaries beginning sixty miles north of the city, became the locus for U.S. atom-bomb tests—for some years a tourist attraction in themselves, as gamblers gathered in Strip hotels to watch the mushroom clouds rising across the desert. After the tests were halted in 1959, the Department of Energy found other uses for the Nye County tract; the DOE remains one of the largest civilian employers in southern Nevada, although Nye County has lost government jobs in recent years.

All of these projects brought tens of thousands of new federal employees and their families to southern Nevada, provided millions of dollars of work for local contractors, and helped fill the casinos and hotels of Las Vegas. The heavy federal presence in the region, in fact, was used as justification for several Washington-financed projects in Clark County in the 1950s and 1960s. The Interstate Highway Act of 1956 paid 90 percent of the cost of building I-15, without which it is impossible to imagine Las Vegas today.

With the end of World War II (and the subsequent boom in the private casino-resort economy), the federal presence in southern Nevada—though still dominant in terms of land ownership and control—began to seem less essential and, to some local citizens, less benign. Casino owners and the civic officials dependent on their prosperity resented the intrusion of the Kefauver Commission (and, following in its wake, the FBI) into their ways of doing business. They resented even more the Tennessee Senator's proposal for a 10-percent federal gambling tax, which Senator Pat McCarran worked ferociously to kill. The city and county strongly resisted federal (and other) efforts in 1968-71 to bring racial integration to their schools and hotels.

Favored by Washington for many years because of what government officials regarded as its red-white-and-blue patriotism (no questions about the value or danger of atomic weapons here: "from the Civil War through World War II, the state of Nevada has always been in the vanguard in the support of such warfare," editorialized the Las Vegas Review Journal), Nevada gradually emerged as one of the leaders of a number of anti-regulatory, anti-federal movements. The "Sagebrush Rebellion," the "County Supremacy" movement (which asserts the primacy of county-based power over state or federal claims), and the "Wise Use Movement" (an industry-supported drive to expand the commercial exploitation of federal lands) all took root, as we shall see, in rural southern Nevada as well as in other Western desert states like Idaho and Montana. At the same time, Nevada's gambling interests were choking on a suggestion of the Clinton administration's to revive the idea of a national gambling tax (a suggestion that died stillborn), and bitterly fought its proposal (adopted in 1995) for a national commission to examine the social and economic impacts of gambling. The long-debated federal proposal to turn Yucca Mountain, 100 miles north of Las Vegas, into the central nuclear dump site for the entire country aroused divided, but largely negative, responses. While the project could create as many as 20,000 jobs, people also worried about their safety (Nevadans had grown more suspicious of nuclear weapons, alive or dead, since 1951), and the unwelcome image of the Silver State being used as the nation's garbage can for dangerous wastes.

In historical fact, Las Vegas has never been a cowboy or even a miner's town, and has little in common with legendary frontier boomtowns like Abilene, Denver, San Francisco, or Tulsa. It began its European-American life as a railroad watering junction, survived as a warehousing and supply center, grew into a spoiled ward of the federal government, and eventually prospered as a destination resort, thanks to its casinos.

But the city is surrounded by millions of acres of both cattle-ranching and mining country, and has persistently drawn its own image and ethos from the lives lived in neighboring rural counties. The very first casino-hotels, both downtown and on the Strip—the Frontier, the El Rancho, the Thunderbird, the Golden Nugget, the Horseshoe—adopted Old West motifs, with antlers and Indian blankets on the walls. Early civic boosters created "Helldorado Days" parades and an imitation frontier village, while at the same time tearing down almost all remaining evidence of the city's genuine past. Casino dealers, cocktail waitresses, and showgirls still wear latter-day versions of historic Western attire. In 1985, Las Vegas bought the National Finals Rodeo away from Oklahoma City; for ten days every December, the city fills up with genuine cowboys and cowgirls and tens of thousands of their fans from all over the West.

This particular image (long symbolized by the thirty-foot neon "Vegas Vic" sign that welcomed visitors to Fremont Street) is now submerged in dozens of other tourist-dazzling themes. An equestrian statue of Benny Binion—former prisoner, admitted murderer, and casino pioneer—was erected at the intersection of First and Ogden Streets after Binion died in 1989. Today, Cowboy Ben is surrounded and dwarfed by faceless, looming parking garages, built to serve visitors to the computerized "Fremont Street Experience" and the casinos it connects. Ben and his horse stand as a symbol of the doomed but defiant "cowboy" spirit of southern Nevada, and its resistance to anyone—particularly the United States government—who tries to fence that in.

To see the archaic concept at its purest, one has to venture out of the city. Two hundred miles northwest of Las Vegas (a skip and a jump, as Nevada measures distances) a collection of angry, hardheaded southern Nevada ranchers and townspeople has refused to accept the notion that the federal government owns their land; that agents of the despised Bureau of Land Management can order them how to raise their cattle and live their lives; that the Old West of legend ever died.

DAVID LITTLEJOHN

■ ■ ■

Roy Clifford Sr. pulled himself slowly, stiffly, from behind the wheel of his old red pickup truck and leaned, half in half out, his rear end on the seat, his feet on the ground, as the dust he had kicked up on his way in blew past. He nodded at us, the boys and me, but didn't say anything. He looked down and spat in the dirt. The boys, Roy Jr. and Cougar, both in their forties, were leaning on a fence a few feet away, watching, waiting to hear how the meeting had gone with Charley Wright, their range man-ager from the federal Bureau of Land Management. But the old man just kept staring at the dirt, watching his spit fade dry.

There were no more answers today than there were yesterday, or the week before, or the week before that. The Cliffords' 300,000-acre grazing allotment, Stone Cabin Valley in central Nye County, Nevada, some two hundred miles northwest of Las Vegas, was still closed. The herd was over on the Ralston allotment, but it would only be able to stay there for a few more weeks; after that, there is a fairly good chance they'll be allowed to move some of the animals into the Toiyabe National Forest, near Hunt's Canyon, in a mountain range the Forest Service calls the Monitor Complex. Of course, the Forest Service will only allow 130 head up there, and only for July and August, so they'll have to feed the rest on their pri-vate land. "And, of course, hay is $185 a goddamn ton...and cattle prices are in the basement... Had to sell nearly the whole damn herd last year. Barely got enough for 'em to buy the hay to feed the rest...," Roy Sr. says.

Life is like that these days for ranchers in Nye County, the third-largest county in the United States, where the traditional economy is largely based on the natural resources of the high desert: forage for livestock and mineral wealth. Nine-tenths of the county is federally owned, adminis-tered by the BLM and the Forest Service, who have the power to close a rancher's grazing allotment or cut his herds in the interests of managing the health of the range. Ranchers can thrive, but only when conditions permit, and the last six years have been hard. "They're like that Chinese boy standing in front of those tanks in Tiananmen Square," said William Champney, a retired professor of agricultural economics at University of Nevada at Reno. "They're about to get squashed."

The total cattle population in the state of Nevada hovered around 500,000 in 1995 and 1996, a fifty-year low, and almost a 30-percent drop from the 1982 peak of about 700,000 head. In Nye County, 30,000 head had fallen to 16,000 over the same period.

Actually, ranchers represent only a small percentage of the overall econ-omy in Nye County, which has a population of only about 18,000—a density of one person per square mile. (The density of Clark County, just to the south, is about 125 per square mile, thanks to Las Vegas.) Almost everyone is feeling the pinch in the central and northern parts of Nye. But ranchers cast a long shadow in the Old Western culture that still dominates so much of people's thinking. Out here, the embattled ranchers have become symbols of persecution—tough, hard-working families, descendants of a long, noble tradition, being driven into extinction by meddlesome federal regulators with screwed-up priorities.

This handful of ranchers has inspired an antifederalist revolution, and made the county famous in the process. Nye County Commissioner Dick Carver, a small rancher in the Great Smoky Valley, has been doing battle with the BLM and the Forest Service at every turn since he was elected in 1988. He claims that federal regulations unfairly and illegally disrupt the "customs and culture" of Nye. His fiery antifederalist rhetoric has made him a hero in the national (and largely western) County Supremacy movement, which seeks to elevate the power of counties relative to state and federal governments, and has been widely associated with militia-type activism. Another rancher in Nye, Wayne Hage, has mounted a $28 million suit against United States over private-property rights on federal lands, and has become in the process a hero in the anti-environmentalist "Wise Use" movement, which seeks open public lands to more private mining, logging, and ranching.

Carver and Hage have been depicted in the liberal press as villains, players in a broad, nationwide network of antifederalist and anti-environmentalist radicals. In the mainstream press they tend to appear as relatively harmless cranks, extreme representatives of the anti-Washington attitude often credited with the Republican congressional sweep of 1994. In the right-leaning press they're portrayed as heroes, freedom-fighters, defenders of liberty. But out here they're just Dick and Wayne, two common-sensical Old Westerners with unusually loud voices.

■ ■ ■

The hub of the cowboy culture in Nye is Tonopah, the county seat, a place where people wear plaid shirts and drive pickup trucks with gun racks visible through the back window. It's also a place where the county's economic decline is plain to see. I helped Jim Wolfe unload a delivery one night at his Ace Hardware store on Main Street. It didn't take long, maybe twenty-five minutes. The 131 boxes represented the first delivery Jim had received in twelve weeks; ten years ago, he got deliveries two to four times that size every week. But then, ten years ago he had ten full-time employees, several part-timers, and two accountants. Now he has one full- and one part-timer, and he gets deliveries about this size once every couple of months.

The population in Tonopah dropped from 4,250 people in 1992 to about 3,100 four years later. One of the area's biggest employers, the Anaconda molybdenum mine, closed in the late 1980s, killing six hundred jobs. The Air Force moved its F117A Stealth fighters from Nellis Air Force Base down to New Mexico in 1991-92.

Tonopah has the look and feel of a space colony in a science-fiction movie, nestled between a bare 6,000-foot peak on the west and lower, rolling, bare brown hills on the east. The place is iridescent at sunset, gray at dusk; at night, the sky is louder than the town below. Maybe it's the wind. Maybe the stars are brighter than the lights.

Main Street is Highway 95, the two-lane highway that runs from Reno to Las Vegas. Travelers stop for snacks and gas; some stay the night in one of the motels. Otherwise, Main Street is pretty quiet. Locals crawl along slowly in their pickup trucks. A few pull into the post office. An old man in an insulated, plaid wool shirt and a hunting cap stops in at the Hock Shop to see if Bob has any bungee cords. The signs in front of the Hock Shop read "Guns&Jewelry," "Antiques," "Tourist Information," "BuyoSell." But no, Bob doesn't have any bungee cords.

Most of the action is up at the top of the hill on the south end of town, at the Station House Casino, Restaurant & Mall. That's where Scolari's Warehouse Market, Family Drug, Oasis Apparel & Gifts, KHWK Radio, the Bureau of Mines, and the Nevada Department of Welfare are all located. Old women and men wearing hats with farm equipment and motor-sports logos mill about in the Station House, smoking cigarettes and feeding quarters into the video-poker games and slots. Others eat grilled-cheese sandwiches and drink coffee in the restaurant.

Tonopah still calls itself "Mining Town, USA," a tribute to its historical roots. "The first great mining camp of the 20th century," it is called in a Convention Center and Visitors Authority brochure. A prospector named Jim Butler struck it rich here in the spring of 1900: an assay showed 395 ounces of silver and 15 1/2 ounces of gold to the ton of ore in the first Tonopah mines. In two quick years, a tent camp grew into a bustling town with churches, saloons, stagecoach lines, and newspapers. The ninety-five years since then have been something of a roller-coaster ride. According to a short historical review on the back of the Station House Restaurant's souvenir menu, "Tonopah's economy tends to swing through bust and boom times. Right now things are pretty rough in town."

If the economy is currently on a downward slide, according to most locals, the reason is clear: the Feds.

■ ■ ■

Nye County is huge, about the size of Vermont and New Hampshire combined, and the federal government—the BLM, the Forest Service, and the military—owns approximately 90 percent of it, or ten million acres. As far as the locals are concerned, BLM and Forest Service employees—range managers, biologists, geologists, archeologists, and all the rest—are an omnipresent nuisance.

"This place is a federal colony," said Trish Rippie, a Tonopah real-estate agent. "It's like India under the British!"

"The BLM office is like Dracula's castle," said convention-center director Jim Merlino. "People used to be afraid to even go in there because they were scared of losing another pint of blood."

No one is more adamant on the subject of federal bureaucrats than Commissioner Dick Carver: "Government is driven by bureaucrats who hold an appointed position, and think they're above God, and above the law, and they can do any damn thing they want!" His voice is high-pitched and nasal, like Mike Tyson's but a little raspier. It peaks at something close to a squeal whenever he says the word "Constitution," which he frequently does. "The Constitution is very specific about the powers of the federal government!…The only power they have to make law has to either deal with the defense of the nation, commerce among the states, communications, or creation of states. It doesn't give them a blank check to make any law they want." (Carver carries a copy of the Constitution in his shirt pocket.)

By July 1994, Carver had had enough: the BLM and the Forest Service were out of control. They were ruining people's lives left and right, and they had to be stopped. "They backed us into a corner," he said. "We had to stand up or bury our heads in the sand, and we chose to stand up."

That spring, runoff from melting snow had washed out an access road in Jefferson Canyon, in the mountains out behind the Carver ranch. Those are Toiyabe National Forest lands, and the Forest Service had decided to close the road permanently. But Carver wouldn't allow it. On the Fourth of July, he drove his D8 Caterpillar out and, with a large, well-armed picnic gathering cheering him on, he bulldozed the road. Forest Service employee Dave Young knew of Carver's intentions ahead of time, and he was there holding a sign: "Stop! Unauthorized disturbance. Dave Young, USFS." Carver didn't stop.

At first, the story of Carver's bulldozer protest receive little coverage beyond publications like *Livestock Market Digest*, in which Carver and his friends were hailed as patriots. But the following year, after the Oklahoma City bombing that killed 638 people, journalists writing about antifederalist activists began making pilgrimages to Nye. Publications like *The Nation* and *The Village Voice* started making connections between depressed areas like Nye County, dependent on their natural resources, and the anti-environmentalist "Wise Use" movement—which its supporters regard as a defense of private-property rights, its detractors as a front for the livestock, mining, logging, and oil industries. From there, connections were made to armed, militia-type resistance, of the sort that seems to have inspired the Oklahoma City disaster. Morris Dees cited Dick Carver as a dangerous example in his book *Gathering Storm: America's Militia Threat*. In a *Nation* cover story of May 1995, David Helvarg wrote, "In the West the militias are using the existing Wise Use network as one of their primary recruiting bases, arguing for military resistance to the government and its 'preservationist' backers."

■ ■ ■

When I visited Carver and his wife Midge in 1997, they estimated that four hundred journalists had been out to see them before me. On a scale of one to ten, they rated most of the resulting stories "minus nine." The only treatments they liked were a documentary made by Danish filmmakers and a feature article in the October 23, 1995 issue of *Time*, the cover of which they have framed and hung in their living room. Over the legend "Don't Tread On Me," the Carvers and a group of friends and neighbors are pictured standing out in the desert, glowering at the camera. The article, "Unrest in the West," recounted the the plowing of the Jefferson Canyon road, and seemed to make a conscious effort not to make Carver look like a wacko. "Some of Dick Carver's critics have tried to link him to militias and white supremacists," wrote Erik Larson in the *Time* survey, "but it is a mistake to dismiss him as just another crackpot. The forces powering the Nye County rebellion are those resculpting the political and social landscape of America at large. They just happen to have converged with their greatest intensity in the West, where private and public interests clash directly and daily, typically over such visceral issues as land and water."

■ ■ ■

In the past, ranchers were the stewards of the range here in Nye, as they were everywhere else in the West. It was in their interest to keep the range in good shape for their own cattle, and for the most part they did a good job. Of course, there was never any question that the primary purpose of western rangeland was to provide feed for livestock. Nowadays, people in Nye believe the bureaucrats spend too much time worrying about unprofitable critters like desert tortoises and wild horses, and not enough time worrying about cattle and their owners.

The history of the people of Nye County runs parallel to the evolution of conservationism in the public-policy arena. In fact, the very word "conservation" meant something quite different when Tonopah was founded than it does to most Americans today. Gifford Pinchot, founder of the U.S. Forest Service, argued in 1910, "The first principle of conservation is development, the use of the natural resources now existing on this continent for the benefit of the people who live here now."

That idea was agreeable to the resource developers of the day, from the miners and ranchers in places like Tonopah to the eastern capitalists who underwrote many of their first ventures. It was also an idea that jibed well with nineteenth-century federal land policy, which was geared primarily towards the goal of "disposal"—the conversion of the federal estate into private property, through mechanisms like the Homestead Act.

The Homestead Act of 1862 had offered new settlers 160-acre tracts of land in territories west of the Missouri River for next to nothing, on the condition that they cultivate and maintain them. Many ranchers and miners moved to the western states and territories hoping to obtain land on similar terms. The Mining Act of 1872 offered a means for miners to acquire title to subsurface minerals, and the Taylor Grazing Act of 1934 allowed ranchers to secure grazing allotments. But deeds to subsurface claims gave miners only the right to mine, as grazing allotments gave ranchers only the right to graze livestock. Unlike midwestern homesteaders, they were never able to acquire full title to the land itself, which remained the property of the United States.

There was more to Gifford Pinchot's definition of conservation than his first stated principle. Conservation, he said, also meant prevention of waste. "The natural resources must be developed and preserved for the benefit of the many, and not merely for the profit of the few." Translated into public policy, this new Progressive Era concept led to a scientific, systematically administered process of resource management, and the end of the old, liberal land-disposal policies. From now on (with rare exceptions), the federal estate was to remain in federal ownership. (In order to acquire available BLM lands surrounding Las Vegas, which still amount to more than 27,000 acres, property developers must offer the federal agency land of equal value somewhere else.) Unlike their luckier farmer-cousins further east, ranchers and miners in places like Nye were doomed to live their lives and run their businesses under the watchful eyes of federal landlords and regulators.

In early days, it didn't matter much. Up through the 1940s and '50s, the BLM (counseled by advisory panels made up largely of ranchers) continued to champion the interests of livestock on Interior Department lands. It wasn't until the 1960s and '70s, when environmentalists gained power in the public-policy arena, that the concept of "conservation" was transformed into that of "preservation." In 1976, the fate of ranchers and miners on public land was sealed when Congress passed the Federal Lands Policy Management Act, which officially gave the BLM authority to manage Interior Department lands with "multiple interests" in mind. In an area like Nye County, for example, decisions regarding the number of cattle allowed on a particular grazing allotment must now be made with the interests of wild horses (or desert tortoises, or underground water sources) taken into account as well.

■ ■ ■

"Most of these operators are still living in the eighteen-hundreds," says BLM range manager Mark Swinney, as he gazes off into the foothills below the Hot Creek Range. "We know more about how to manage the range now."

Swinney is a short, stout man in his early forties who talks with a harsh midwestern twang, his conversation peppered with acronyms like ESIs, WSAs, and AUMs (Ecological Site Inventories, Wilderness Study Areas, and Animal Unit Months). We are ten or fifteen miles north of Highway 6, on a dirt road in the middle of the Cliffords' Stone Cabin Valley grazing allotment—which, Swinney says, was closed because it had been "beat to snot" by drought and overgrazing. We are looking for cattle and wild horses, the stragglers and roamers that ranchers lose track of (on a 300,000-acre allotment, it's not hard to lose track of a few head), and horses that habitually wander back to the watering holes they're used to.

"There we go," Swinney says, focusing his field glasses. Off in the distance, five cows stand knee-deep in forage, chomping away. "Those'd be Tom Colvin's." He hands me the binoculars. "See the dewlaps." Each of the animals has a pendulous fold of skin hanging under its throat, a flap that was cut as a marking (instead of a brand). Swinney marks their location on his map. The Colvins are allowed twenty-five strays out here; if Swinney finds more than that he can give them a citation.

We turn and head back down towards the highway, passing a heavily grazed and beaten area near a watering hole which looked like a dirt parking lot. "This is why we had to close this allotment," Swinney says. Once cattle and wild horses get used to drinking from a watering hole, they will keep coming back and destroy the grasses and brush.

Near the highway, four cows turn tail and run from us. Swinney gnashes his teeth. "Now this really rankles me," he growls. "You'd have to be half-blind with dirty glasses not to see these animals next to the damn highway." He pauses and marks their location on the map.

Away from the water holes, the forage is healthier and appears to be making a comeback. But the allotment is still not ready to be reopened. "I don't know what the solution is here," Swinney says. "I think we'll probably have to keep this allotment closed. The best thing for us, in terms of avoiding controversy, would be a dry spring and summer." That way, it would be hard for anyone to question the decision to keep the allotment closed. "But eventually we'll have to address the issue."

Modern range science is bunk, as far as a lot of the ranchers around here are concerned, especially those whose families have been here for a century or more, and grew set in their ways before the BLM and the Forest Service were ever created. "Cowmen know how to take care of the range better than bureaucrats," they will tell you. "We've been doing it for generations, through good times and bad." Some feel that their family history, in and of itself, gives them title to the land. Others go to their safes and pull out stacks of deeds, or records of of the inheritance taxes they had to pay when their parents or grandparents died. "Look," they say, pointing at their papers. "If this doesn't prove we have private-property rights out here, then what does?"

■ ■ ■

Roy Clifford Sr.'s grandfather, Ed Sr., had already been in the area for thirty years when Jim Butler struck it rich and the town of Tonopah was created. Ed Sr. arrived in Stone Cabin Valley, about thirty miles east of Tonopah, in 1872. According to family legend, he got off the boat from England, walked out to Nevada with a wagon train, and built the original stone cabin after which the valley was named. In time, he and his descendants built up a small ranching operation.

Now two generations of Cliffords live out in the hollow near the original stone cabin. Roy Sr. lives in a three-room wood-frame bungalow built in 1916. Roy Jr. and Cougar have trailer homes of their own. Cougar's mother, who is Roy Jr.'s Aunt Gladis, lives alone in a cottage of her own; her husband, Ed, died of leukemia, which her nephew blames on radioactive dust from the nuclear blasts that took place eighty miles south in the 1950s. "You used to be able to look down that way," Roy Jr. says, pointing down towards the test site, "and see huge mushroom clouds fill the sky."

The Cliffords' closest neighbors, the Fallinis, who live about twenty miles east, have been here since the early days, too. Take Highway 6 over the pass between the Hot Creek Range and the Kawich Range, past the boarded-up bar and restaurant at Warm Springs, turn right on Highway 375 (now officially labeled the "Extraterrestrial Highway" because of the persistent legend that creatures from outer space landed nearby in 1947), and you'll see the Fallini ranch house on the left, at the foot of the Pancake Range. Other than the ranch house, the sheds, and the corrals holding several hundred head of cattle, there's nothing else for miles around.

Joe Fallini's grandfather, Giovanni (a.k.a. Joe) Fallini, arrived in the area sometime around 1860. Giovanni was born near the Swiss-Italian border and worked his way across the Atlantic on a ship to New York City. He later took a train out west (he had relatives in Eureka, California) and began working in the mines. He married an Italian girl and started hauling wood and freight for a living. The freight business took him down to Eden Creek, at the foot of the Kawich Mountains, on the southwestern part of the Fallinis' present range. Giovanni ran a store down near the Reveille mill site for a while, and began building up the ranch near Eden Creek one cow at a time. When the biggest ranching operation in the area, the Reed family's United Cattle and Packing Company (which covered three million acres), fell apart due to droughts and bad cattle markets in the 1920s, the Fallinis, the Cliffords, and several others bought the grazing and water rights to the range. Today, the Fallinis' grazing allotments cover 600,000 acres. The Cliffords' Stone Cabin Valley allotment is about half that size, and they share it with another, bigger rancher, Tom Colvin.

■ ■ ■

"We never wanted to be a big outfit," Roy Sr. told me over Pepsis in his small living room, whose walls are lined with deer and elk heads. "We just wanted to make an honest living. We used to run a hundred fifty or two hundred head of cattle—whatever we figured we could make a living on. It was just a nice little operation."

Roy Sr.'s dad, Joe, and Joe's brother Ed, survived that way up into the 1970s, never building up a herd of more than about five hundred head, mining in the winters to make ends meet. But as cattle prices dropped sharply in the '60s and '70s, they needed bigger herds to survive. In 1978 they bought the grazing rights for the Hunt's Canyon allotment on the western slopes of the Monitor Range, and built their herd up to about 1,200 head. Since 1989 there have been six years of bad droughts, which are hard on the forage, so the BLM has made ranchers cut their herds. At this point, it looks like the Cliffords might not make it.

The Fallinis aren't in any immediate danger of going under. For one thing, they are a bigger operation; in normal years, they run about 2,200 head. More important, they can afford to fight the BLM in court. In Joe's comfortable upstairs office in the sprawling Fallini ranch house there are sixteen large file cabinets, most of them full of records from his lawsuits. Joe has sued the BLM thirty-three times, and won more often than not. His biggest victory came on the issue of wild horses, a particularly annoying burr under local ranchers' saddles.

After the Wild and Free-Roaming Horses and Burros Act was passed in 1971, the unowned horses' numbers were allowed to grow. ("I actually prefer to call them 'feral' horses," Mark Swinney said, during our cruise through the Stone Cabin Valley allotment.) Consequently, cattle herds often had to be cut, because there was only so much forage on the range to go around. This made ranchers furious. After all, they remind you, ranchers were the ones who released these horses (or their ancestors) in the first place, around the time Model-Ts and tractors took their place. "Hell," ranchers say, "the damn things wouldn't be able to live out there in the desert if we didn't develop the wells and the water pipelines. Now the BLM's letting them eat us out of house and home."

Joe Fallini has proof of the damage they've done. He led me downstairs to the den, where enlarged copies of eighty-year-old family photographs hang on the walls. In a corner of the room stands a refrigerator-size safe, like an old-time bank vault. Joe opens it and begins digging through boxes of family photos and stacks of old deeds (signed by, among others, Warren Harding, Calvin Coolidge, and Franklin D. Roosevelt). He finds what he was looking for.

"Okay," he says. "You want to see what those wild horses did out here? Look." He spread out four color photos, all of the same view of the southeastern part of the Fallini grazing allotments. The first picture, taken in July 1980, shows the valley green and lush; the second, taken in July 1982, shows the forage sparse and stressed; the third, July 1983, shows the valley bare and dead-looking. In the fourth, dated July 1984, the valley looks about the same as it did the previous year.

Those were pretty decent rain years by high-desert standards, with an average of 8.43 inches of precipitation. (Six inches is normal. The drought years of 1985, '86, '90, and '91 each averaged 3.52 inches; the average in Las Vegas is just over four.) But between 1980 and 1984, the herds of wild horses were allowed to grow to their highest numbers in history.

Back upstairs in his office, Joe pulls out figures from a study he had prepared for his wild-horse lawsuit. When the Horse and Burro Act was passed in 1971, there were 126 wild horses on the Fallinis' Reveille grazing allotment. By 1980, when the first of the picture of Railroad Valley was taken, there were 1,233. By 1984, when the last picture was taken, the number had swelled to its 2,306. Joe sued in 1983, and three years later a judge ordered that the BLM had to keep the horses' numbers down to their 1971 level. But the cost of this and the other court battles made the victories bittersweet.

Joe's face tenses with anger. "Ever since the BLM has been in existence, they have done everything possible they could to destroy this operation. They're continually badgering us....The wild horses knocked down one of our corrals down at Cedar Park, and the BLM gave us a notice to fix it. Then we fixed it and they gave us a notice of unauthorized improvements!...They tell us we're not good range managers. That's bull. If we weren't good range managers, they never would have been able to have that many horses out there."

■ ■ ■

Last summer, Ron Huntsinger, the new BLM field-station manager for the Tonopah district, sent all of the ranchers in the area a warning that the previous dry winter and early hot summer were adding up to trouble. "The climactic conditions have the vegetation in a stressed condition and water sources are in a limited supply in many areas," he wrote.

> Due to these early drought conditions, I wanted to ask livestock operators to assess the effects on the range. We could be facing possible allotment closure(s), if the hot and dry weather conditions persist as they have early in the grazing season. We are looking to mitigate any impacts on operators whose livestock depend on public lands to meet their forage needs. In order to prevent long term damage to the range, which could result in future reductions, we suggest that operators consider such voluntary measures as water hauling, water control management, herding with pastures, early removals and reductions in herd size when needed.

Outraged at being told how to manage his land, Joe Fallini fired back, "The Twin Springs Ranch has existed since the 1860s and it was developed long before there ever was a Bureau of Land Management."

Through the years we have learned many things including how to manage, on our own, the range in a productive manner. We learned how to do this without the modern day Bureaucrat that now controls every move we make. Contrary to what you may think, it is not to our benefit to destroy the range we use. We have known there would be droughts and we know there always will be. In the past we have taken measures to protect ourselves from these droughts by maintaining at least two years of feed on what is now the Reveille allotment. We also, through the rotation of cattle and the diversification of water, maintained a thriving ecological balance on the range land. Now the Bureaucrat enters and starts destroying this concept of two years of drought feed. Due to this fact we no longer hold the peace of mind of having this extra feed. Ironically, if the Bureau of Land Management would have stayed out in the first place, we would not be in the position we are today.... Through mismanagement the BLM allowed the horses to increase from 126 head to 2,306 in 1984. This destroyed the Twin Springs Ranch management practices....

"There's no question," says Mark Swinney, as we near the end of our tour through Stone Cabin Valley, "the horses did a lot of damage. But their numbers have been down for eight years." The reason some of Fallini's allotments are still "beat to snot," in Swinney's opinion, is that Joe doesn't rotate his herd properly.

In 1991 Joe put in a request for permission to make five new water improvements on his allotments. He wanted to dig one new well and add pipelines from four other sources to make new watering holes. By creating as many different places for the livestock to drink as possible, and spreading those spots evenly over the range, he believed that both cattle and horses would be encouraged to move around, so they wouldn't trample any one area excessively.

No. No. No. Swinney shakes his head. That's not the way to do it. You have to rotate the herd, like crops on a farm. Turn off or fence off the water everywhere except for a few areas. Keep the animals in those areas for several seasons while the forage recovers everywhere else. Then rotate.

Range conservationist Charley Wright recommended that most of the Fallinis' requests for new watering holes and conduits be denied. Fallini appealed the decisions and won one of them, for a four-mile pipeline extension from a source known as Charlie's Well. The family had just gotten the news when I arrived, and they weren't going to waste any time getting the work done. "You never know. The bastards might try to change their minds." So I squeezed into one of the family's pickup trucks with Joe and his youngest daughter, Anna, and we headed out to Charlie's Well to get started.

We turned south off the Extraterrestrial Highway and bounced down a dirt road in the middle of Reveille Valley, a "fifty-year flood plain"—a flat-land where a flood can be expected at most once every fifty years. The Kawich Mountains, to the west, were purple in the afternoon light, the greasewood and button sage in the valley mostly a brownish gray. Rolling down his window, Joe saw rice grass and greenish signs of spring.

There are more than two hundred water developments on the Reveille allotment. The Fallinis have put most of them in over the last two generations. In addition to Charlie's Well, there's a Joe's Well and a Ray's Well, all named after the fellows who dug them; Witch's Well got its name when one of Joe's aunts found the site using a dowsing rod. "There wouldn't be any goddamned animals out here if it weren't for us developing the water," Joe asserted once again.

After about twenty minutes (it would take two-and-a-half hours to drive the full length of the Fallinis' allotment), we turned off the dirt road. Joe paused, reset his trip odometer and shifted into four-wheel drive. We began crawling east, driving straight over the range, at about five miles an hour. After a quarter of a mile, we stopped. The forage was three feet high and had barely been touched. There were only a few scattered cow pies on the ground, all old and as dry as shredded wheat. There was no incentive for animals to come here yet.

A stake with a red ribbon tied to the end was lying on the ground right where Joe had planted it six years ago, when he originally requested permission for the pipeline. That's where the new twenty-thousand-gallon holding tank was to go, fed by the water in the new pipe that would come straight up from Charlie's Well, four miles due south.

Joe turned the pickup and we headed for Charlie's Well, following the pipeline's future path to get a feel for the ground. "It feels pretty soft. You should be able to rip the whole four miles this afternoon." Anna nods. She is a junior at California State Polytechnic University in San Luis Obispo, majoring in agricultural economics, and she hopes eventually to take over the ranch from her parents. She's already pretty good with the Caterpillar; next she wants to get her industrial driver's license, so she can haul water in the eighteen-wheeler. Then she'll learn to fly the chopper. Joe, who has a degree in agricultural mechanics (UN-Reno), is licensed as a fixed-wing and helicopter pilot, a heavy-machinery operator, and a building contractor. He has plenty to teach his daughter.

Joe's massive D8 Cat is parked and waiting next to Charlie's Well. Its treads come up to Joe's chest and Anna's shoulders. The two climb up into the cab. Joe pushes back his Cal Poly "Ag Engineering" cap, pulls his dime-store reading glasses low on his nose, and squints, tinkering with the starter. Anna stuffs plugs into her ears.

A pair of Air Force C130s passes slowly overhead, a few hundred feet off the ground, but they don't seem to bother the three cows that have been watching us intently from a few hundred yards away. The cows scatter, though, when the bulldozer roars to life and Anna begins ripping a trench in the direction of the stake with the ribbon. She muscles along at two or three miles an hour, dragging a long, four-inch blade that looks something like a bucked tooth, cutting two feet into the ground behind her as she goes.

Joe watches for a few minutes. "She'll rip a four-inch trench north today. Tomorrow we'll rip deeper coming back south. Then we'll rip north again, laying the pipe in thirty-two inches deep as we go. The whole thing will take three days." He stands with his short, strong arms crossed over his chest, resting on top of his round belly. Then he shakes his head and lets out a disgusted chortle. "Six years' wait for three days' work."

It was going to take Anna at least an hour to rip the four miles out to the stake, so Joe and I drive down to the place Giovanni built at Eden Creek in the 1890s. Part of the way there, I notice a cow's skeleton. "We lose them to coyotes or vehicles," Joe says, "or lice—we call that the BLM disease: a bunch of saprophytes sucking the life out of a body." Other than the skeleton and the three cattle we saw at Charlie's Well, there were no others in sight.

"Yeah, we pulled the cattle in for the benefit of the range, and we didn't need the goddamned BLM to tell us to, either," Joe says. "You know what gets me? You can spend your whole life out here—four generations—and the goddamned bureaucrats come out here and suddenly they're the experts and we don't know anything. There wouldn't have been a ranch here for a hundred and twenty years if we didn't know how to manage the range. It's degrading when you've built up your livelihood, then the government comes in and tells you you don't know anything. Bureaucrats work seven to four or whatever, and take vacations. It's not like that for us. We work twenty-four hours seven days a week. They come in, chart your destiny for the rest of your life. Even if they're only there for two or three months, we have to live with what they do."

The walls of Giovanni's cabin at Eden Creek are made of stone and cement. The wooden floors and the back step are falling apart. Behind the cabin, piñon and juniper trees grow on the slope leading up into the Kawich Mountains. "Granddad is buried up there."

On our way back to meet Anna, we stop to check on several other pipelines: Cedar Pipeline, which Giovanni and the United Cattle

Company put in, which is indeed made of wood ("Those old-timers did whatever they had to do to get things going"); Five-Mile Pipeline, which Joe's father and uncle laid right after World War II; and George's Pipeline, which is only twenty-five years old. "God I love progress," Joe says. "I hate it when people try to shut it down."

Anna's face is caked with dirt when we meet her; she is twitching her nose and trying not to sneeze. "Daddy, next time I'm gonna wear one of those ventilators," she says, taking the plugs out of her ears. The sun had fallen over the Kawich Range and the wind was beginning to blow cold. Anna looks back at the fresh trench and shivers. "Pretty good timing."

In 1995 Congress debated overhauling the Taylor Grazing Act of 1934 and raising grazing fees, which are currently $1.34 per "Animal Unit Month"—the cost of grazing one cow and one calf per month. Eastern politicians talked of "welfare ranchers" getting a free ride on public land; I asked Joe what he thought of that.

"I'd love to see them come give it a try. And it ain't all that damn cheap when you add in the costs of maintaining the water and the fences and buying the feed and all the rest of it. At this point it would be cheaper and less worry for us to go somewhere else and lease someone's private land for ten dollars per AUM and have them take care of everything."

But the Fallinis won't do that. They're dug in too deep. Anna already has a place picked out where she wants to build a house, down by Giovanni's old cabin at Eden Creek.

■ ■ ■

There is a shared sense among folks in Nye County that they have been closed out of the land-management planning process; that they have had to deal with fundamental injustices; and that their economy has been destroyed as a result. In their anger, and in their rebellion, some of them have built up a sort of mythology, a view of American history and law to justify their position.

Dick Carver thinks the framers of the Constitution intended county governments to take priority over state and federal government. His theory is based in part on his understanding of the "equal footing" doctrine defined in the the 1777 Articles of Confederation—an interpretation shared by few politicians or constitutional scholars.

Part of the reason Carver has attracted so much attention is that he has taken his theory on the road, preaching what he calls the Counties Movement to radically antifederal, ultraconservative, populist, anti-environmentalist, and so-called Patriot groups in twenty-six states. He speaks at symposiums organized by Wise Use advocacy groups, like the Western States Coalition, People for the West!, and the National Federal Lands Conference, which has come out in support of private militias.

But Carver is no bomb-thrower. He is an earnest, proud American, intensely loyal to his friends and neighbors, and deeply convinced that there is something profoundly wrong with a government that has assumed so much power in their lives. His is a loud voice in Nye County, but he by no means speaks for everyone.

■ ■ ■

As far as Wayne Hage is concerned, Carver's county-supremacy theories are just as bad as the current federal regulatory apparatus. The issue, as he sees it, is not whether the federal government, the state government, or the county government should control public lands; he regards any form of government ownership as socialism, and thus as un-American.

Wayne Hage and I have spent four hours in the Station House Restaurant, drinking coffee and talking about the legal history that led up to the "range wars" of the 1980s and '90s. Unlike the folksy Carver, Hage is stern, intimidating, and deliberate. He speaks in a baritone voice with slow, measured precision. The real issue, he says, is not which level of government should oversee the western rangelands, but whether private citizens have rights to manage them at all. In his book, *Storm Over Rangelands: Private Rights On Federal Lands*, Hage argues that they most certainly do. He insists there are long-established private rights to forage, water, and mineral wealth, and that *Hage v. United States* could decide the matter once and for all.

After Dick Carver, Wayne Hage is the second-most-vocal figure in Nye County on the subject of the emotional and legal state of war that exists between local citizens and the federal government—"the Lands Issues," as all of its subordinate battles have come to be called. Dick Carver may be the George Washington of the Counties Movement, but Wayne Hage's prolonged fights with the federal government over private-property rights have made him a hero of the advocates of what has come to be called "Wise Use."

Hage and his wife, Jean, bought a ranch in Pine Creek, east of the mountains behind Carver's place, in the spring of 1978. They bought it from the Arcularius brothers, who wanted out after years of struggling with Forest Service regulations. The Forest Service won't comment on the case, but by all accounts Hage and the Forest Service were like the Hatfields and the McCoys from day one.

They started out fighting over a spring in Meadow Canyon. Hage said he owned the rights to the water there, and had two court decrees to prove it. The forest ranger disagreed, piped water from the spring into a ranger station, and then fenced the spring off completely so no livestock could get to it. Then the Forest Service began serving Hage with citations, declaring that his cattle were roaming off his allotment.

The climax came in July 1991, when the Forest Service confiscated 108 head of Hage's cattle, sold them at auction, and billed Hage for their costs. Two months later, Hage, who had already fought and beaten the Forest Service three times in administrative appeals, filed his $28-million "takings" case against the United States. In March 1996, Judge Loren Smith denied a government motion for summary judgment, ruling that Hage might be able to prove the existence of range rights—if he could prove that the rights were in existence prior to the withdrawal of the land for a national forest, and that his rights have their origins in Nevada state law. After seven years of delays, during which time Hage spent more than a million dollars on litigation, his case was finally heard in court in October 1998.

Hage's historical and legal argument goes like this: while the Homestead Act created a neat process of federal land disposal in the Midwest in order to encourage agriculture and populate the region, the Mining Law of 1872, the Taylor Grazing Act, and other laws combined to create a more complicated process in the West. Here, federal lands were divided into what Hage calls the "split estate." There is a mineral estate—the mineral wealth under the land—and there is a surface estate, which includes water rights and forage for livestock. Miners were thereby able to make mining claims in much the same way homesteaders were able to carve farms out of the public domain, and ranchers were able to establish private ranges for their livestock. All of the western states have in their constitutions "disclaimer clauses," which in Hage's analysis were meant to guarantee the U.S. government the right to first disposal of the federal domain. Before 1864, when Nevada was not yet a state, miners made their claims and paid their fees to the federal government. After Nevada became a state, the deed to that claim was recognized under state law as private property. The same process, Hage insists, applied to grazing and water rights. Judge Smith has acknowledged that Hage might have a valid argument.

It's certainly a popular view with the ranchers in Nye. When they look out over the range, they don't see federal lands on which they live as government tenants: they see private property, cultivated and developed with their own families' money and sweat. Joe Fallini sees hundreds of wells and water pipelines that his father, grandfather, aunts, and uncles developed at their own expense. He sees vast grazing allotments, on which he had to pay inheritance taxes when his parents died, a total of more than $830,000.

When we finish talking, the lunch counter and tables in the Station House are filled with the late-afternoon coffee crowd. The ambient chatter, interrupted only by a bus boy's periodic crashing and banging, keeps returning to the same themes.

"What's the BLM good for? Target practice, that's what."

"They're driving us into extinction."

"The bastards are empire building."

"It's eastern people running western people's lives."

"These federal agencies are just a damn jobs program."

"The hospital is about to go under and there's no new construction in town, but I betcha they'll still have the money to build a new BLM building."

"I'm proud of Dick Carver. At least he shoved it back in their faces."

"Yeah, but that isn't the right way to do it. You should go through the courts, like Hage and Fallini and them."

"What kind of crap is that? You have to be able to afford good lawyers to survive?"

"Look, we can't have *no* land management."

"Nobody's saying you should. But the cowmen have been doing it for a hundred and fifty years. They know what they're doing."

"Well, most of them are over fifty. It's a dying lifestyle."

Epilogue

LEARNING MORE FROM LAS VEGAS
David Littlejohn

This is obviously not the last word on Las Vegas. It is not even the last word on Las Vegas today—which, for this team of reporters, means Las Vegas as we found it between fall 1996 and fall 1998—let alone Las Vegas yesterday or Las Vegas tomorrow. Those interested in the history of this city should read Eugene Moehring's *Resort City in the Sunbelt: Las Vegas 1930–1970* (as updated in 1995), and the Las Vegas chapters of John M. Findlay's *People of Chance: Gambling in American Society from Colonial Times to Las Vegas* (1986). In addition to the millions of words that have been written about the casino-hotels of the Strip and Downtown, as well as the entrepreneurs, entertainers, gamblers, tourists, athletes, and criminals identified with them, popular articles and academic studies have addressed the city's water shortage, environmental problems, racial minorities, labor relations, new housing developments, and feeble efforts at planning.

This collection is not even as complete as we would have liked to make it. The realities of book publication obliged us to omit Becky Quinlan's chapter on the beleaguered Clark County School District—now the nation's ninth- or tenth-largest, growing by twelve thousand students a year, the equivalent of one new elementary school every month. In order to reduce a swollen introduction, I cut out segments dealing with professional and amateur sports, the local cultural scene, and Clark County's efforts to expand its economic base. After many months of work, Michael Stroh felt obliged to abandon the most elusive subject of all: an overall assessment of the social effects of a gambling-based economy. The final report on this subject by the National Gambling Impact Study Commission, appointed by President Clinton and congressional leaders in 1997, was due to appear in June 1999, after this book had gone to press. But given the sharp ideological split in the commission's membership—what one member saw as moral and social decay another saw as legitimate entertainment and a source of economic revival—I am presuming that the NGISC was no more able than was Mr. Stroh to draw any clear-cut and convincing conclusions.

I regret in particular the absence of two proposed sections: one dealing with the University of Nevada at Las Vegas, the other with the role of Mormons and the Mormon church in southern Nevada. After talking or corresponding with many members of the university's faculty and administration, and evaluating as best as I could the quality of work being done there, I concluded that UNLV was a far more interesting and productive place than its reputation would lead one to believe. That reputation was nationally enlarged (then darkly tarnished) by UNLV's years as a basketball power under coach Jerry Tarkanian (1973-92; NCAA champions 1990).

"Las Vegas is an easy place to ridicule and a hard place to take seriously," complained Leonard Zane, professor of physics and head of the honors program at UNLV, where he has taught since 1973. Even so, he added, "We can become and in some ways we already are a major university not only in the southwest but nationally." Prof. Boyd Earl of chemistry, a former department chair, extrapolating the growth and change he had seen since 1976, insisted that "UNLV will be a major university within a few decades, despite the gaming industry." In fact, he wrote, "While in many respects UNLV has improved since I've been here, for the most part Las Vegas has not. From being a university that, in many people's minds, was not good enough for Las Vegas, UNLV is going to be a university that's too good for Las Vegas."

Many of us encountered the Mormon presence in the course of our investigations, which is not surprising. Holding today a power far in excess of their numbers (which are estimated at about 7 percent of the population), the Latter-day Saints were the city's first white settlers, on a mission from Salt Lake City in 1855. Although they do not (officially) smoke, drink, or gamble—and can thus play no direct role in the Industry (a special dispensation permits Clark County Mormons to work in casinos)—they tend to dominate areas such as banking, property development, education, and several branches of local and state government. But it is difficult for non-Mormons to learn much about the operations, connections, and attitudes of this unusually secretive group. The least one can say is that Mormons in positions of influence in southern Nevada seem to be especially comfortable hiring, promoting, and dealing with one another, which sometimes gives to their interlinked operations the aspect of a powerful private club, fraternal order, or alumni network.

■ ■ ■

Methodist preacher Tom Grey, founder and director of the National Coalition Against Legalized Gambling, constantly cites Las Vegas and its problems as a warning to other cities, counties, and states contemplating the legalization of casino gambling. As I wrote at the outset, however, Las Vegas is too special, too singular—it is, after all, the only American city *created* by casino gambling—to offer any clear-cut lessons to other places thinking of going that route.

But that does not mean that Las Vegas is in no way paradigmatic, a possible model of what many other American cities are or are becoming. In a November 1994 *Time* cover story on Las Vegas, Kurt Anderson expressed what has now become a commonplace: if this city no longer shocks or surprises, it is because so much of the rest of the country has adopted its values and style. "Las Vegas has become Americanized," he wrote, "and, even more, America has become Las Vegasized." Among the evidence he cited were new sex clubs and casinos across the country; the gigantic Mall of America; Vegas-style entertainment at pop concerts and on Broadway; and the global spread of the Strip aesthetic.

There remain urban critics who perceive, in the ever more spectacular tourist precincts of Las Vegas, a model for, or a mirror of, the rest of the United States. Twenty-five years after Robert Venturi and his associates drew lessons for architects and planners from an earlier generation of casino-hotels, the photomontages of *Learning from Las Vegas* look almost rustic in their simplicity. Gridlocked traffic on the Strip has made absurd the Venturis' concept of giant signs designed to be read by people driving by at "high speed." Even so, Jean-Louis Cohen concluded in 1997, "None of the analyses [they] made in 1972 would be contradicted by the astonishing acceleration in the pace of construction and the inflation in the size of the architectural structures that were to follow."

One of the most ardent contemporary followers of Venturi et al. is architect and critic Alan Hess (*Viva Las Vegas*, 1993). "The Las Vegas Strip has never stopped changing," he wrote in a review of the New York New York Hotel in 1997. "But now, with suburban areas growing denser and more varied, with entertainment venues growing in importance, with themes emerging as a multifaceted approach to architecture, and with gambling a national interest, the rest of the country is finally catching up to Las Vegas....For better or worse, the Las Vegas Strip provides a new model for public places."

But no new American entertainment venue or gambling precinct is ever likely to catch up to those of Las Vegas. More pertinent may be critics and observers who venture beyond the Strip, and see in the "real" city a replica of developments taking place elsewhere, and a portent of cities to come. Frances Anderton and John Chase write,

> While the Strip is celebrated for its brazen exhibitionism, the power of its imagery has also acted to mask the human and experiential aspects of living and working in Las Vegas, and the impoverishment of urban design and daily life in the remainder of the city....
>
> Las Vegas itself, aside from the Strip, is shockingly ordinary and prosaic, representative of other American cities and of suburban aras of American cities which have experienced most of their growth relatively recently. Indeed, the non-Strip, non-Fremont Street Las Vegas is no more mythic or fantastic than Salt Lake City, Utah or Boise, Idaho. Because much of its growth is so recent, and there was so little previous development of infrastructure to shape it, its low-density, car-oriented urban fabric demonstrates more clearly than other US cities the current American attitudes to urban design. The dominant factor determining building and city planning in Las Vegas is expedience, whether that is building with blocks in simple volumes or large slab casino towers. An individual building is simply the least expensive enclosure of space that will keep the occasional rainstorm out and the ever-present air-conditioned air in.
>
> The city of Las Vegas consists of mile upon mile of residential neighbourhoods. Until recently, one-story single-family homes made up most of the housing stock. But even in a sprawling metropolitan area such as Las Vegas, only 50 per cent of citizens now live in single-family houses, with 7 per cent living in detached mobile homes and 40 per cent in apartments or condominium townhouses. The new townhouse communities of Las Vegas are walled and gated subdivisions, many of them master-planned around golf courses, artificial lakes, shops and schools.
>
> Driving down the boulevards through these communities one passes row after row of walled-off backyards—no front doors, no front porches, no sense of communication between the motorist and what he or she is driving through. Gated communities are equally attractive to wealthy homeowners who want to be physically separated from the rest of the city as to senior citizens who like the security and to young working families for whom property is affordable. The popularity of these fortified residential neighbourhoods testifies to the pervasive urban paranoia that characterises Las Vegas....

None of the features of planned communities such as the Lakes is unique to Las Vegas—they can be found in many other American urban areas, particularly Sunbelt communities such as San Diego and Palm Springs. But is safe to say that Las Vegas is probably the largest American community to have such a high proportion of its citizens living behind gates and walls. (*Las Vegas: The Success of Excess*, 1997)

In many ways, the "real," the locals' Las Vegas recalls other recently evolved cities throughout the southern half of the United States. Like Las Vegas, these depend for their survival on "unnaturally" imported water. Auto-dominated living and planning lead to intolerable traffic congestion and air pollution as populations grow. Strip malls along six-lane boulevards punctuate walled and gated housing tracts. Large, ancillary "third-world" service economies grow, made up of corporate domestic servants and round-the-clock telephone answerers. In the end, some of these cities depend on a tourism as absolute as the Caribbean's or Tahiti's, in which minimum-wage locals survive by waiting on and cleaning up after extravagant, short-term visitors.

"Postmodern" cities like these have been analyzed by a new generation of urbanologists, taking their clues from French theorists like Michel Foucault and Jean Baudrillard. Such people often profess scorn for old-fashioned, value-laden, "historicist" critics who find fault with things like giant billboards and parking lots, strip malls filled with chain stores, or "what used to be called 'urban sprawl.'"

The focus of postmodern urban theory remains fixed on Los Angeles, which is seen not as a place to be derided, but as a present and future reality, a phenomenon to be studied—or at least upon which to construct new theories. Several urban theorists seized upon John Portman's 1986 Bonaventure Hotel in "downtown" Los Angeles—a complex of five bronzed-glass cylinders enclosing wedge-shaped rooms, numerous shopping and eating places, and a high, hard-to-read internal atrium—as the iconic postmodern place, a "new hyperspace" (as Michael Jameson wrote in 1991) that "we do not yet possess the perceptual equipment to match."

But any one of a dozen hotels in Las Vegas, let alone the city itself, would have suited as well, meeting as they do the requirements for Michel Foucault's 1967 concept of a "heteropia": a totally alien, disconnected space, in which "the juxtaposition of heterogeneous elements is so incongruous and disuptive to our normal sense of order that we are unable to realize such perversity within a coherent and familiar domain."

Edward Soja, an American member of this school, prefers to focus on Los Angeles as "the quintessential postmodern metropolis" because one can still trace in it the shift from a port- and factory-based "modern" city to the prototypical American city of the future: a metropolitan area dependent on leisure and service industries, with their legions of low-paid, often immigrant workers; a city spreading like a runaway cancer, spawning in the process instant new urban-suburban nodes, with their own social disorders and instantly congested new freeways. Soja focuses on another interesting aspect of the transformation of the Los Angeles conurbation from a modern into a postmodern metropolis: the overwhelming spread of the artificial in place of the real, from film and television studios to mammoth theme parks, then to stage-set streets, malls, and buildings all over the area.

Las Vegas, like a number of other born-yesterday boomtowns of the Sunbelt which are younger than L.A., never went through the traditional phases of urban growth. By the time it became a city—of half a million in 1979, of a million in 1996—all these paradigms were already in place. In many ways, Las Vegas seems to me ahead of L.A. in the race to become the first purely postmodern city—antihistoric, uncentered, prisonlike, and purposely disorienting. It was into supersurveillance and guard-gating, let alone the ubiquitous derealizing of the real, well before Los Angeles was.

To me, it makes both economic and symbolic sense that the largest private employer in Clark County outside the casino-hotels is a paternalistic, employee-friendly credit-card processing factory, the "service industry" par excellence. Inside a wide-spreading, white, blue, and glass building full of fake cactus and southwestern art nine miles out on West Sahara, 1,400 workers (teens and seniors welcome; no college degree required) answer 100,000 phone calls and "process" 600,000 statements or payments every day. Under tight security, they control machines that imprint and issue 15 million new pieces of plastic a year. Credit-card holders around the country believe that this classic heteropia is located in a nonexistent city called The Lakes, Nevada. But then, no one ever knows where the respondent to an (800) phone call may be sitting.

■ ■ ■

I cannot pretend that our team of reporters and photographer—most of us from older, more traditional cities and towns—found Las Vegas, on the whole, attractive or appealing. But a great many people, including natives, newcomers, and visitors, see in this unique place the model of a liberated American city, free of the heavy hands of the Past, the East, and the Proper. One of the most provocative new defenders of Las Vegas is art critic Dave Hickey, who arrived here in 1990 from Fort Worth by way of

San Diego. In an anti-establishment, bad-boy style that recalls both Hunter S. Thompson and Tom Wolfe (with a Texas bite and a bounce all his own), Hickey makes a point of defending the Las Vegas ethic and aesthetic against the imagined values of stuffy East Coast curators and critics ("Better vulgarity than entrenched ideas about taste"), or the American heartland, or his own discontented colleagues at UNLV.

> Since I must regularly venture out of Vegas onto the bleak savannas of high culture, and there, like an aging gigolo, generate bodily responses to increasingly abject objects of desire, there is nothing quite as bracing as the prospect of flying home, of swooping down into that ardent explosion of lights in the heart of the pitch-black desert—of coming home to the only indigenous visual culture on the North American continent, a town bereft of dead white walls, gray wool carpets, ficus plants, and Barcelona chairs—where there is everything to see and not a single pretentious object demanding to be scrutinized. (*Air Guitar: Essays on Art and Democracy*, 1997)

Hickey has written cheeky essays in defense of the ineffable Siegfried and Roy and their cultural progenitor, Liberace. He insists that he prefers his view of the Strip by night (he lives in a high-rise on Desert Inn Road) to the boring sunset behind it.

> It's spectacular, or course, and even, occasionally, sublime (if you like sublime), but to my eyes that sunset is always fake—as flat and gaudy as a Barnett Newman and just as pretentious....One either prefers the honest fakery of the neon or the fake honesty of the sunset—the undisguised artifice of culture or the cultural construction of "authenticity"—the genuine rhinestone, finally, or the imitation pearl.

Despite Hickey's bravado, I know of no other U.S. metropolitan area of Las Vegas's size and prosperity so lacking in established cultural institutions. The overweening presence of an industry that earns $6 billion a year selling what it calls entertainment—entertainment that, unlike movies, records, sports, theater, or music, is based exclusively on the handing back and forth of cash—may have something to do with the low esteem in which more subtle and less profitable forms of diversion are held.

This is not to say that Las Vegas should aspire to be Minneapolis (a city Mayor Jones sometimes cited as her role model), or Phoenix, or Santa Fe, or anywhere else. Although they may be imploded and replaced from time to time, the casino-hotels of the Strip are not going to disappear. Whatever Las Vegas becomes when it grows up—and this applies to its cultural as well as its economic and educational self—it will have to come to terms with the Industry, capitalize on it, take it into account. I doubt that any city as lively as Las Vegas will remain unidimensional. But as Professor Zane of UNLV reminded us, "I believe some people are still try-ing to evaluate Las Vegas by a set of standards that were developed for a different century. Las Vegas is different and will remain different as long as it exists. To say it lacks the culture of this place or that is to miss the point."

Many conditions recorded in this book will be recognized by Americans from other states and cities: vaguely religious, feel-good megachurches; Third World immigrants doing most of the hard work; a rapid accommo-dation to an increasingly "invisible" homeless population; teenage anomie, with its attendant drug use, careless sex, casual crime, and suicide; old peo-ple living out their lives in enclaves where young people never intrude; and families, or what is left of families, retiring to isolated and gated suburbs, their days broken by longer and longer automobile commutes and by trips to strip malls and fast-food outlets along traffic-clogged boulevards. All this occurs, in Las Vegas as in other places, in a postmodern urban nexus surrounded by golfing greens but devoid of a center, with a retail economy almost entirely created by corporate decisions made elsewhere.

In many ways, Las Vegas—quite apart from its dominant industry—does represent the future, and increasingly the present, of the urban and suburban United States. The population of this country has tilted toward the cities of the Sunbelt, now a major locus of both tourism and domestic and foreign migration. This, after all, is where the jobs are, as well as the sunshine, secu-rity, and creature comforts sought by ever-increasing legions of the old. The geographic isolationism, political unconcern, and economic selfishness of Las Vegans, their increasing willingness to live in gated communities of the mind, are hardly conditions of fin-de-siècle American life unique to Las Vegas.

As we have seen, the heavy hand of the Industry affects the lives, atti-tudes, and expectations of thousands of Las Vegans, whatever may have brought them to the city in the first place. Bingo halls, neighborhood casi-nos, the slot and video-poker machines in hundreds of local stores tempt most of the population to gamble regularly. The still-growing job market of the megahotels absorbs vast numbers of new residents, demanding for the most part a hardworking but uneducated workforce. It persuades many young people to stop their education early, and, perhaps most important, has made much of Las Vegas a three-shift, 24-hour-a-day town, with all the implications that situation bears for family life, school schedules, and teenage behavior. More than 30 percent of the county's public schoolchildren change schools every year, largely because of high job turnover and transience in the adult population.

The overwhelming presence of the Industry has not made it easy for

Clark County to attract other kinds of business, or for UNLV to flourish as it might in a city with a different economic base. Because of its role as the national center of sports gambling, Las Vegas has never been permitted to house a major-league baseball, football, or basketball team. One reason often given for the city's relatively thin cultural offerings (along with the demographic imbalance caused by undereducated service workers and cocooning retirees, neither of whom are much into the arts) is that they could never compete with the showrooms on the Strip.

Tens of thousands of workers and their families are drawn by the new jobs that open up when new casino-hotels are built and staffed. But even more tens of thousands are drawn to Las Vegas, as to other American sunbelt cities, because it seems to them cheap, healthy, and warm, a good place to work, to raise children, or to retire. The Clark County School District has to hire more than 1,400 new teachers a year, most of whom it draws from other states by means of good salaries and promises of job security and "instant" seniority: after all, there will be another 1,400 teachers behind them next year. Architects, engineers, and other professionals are often able to find more stable and better-paying jobs here than they are in older, more traditional American cities; during California's recession in the late '80s and early '90s, great numbers of them moved to Nevada. Small businesses blossom, sprouting at every intersection mall as the city expands into the desert.

The boom that is Las Vegas may have had its seed in the expansion of the casino-hotels and their servant industries, but it has long since assumed an independent life of its own, and today is little different from similar booms in Phoenix, Fort Lauderdale, or Houston. More workers are employed building new houses than on the swarming, relatively short-lived construction sites on the Strip.

As it passes the one-million population mark, even a widespread, essentially unplanned agglomeration like Las Vegas may begin to feel and act more like a city. Its citizens may begin to care more about things like the proper dispersion of political power; the presence of genuine and indigenous cultural amenities; the value of good architecture, and the importance of parks; the quality of public education; and an honest coming to terms with the environment, typified by the new Clark County Government Center and the desert-friendly planning in Summerlin.

To learn its lessons, we must look closely at *all* of Las Vegas, away from the Strip and Downtown. Unless something singular and unpredictable happens to alter the bend of history, this is what the United States may well look like for a majority of its citizens sometime in the next century. But because of its uniquely gambling-dominated past, present, and almost certain future, Las Vegas will remain, for better or worse, one of a kind.

LIST OF ILLUSTRATIONS

Advertising: nude club, wedding chapel
Billboards and school bus, Las Vegas Boulevard North
Arrest at a strip mall
Homeless on the street
Cell A2, Juvenile Detention Center
Teenagers at Red Rock Canyon
Teenagers at strip mall
Change girls at neighborhood casino
Information center at Latino swap meet
Strip mall bar in afternoon sun
Pool players in Mexican bar
Pastor at Sunday service, Greater Philadelphia Church
Choir at Greater Philadelphia church
Homeless man in his private shelter

NOTES ON CONTRIBUTORS

David Littlejohn (editor), of San Francisco, studied architecture and English at the University of California at Berkeley, and received his Ph.D. in English at Harvard in 1963, the year he joined the Berkeley faculty. From 1969 to 1997, he taught in the Graduate School of Journalism. Between 1965 and 1975, he served as "Critic at Large" for KQED (San Francisco) and the PBS network, for whom he wrote and broadcast more than 200 programs or reviews. He was a West Coast arts correspondent for the London *Times* from 1975 to 1989, and has been serving a similar role for the *Wall Street Journal* since 1990. He has published more than 300 articles and reviews for newspapers and magazines in the United States, England, Italy, and France. Littlejohn has written or edited twelve earlier books: six on literary subjects; two novels; a genealogical-historical essay; *Architect: The Life and Work of Charles W. Moore* (1984); *The Ultimate Art: Essays around and about Opera* (1992); and *The Fate of the English Country House* (1997). (dtl@uclink4.berkeley.edu)

Eric Gran (photographer), of San Jose, California, received his B.A. and M.J. degrees from the University of California at Berkeley. He has travelled and photographed extensively in Eastern Europe, Asia, and the United States since 1985. After being awarded the Dorothea Lange Fellowship for Documentary Photography in 1995, he photographed life in the Indian state of Orissa for a forthcoming book, *Jagannath*. Recent projects include a story on explorers attempting to walk across the frozen Bering Strait *(Alaska Magazine)*, the decline of the movie industry in Hong Kong *(Los Angeles Times)*, and the efforts of an Oregon treatment center to uncover the roots of violence in children (PBS Frontline online). He received a grant to photograph the WWII generation of shipyard workers from the South in Oakland, California, and is at work on a documentary study of the Silicon Valley. He also serves as lab assistant and printer to photographer Wayne Miller. (ericgran@excite.com)

The following contributors have all received Master of Journalism degrees from the University of California at Berkeley, where most of the research for this book was undertaken.

Randolph Court, of Richmond, Virginia, has a B.A. in American studies from the University of California at Santa Cruz. He has been a writer and editor at *Hyper Age* and *Wired News* in San Francisco; an intern at Pacific News Service; a staff writer for the *San Diego Daily Transcript*; and a researcher/writer for the Center for Investigative Reporting in San Francisco. He is now a technical policy analyst at the Democratic Leadership Council Progressive Policy Institute in Washington.

Bill Dauber, of Whittier, Calif., has a B.A. in history from the University of California at Irvine. A bilingual reporter of Mexican heritage, he has worked as an assistant editor for *La Voz Mestiza*; a staff writer for *The New University* at Irvine; an intern at the *Seattle Times*; and a sports writer for the *Orange County Register*. He is now a reporter for the *Whittier* (Calif.) *Daily News*.

Malcolm Garcia, of Santa Rosa, Calif, has a B.A. in English from Coe College, Iowa, and an M.S.W. degree from San Francisco State University. He has worked for thirteen years with homeless people and refugees in San Francisco, where he founded and edited *By No Means*, a monthly magazine by and for homeless people. The author of *Division Point* (1991), a collection of short stories, he has also worked as a reporter for the *S.F. Weekly* and written for the *San Francisco Chronicle*. After working as a reporter for the *Philadelphia Inquirer*, he is now at the *Kansas City Star*.

Maia Hansen, of San Francisco, received her B.A. in English from Dartmouth College. She has worked as a writer for the Berkeley Guides series, *Seattle Weekly,* and *Northwest PhotoNetwork,* and as a desktop publisher and editor at The Learning Company. An extensive traveler, she is now an editor for the Lonely Planet series of travel books.

Joe Heim, of Philadelphia, has a B.A. in English from Villanova University. He has worked as a correspondent for the *West County Times* and *Contra Costa Times* in California; an editorial assistant for *Cancer Research*; a senior program administrator for the South African Education Program (Institute for International Education, Washington); a tenant advocate in Baltimore; and a freelance music critic. He worked as a critic and reporter for the *Seattle Times,* and a reporter for *Education Daily* in Washington, D.C.

Andrea Lampros, of Portland, received her B.A. in American history from Mills College. She has served as a Congressional intern; a coordinator for the Washington, D.C., Committee in Solidarity with the People of El Salvador; a production assistant for a Time/Life Television documentary on Incan civilizations in Peru; an associate director of the National Sanctuary Defense Fund in San Francisco; and as a reporting intern at the *Reno Gazette* and the *Sacramento Bee.* She is now the education reporter for the *Contra Costa Times* in California.

Lori Leibovich, of Newton, Mass., has a B.A. in American history from the University of Wisconsin at Madison. She has worked as a fact-checker for *U.S. News & World Report* and a reporter for the *Monterey County Herald.* Her writing has appeared in the *East Bay Monthly, San Francisco Focus, Mother Jones,* and the *San Jose Mercury News.* After serving as associate editor at the online magazine *Salon,* based in San Francisco, she joined the staff of *Talk* magazine in New York.

Michelle Ling, of Los Angeles, has a B.A. in anthropology from the University of California at Berkeley. She has worked as a marketing representative for EMI Records; a legal assistant at a San Francisco law firm; a reporting intern at the *Point Reyes Light* (Calif.); and an internet reporter for the "State of the World Forum," held in San Francisco in 1996. She is assistant editor of *California Monthly,* the University of California alumni magazine.

Nefretiti Makenta, of Washington, D.C., is a graduate in English from Utica College of Syracuse University. She has been an English teacher in the Upward Bound program at the University of California at Berkeley. In Washington, she co-produced and hosted a television program of video-music criticism, and worked as a writer and fundraiser for the city's Department of Recreation and Parks. She has served as managing editor of the *Bay Area Black Student Journal*; a writer for *Non Profit Times* and the *Oakland Post*; and a reporting intern at the *Washington City Paper*. In 1998-99, she produced an independent video documentary about the black poetry revival in Washington.

Lisa Moskowitz, of St. Louis, has a B.A. in political science and history from Duke University. She has worked as a staff assistant to Representative Joan Kelly Horn (D.-M.), a press intern to Senator (now Representative) Richard Gephardt (D.-M.), and as a marketing-communications specialist for the Federal National Mortgage Association (Fannie Mae) in Washington. She has written for the *Grants Pass Daily Courier* (Ore.), *Adweek*, and the online magazine *Salon*. Having worked for a year as an editor for *PC World Online* in San Francisco, she now writes for a number of publications, and works as a Web content consultant.

Marie Sanchez, of Stockton, Calif., a native Spanish speaker, received her B.S. in Biological Science from the University of California at Davis and her M.A. in Latin American Studies from the University of California at Berkeley. After a career as a grants administrator and writer at the University of California at San Francisco and a human-resources manager at Pacific Bell—as well as a volunteer teacher in migrant-labor camps—she worked as a reporter for the *Salinas Californian* and the international diabetes Web site. She now writes on health and science for the *Boston Globe* and other publications.

Virginia (Jenna) Ward, of San Francisco, received her B.A. in history from the University of California at Santa Cruz. She has worked as a reporting intern at the *Sonora Union Democrat* (Calif.), a staff writer for the *Santa Rosa Press Democrat* (Calif.), an intern and stringer for the *New York Times* (San Francisco Bureau), and a writer for *The Recorder*, San Francisco's legal newspaper and the *Legal Times* of Washington, D.C.

Heather World, of Seattle, received her B.A. in history from UCLA. After working for the *Guardian Newsweekly* and WNYC Radio News in New York, she wrote for a number of New York publications. In San Francisco, she worked as a production assistant at *S.F. Weekly* and a writer for *Callboard* magazine. She is a reporter for the *San Mateo County Times*.

INDEX

As all of the essays in this book deal with Las Vegas (Greater Las Vegas, Las Vegas Valley), Clark County, or Nevada, there are no index entries for these geographical areas. References to areas such as the Strip (Las Vegas Boulevard South) and Downtown, individual city streets, and such common topics as casinos, gambling, hotels, and tourism, generally, are also unindexed.